Praise for *Front Row at the Trump Show*

"Jonathan Karl gives us much more than program notes for the Trump Show in this revealing and personal account of his relationship with our 45th president. We learn what it is really like to be on the White House beat, about the peculiarities of dealing with the personality in the Oval Office, and ultimately the risks and dangers we face at this singular moment in American history."

—Mike McCurry, former White House press secretary (1995–1998), and director/professor, Center for Public Theology, Wesley Theological Seminary

"The Constitution is strict: It says we must have presidents. Fortunately, we occasionally have reporters as talented as Jonathan Karl—an acute observer and gifted writer—to record what presidents do. Karl is exactly the right journalist to chronicle the 45th president, who is more—to be polite—exotic than his predecessors." —George F. Will

"No reporter has covered Donald Trump longer and with more energy than Jonathan Karl. It pays off in his account of what he calls the Trump Show with some startling scoops. What did the president scrawl across the rejected resignation letter from his attorney general? He tells us."

—Susan Page, Washington bureau chief, *USA Today*

"Jon Karl is fierce, fearless, and fair. From cub reporter at the *New York Post* to chief White House correspondent for ABC News, he's covered Donald Trump—and the White House—for a generation. He knows the man, and the office. *Front Row at the Trump Show* takes us inside the daily challenge of truthful reporting on the Trump WH, revealing what's at stake with vivid detail and deep insights." —George Stephanopoulos

"Jonathan Karl is a straight-shooting, fair-minded, and hardworking professional, so it's no surprise he's produced a book historians will relish. It's about good old-fashioned news-getting—about the process and the rules and how it works. Overlaying it is this most amazing moment in American political history. Underlying it is a story about waking up each morning and trying against the odds to find out what's true."

—Peggy Noonan, *The Wall Street Journal*

FRONT ROW
AT THE
TRUMP SHOW

JONATHAN KARL

DUTTON

DUTTON

An imprint of Penguin Random House LLC
penguinrandomhouse.com

Previously published as a Dutton hardcover in March 2020

The Library of Congress has catalogued the hardcover edition of this book as follows:

Names: Karl, Jonathan, author.
Title: Front row at the Trump show / Jonathan Karl.
Description: [New York]: Dutton, [2020] | Includes index.
Identifiers: LCCN 2019046582 (print) | LCCN 2019046583 (ebook) |
ISBN 9781524745622 (hardcover) | ISBN 9781524745646 (ebook)
Subjects: LCSH: Trump, Donald, 1946– Press coverage. |
Presidents—United States—Election—2016. |
Presidents—Press coverage—United States—History—21st century. |
Press and politics—United States. | United States—Politics and government—2017– |
Karl, Jonathan. Classification: LCC E912 .K37 2020 (print) | LCC E912 (ebook) |
DDC 973.933092--dc23
LC record available at https://lccn.loc.gov/2019046582
LC ebook record available at https://lccn.loc.gov/2019046583

Dutton trade paperback ISBN: 9781524745639

Printed in the United States of America
1   3   5   7   9   10   8   6   4   2

Book design by Nancy Resnick

For Maria, Emily, and Anna

CONTENTS

NOTE FOR THE PAPERBACK EDITION

Like most people, I watched in horror as a mob of rioters, many of them waving Trump flags and chanting "Fight for Trump," rampaged through the U.S. Capitol building on January 6, 2021. The scene was shocking, but it wasn't surprising.

The events described in this book foretold the grim final chapter of the Trump presidency. In 2015, when Donald Trump joked about killing journalists in Grand Rapids, Michigan, the crowd laughed along with him. After he directed his rage at a lone cameraman at a crowded and boisterous rally in Mississippi in 2016, his campaign manager laughed when he was warned that the incitement was dangerous.

As I recounted in the hardcover edition of this book, I met with the president in the fall of 2019 and told him his rhetoric was dangerous. "Some sick person might take your words to heart," I said. His response haunts me today after watching an insurrection in the Capitol building triggered by the president's words: "I hope people take my words to heart."

I wrote this book with an eye to history. My goal was to write something that could be read decades from now to help answer a simple question about this strange era in American politics: What was it like?

The reaction to the hardcover version of this book that surprised me most was Donald Trump's. It wasn't so much what he said, but when he said it: at a meeting of his top economic advisors during the darkest days of the economic downturn triggered by the coronavirus pandemic. The economic outlook was grim, but when he spotted me by the cameras in the back of the room, he turned to a different subject. "Your book was very good, by the way," he said. "It was better about me than I thought it would be. You've known me for a long time." Just a few weeks earlier, he had lashed out at me during a nationally televised press conference. "You're a third-rate reporter," he said, angrily adding, "You will never make it." Neither the insult nor the strangely timed compliment would have surprised anybody who has read this book.

Animating these pages, and all of my reporting of the Trump presidency, is a desire to let the facts speak for themselves. I firmly believed, and still do, that as a reporter, my political views should be irrelevant to the way I do my job. No human being is purely objective, but as a reporter, I aim to be fair and accurate. As Trump became a political force, I was determined to treat him the way I had treated every other political figure I had covered: I would approach him with skepticism and never shy away from asking tough questions, but I would also treat him fairly. This was a challenge: Donald Trump branded me and my colleagues as the opposition party and, even worse, as traitors to the country we love. He told his supporters we were liars. Using the most powerful platform on the planet, he relentlessly sought to undermine good journalism and the very idea of a free press.

As the Trump Show draws to an inglorious end, the same objective method drives my reporting. But I am left with an unmistakable conclusion: Donald Trump has undermined our democracy. I'm not just referring to his effort to undermine public faith in a free-and-fair election (and one that broke a US record for turnout). This is bigger than that. Donald Trump used the power of his presidency to wage a war on truth.

"A lie can get halfway around the world before the truth can get its shoes on" is a quote often attributed to Mark Twain, but it is also something Twain scholars insist he never said. Good luck correcting that one. Unfortunately, lies travel faster than they ever have; many of the lies of the Trump era will be just as enduring, but far more damaging, than a misquote of Mark Twain.

My original epilogue to this book ended on a note of optimism. My new afterword explores the darkest moments of the Trump presidency, when the war on truth turned deadly and shook the foundations of our democracy. In the end, people did take Trump's words to heart, incited by his self-indulgent rage to assault the symbol and workplace of American democracy. His presidency is over, but rage remains. He has done lasting damage. I still believe in the strength of our institutions and the values enshrined in dusty old documents written by profoundly flawed men. But we have serious work ahead—as journalists and as Americans—to regain the trust of those who have been told over and over again not to believe what they see with their own eyes.

Jonathan Karl
January 2021

didn't have his phone number, so I dialed the one listed in the phone book for the Trump Organization.

"Can I speak to Donald Trump?" I asked.

It was an audacious call. I had been working as a reporter in New York City for less than a year. I had never met the man, and at this moment Trump's home and office were the epicenter of the most intense media frenzy I had ever witnessed.

"What do you want?"

The woman on the line was Norma Foerderer, Trump's longtime gatekeeper and someone so integrally involved in all his dealings—business and personal—that *The New York Times* had reported a few years earlier, "Some suspect she runs the company."

At this point, all I knew about Donald Trump was what I had read in the newspapers or seen on television. But I figured I knew enough to say exactly the right thing to get him on the phone.

It was August 1994, and the public was fixated on the tabloid story of the decade: Michael Jackson had just secretly married Lisa Marie Presley—the King of Pop together with the daughter of the King of Rock 'n' Roll. And the newlyweds, who had not yet been spotted together in public, were trying to stay out of sight right in the middle of Manhattan—at Trump Tower.

The news had brought a mob of paparazzi, Michael Jackson fans, Elvis Presley fans, and a parade of onlookers hoping to catch the first glimpse of the married couple. So many people had surged to Trump Tower that the NYPD had cordoned off the sidewalks around the building, forcing the growing crowd to watch from across the street.

I was a twenty-six-year-old reporter more interested in politics than celebrity sightings and spent most of my time reporting on a new mayor in City Hall named Rudy Giuliani, but I was working for the *New York Post* and on this particular day, my editors only cared about one story.

So I made what I believed would be a slam-dunk pitch to get Trump on the phone:

"I want to do a story on why the most famous newlyweds in the world would have their honeymoon at Trump Tower."

And sure enough, I got a quick call back. Donald Trump was on the line telling me to come on over. Along with *New York Post* photographer Francis Specker, I hustled uptown to Trump Tower. Walking past the police cordon set up to keep the paparazzi mobs away, I was whisked up to meet Trump in an office on the twenty-sixth floor filled with framed magazine covers featuring his favorite subject: Donald Trump.

It was a whirlwind from the start, a private tour of Trump Tower given by the man himself. The ground rules were simple: He would show me everything, I could use all the information he gave me, and I could quote him as "a source in the Trump Organization." We met with Michael Jackson's bodyguards and photographed the basement tunnels Jackson and Presley were using to get in and out without being spotted by the mob outside. He showed me a blue van with tinted windows in the garage—the couple's secret getaway car.

He showed it all off—from basement to penthouse—and along the way my source in the Trump Organization gave me all the gossipy details. I learned the terms of Michael Jackson's lease of the apartment directly below Trump's own. He wanted me to know that Michael and Lisa Marie had lots of famous neighbors. Steven Spielberg had an apartment on the sixty-fourth floor, Andrew Lloyd Webber on the sixtieth. My source pointed out apartments he said were owned by Elton John, King Fahd of Saudi Arabia, Sophia Loren, and the British royal family. He told me of a woman who bought one apartment for several million and then bought the one below so she could put in a swimming pool. "It's the most expensive pool in the world," a source in the Trump Organization told me.

None of this was serious, but my editors at the *New York Post* ate it up. They had a screaming front-page headline—"INSIDE MICHAEL'S HONEYMOON HIDEAWAY"—and four separate articles inside the newspaper, including one headlined "Tour Bares the Secrets of Lisa and Michael's Honeymoon Nest." If any of the residents of Trump Tower were unhappy with the *New York Post*'s printing a graphic of the building with arrows pointing to where they lived, they would need to take it up with a source in the Trump Organization. The *Post* had a big exclusive for the front page and I had a new source.

At one point while he was showing me his apartment on the sixty-eighth floor—the same floor plan and décor as Michael's, he told me—Trump stopped, turned, and asked if I wanted a picture. At first, I was a little confused. Didn't he notice I had come with a photographer who had been snapping photos the entire time? But I quickly realized he was asking if I wanted to get a picture taken with him. And with that I stood next to Donald Trump and faced photographer Francis Specker.

At some point while I was still in New York, I put the photo in a frame, but when I moved to Washington some two decades ago, I tossed it in a box of other old photographs. And for more than a decade it has been in the box down in my basement. Looking at the picture now, it appears to me as if it just came out of a time capsule. I am wearing a heavily wrinkled suit and a tie I almost certainly bought for three dollars from a New York street vendor. The background is pure Trump: a crystal chandelier, glossy marble, a decadent ceiling adorned with carved stone, and gold—lots of gold. I have long hair and the awkward grin of a reporter trying to figure out why the guy he's interviewing suddenly stopped to pose for a photograph with him. As for Trump, he is considerably slimmer than he is now, but it is striking how little about his appearance has changed: He's wearing the same style of dark suit he wears now, the same long red tie, the same facial expression I have seen in a thousand other photos.

As my secret tour of Trump Tower ended, I figured this wouldn't be the last time I'd call him and get a quick call back, but I had no idea where it would lead. I was a cub reporter for a New York tabloid. He was a flamboyant real estate developer with a scandalous personal life. As I shook his hand, I couldn't have begun to imagine his journey would ultimately lead to the White House, and so would mine.

INTRODUCTION

I arrived at the White House just a few minutes after the new president.

As the Trump family surveyed the White House residence for the first time, I took a walk through the West Wing. Hours earlier, the walls had been adorned with photos of Barack Obama and his family. Now all that remained was empty picture frames. I ducked into the office of the press secretary, the door open but the room barren except for a large brown bag on the floor in front of the desk, a so-called burn bag used by White House officials to discard paper meant to be incinerated rather than preserved for history. Desks were empty, most of the computers gone, a few empty boxes tossed about. An old workspace. A new administration. Eerily dark and calm before the storm to come.

Sean Spicer, the new press secretary, scurried by as I walked down the hallway outside his new office. All smiles and almost giddy about his new surroundings, he expressed amazement about the emptiness of the place, confessing he still had to figure out where the bathrooms were and how to get his computer hooked up.

Downstairs in the White House briefing room, I ran into Steve

Bannon, the president's newly minted "chief strategist." It was the first time Bannon had ever set foot in the briefing room. It would also be the last. He would become a surprisingly accessible source to some White House reporters, but Bannon would also brand the press "the opposition party," a label President Trump would fully embrace. Bannon would never again physically venture behind enemy lines, even though the briefing room and the adjoining workspace for the White House press are a mere twenty-five paces from the Oval Office.

With the inaugural parade still going on outside, there weren't many reporters in the White House yet. In fact, the group of reporters in the press pool, which is supposed to be with the president at all times, had been left behind at the Capitol building by Trump's press handlers. It would take them a couple of hours to navigate through security and make their way to the White House. Aside from Bannon, Spicer, and a few others, many members of the president's senior staff had not arrived at the White House yet.

With Obama's team gone and much of Trump's team not here yet, there was a home-alone feel to the moment. An ABC camera was positioned in the middle of the North Lawn, directly in front of the White House, to capture live video of the president walking out of the White House and to the viewing platform on Pennsylvania Avenue. There was nobody to tell me I could not go right to the temporary wooden walkway connecting the main entrance of the White House to the presidential viewing area, so at the last minute, I hustled out and positioned myself right behind the military servicemembers lining the walkway with ceremonial rifles. ABC was carrying the entire parade live, so I called into the control room and told special events executive producer Marc Burstein, "I have a feeling the president is about to walk right past me."

About five minutes later, while I was on live television, there came the new president, walking right toward me. He had taken the oath of office just a few hours earlier. The whole thing caught me by surprise—what would I do? In more than twenty years as a correspondent in Washington, I've learned to always be armed with questions for anybody in power, especially the president. But he had just taken the oath of office and toured the White House residence for the first time. I was standing on the lawn of his new, if temporary, home. He was walking out to see a parade commemorating his place in history as the forty-fifth president of the United States. I wasn't even entirely sure I was allowed to be where I was. He nodded at me as he walked by.

"Mr. President, how are you feeling?"

"Really great. Thank you," the president responded.

As it played out on live television, George Stephanopoulos quipped, "Jon Karl, your first interview with the president."

There would be plenty of tough questions to come, but this was a day of ceremony, a day meant to celebrate the defining miracle of American democracy: the peaceful transfer of power from one party to another.

John Adams left Washington the night before Thomas Jefferson was sworn in as the third president. But for every newly elected president since then, with the sole exceptions of Adams's son John Quincy and the bitterly impeached Andrew Johnson, the outgoing president has been there for a generally orderly and choreographed transition. Since Ulysses Grant turned power over to Rutherford B. Hayes after the hotly contested election of 1876, the outgoing and incoming presidents have actually spent the morning of the inauguration together, meeting at the White House and sharing the two-mile ride to the Capitol building for the swearing in. In the election of 1888, President Grover Cleveland was beaten by Benjamin Harrison, but as the rain came down on the inauguration, Cleveland held an umbrella over Harrison's head while he took the oath of office. It was a temporary truce. Cleveland would beat Harrison in a rematch four years later. During the depths of the Great Depression, Herbert Hoover and Franklin Delano Roosevelt rode together from the White House to the Capitol. The two men so detested each other they barely spoke. But it was a cold day and they were riding in a convertible, so they shared a blanket to keep warm.

Donald Trump and Barack Obama shared a level of mutual contempt that made Hoover and FDR seem like old friends. But on January 20, 2017, they too shared that ride. Consider for a moment how few people have done that: In all of American history there have only been twenty-four transfers of power where a president-elect from one party replaced a president from another. I have had the privilege of being present for three of them. Each of them remarkable. Each, by definition, historic—but none like this one.

Harry Truman once said, "The only thing new in the world is the history you don't know." But almost everything seemed new about the arrival of Donald Trump at 1600 Pennsylvania Avenue.

The 2016 campaign had been an adventure that turned upside down just about everything I thought I knew about politics. I had known Donald Trump since I was a twentysomething cub reporter for the *New York Post* in the early 1990s. He was a big name but always accessible, willing to take a call from an unknown and very green reporter for a New York tabloid.

Back then, on a slow news day, I could call up Norma Foerderer,* who sat right outside his office on the twenty-sixth floor of Trump Tower. Without fail, Norma could connect me to Trump, often within minutes. This relationship started when I had been a reporter for only a few months and I pitched him on doing the story about Michael Jackson and Lisa Marie Presley staying at Trump Tower

---

*Norma Foerderer died in 2013, two years before Donald Trump launched his presidential campaign.

shortly after they secretly got married. Trump loved my pitch because it turned a story about the world's biggest pop star into a story about Donald Trump.

As I moved on to the City Hall beat and reported on a first-term mayor and future Trump lawyer Rudy Giuliani, Trump was somebody to call for a colorful quote from time to time. He'd go along with just about anything. On a whim, I once called for help with a book party invitation. I had just written my first book and I was putting together a party to celebrate. As a goof, I included endorsements of the book on the invitation from some of my friends, including my buddy Douglas Kennedy, Frank Luntz, and legendary *New York Post* rewrite man Bill Hoffmann.

Hoffmann had a hand in just about every Trump headline in the *New York Post* in those days, including the most famous one of all. It's Bill Hoffmann's byline on the "The Best Sex I've Ever Had" story during the height of the tabloid frenzy over Trump's affair with Marla Maples. Trump called him "Wild Bill" and would regularly reach out to him with stories. Trump couldn't pretend to be his own spokesman when talking to Bill—no pretending to be "John Barron," as he did with some reporters in those days—but with Bill he almost always had the same ground rule: "You can quote me," he'd say, "but only as a source close to Donald."

When I was making my book party invitation, Bill suggested I call Trump to see if he'd give me a quote too. Why not? So, once again, I called up Norma Foerderer.

It wasn't a particularly serious request. I wasn't asking for a quote to put on the book cover. I was sending out invitations to family and friends for a small book party at the Heartland Brewery in New York and thought it would be funny to have a quote from Donald Trump on the invitation.

Norma got Trump on the phone, and he told me to send him a

copy of the book. A couple of days later I got a call back. He told me to write a quote, and if he thought it was okay, I could use it.

And with that, I became a ghostwriter for Donald Trump. Here's the quote I penned for him and he approved: "What a book! Jonathan Karl is the best in the business: Tough, fair and brutally honest."

He went along with it and everybody got a good laugh. I wasn't the only one to find Trump entertaining in those days. Heck, Bill and Hillary Clinton went to the wedding when Trump married Melania in 2005. He seemed like a cartoon version of a rich developer. He was fun to be around. There was a sinister side to Trump, but at the time, I did not see it.

When I left the *New York Post* and became a reporter with CNN in Washington, it never occurred to me that I would cross paths with Trump again, or that the guy whom I'd called up to give me a quote for a party invitation would end up the president of the United States.

In some ways, Trump the president can still be as entertaining as Trump the flamboyant developer was.

But it's hard to believe this is the same Donald Trump who called "Wild Bill" Hoffmann with little scoops or showed me around Trump Tower, offering quotes as "a source in the Trump Organization." Back then, it seemed like it was all in good fun. He was America's greatest egomaniac. Is that an exaggeration? Maybe, but Trump exaggerated about everything. But what did it matter? He was a guy who wanted to slap his name on everything, and somehow, he managed to find a way to do it even while going bankrupt along the way. He still has the power to be entertaining, but now the stakes are entirely different. His dark side is on full display, and there are real consequences, even though he often seems to worry about little beyond what he has always seemed to cared about most: himself.

In the White House, Donald Trump engages the press as much as he ever did. But a reporter in the Trump era faces a president who seems to have no appreciation for or understanding of the First Amendment and the role of a free press in American democracy. Donald Trump muses about changing libel laws, presumably so he can sue reporters who write stories he finds objectionable. He talks about punishing newspapers and book authors who criticize him. He provokes his supporters at rallies to taunt and jeer at the reporters who are covering him.

He declares us disgusting. Dishonest. Traitors. Enemies of the people.

When faced with such an onslaught from the most powerful man in the country, it is tempting to fight back. And, as a reporter, sometimes you need to fight back. If the president declares real stories fake, the record must be corrected. If a president attempts to block reporters from covering the work of his administration, we need to fight back. If a president attempts to use the tools of law enforcement to target reporters for doing their jobs (something Trump talks about and the Obama administration actually did), reporters and news organizations need to fight back.

But a free press is not the opposition party. Our role is to inform the public, seek the truth, ask tough questions, and attempt to hold those in power accountable by shining a spotlight on what they are doing. We are not the opposition, but in the Trump era, the free press has sometimes appeared like the opposition. For some, that's fine. There's nothing wrong with being an advocacy reporter. The best opinion journalists are those who actually do reporting and offer some real information to back up their views. But there is a crucial role for reporters and news organizations who strive for objectivity and balance. Our opinions—and we all have opinions—should be irrelevant. Even when the person you are covering treats you unfairly or brands you disgusting or a traitor or fake, a reporter should strive to treat him or her fairly. Even if you personally find the policies of a president repugnant, a reporter should report the facts and leave the judgments to others.

This book is about what it is like to be in the front row at the Trump Show—to be taunted by the president and courted by him, to be targeted by his enforcers and then watch him target them. My vantage point is unique—and not just because of where I sit at presidential press conferences. I've known Donald Trump longer than almost all of his top advisors and the reporters who cover him. And I know firsthand what it's like inside a Trump-free White House. I sat in a front-row seat at the White House full-time during the entire second term of President Obama and for periods of time during the presidencies of George W. Bush and Bill Clinton (all presidents, by the way, who also bitterly complained about the press coverage of their administrations even if they didn't publicly threaten or slander reporters the way Trump has).

I also happened to be in the Oval Office when, just two days after the 2016 election, Donald Trump first met Barack Obama. In writing this book, I mined my notebooks, my journals, and my experience to tell a story that is impossible to convey in the crush of day-to-day reporting on the Trump White House: what it is really like to do this job and interact with this president. I have also gone back to interview the key players to learn what was really going on behind the scenes during the most consequential moments of the campaign, the transition, and the Trump presidency.

I call it the Trump Show because that is the way President Trump sees it. He tracks the ratings and the crowds. He follows the reviews. He slams the critics but craves their approval. And when he can't get their approval, he sets out to prove them wrong by pointing to his adoring fans and showing that he can command the world's attention by changing the story line any time he wants to change it.

Donald Trump is the creator, chief publicist, executive producer, and star of the Trump Show. He may be at war with the news media, but he is also in love with the news media. In fact, we have never had a president who so eagerly consumes so much TV news. For Donald Trump, the taunts and personal insults are part of the game. He sees the public jousting with the press as a critical component of the Trump Show's success. But this is a dangerous game. A president's rhetoric, especially rhetoric that incites hatred or willfully distorts the truth, has consequences. I will spell that out, but what you will also see on the pages to come is a president who engages the press directly—and loves doing it. This may be a president who has no appreciation for the role of a free press in American democracy, but he certainly appreciates the role a free press has in promoting the Trump Show.

In fact, there's nothing more fake in the Trump era than Donald Trump's attack on "fake news." Donald Trump rails against the "failing *New York Times*," for example. Don't believe it. He doesn't. Spend time with the president and you won't have to wait long to hear him marvel at how often he dominates the front page. He loves seeing his name on the front page—whether the stories are negative (as they usually are) or positive (a rarity). Occasionally he admits he still loves *The New York Times*. He often lies about the paper losing money, but sometimes he acknowledges it is actually thriving, not failing (circulation is up, and so are profits, since he was elected president), and he takes full credit for its success.

"The *Times*, I think they are going to endorse me," President Trump declared at a September 2018 press conference in New York. And pointing at me, he predicted an ABC endorsement too.

"I think ABC, CBS, NBC, the *Times*—they're all going to endorse me, because if they don't, they're going out of business," he said. "Can you imagine if you didn't have me?"

For the record, the networks don't endorse candidates. And there is no way in hell *The New York Times* will endorse Donald Trump. But tucked inside that presidential untruth are two fundamental truths about the Trump era: 1) Donald Trump craves the attention of the news organizations he attacks and relishes the attention he gets even when it's negative, and 2) reporters and many of the news organizations we work for are thriving thanks to Donald Trump and the intense interest in his actions that is shared by those who love him and those who believe he is a threat to the republic.

But, again, this is a dangerous show. Thanks in part to the president's relentless verbal attacks, White House reporters routinely get death threats. The threats have come through social media, in letters to our homes, and in taunts from people at Trump rallies. Others have had it much worse. Bombs were mailed to CNN in 2018, a murderous intent thwarted only by the incompetence of the fervent Trump supporter who sent them. But there is an even more profound threat than the threat of violence. The president is waging a war on truth, helping to convince millions of Americans that real news is fake, that journalists are partisans out to get him.

Donald Trump has gone to war with the press primarily because he feels personally slighted. He lives in the White House, but he doesn't believe he has received sufficient credit for pulling off the greatest political upset in American history, which he did. And now that he is president, he doesn't think he gets any credit for what he has done. It may be silly for somebody who goes to work in the Oval Office every day to feel insufficiently appreciated, but the truth is that the mainstream media coverage of Donald Trump is relentlessly and exhaustively negative. His accomplishments—and there are accomplishments—are either ignored or overshadowed by the drum-beat of outrage fueled by his own outrageous behavior.

There are reasons a large swath of the American people applauds Donald Trump and doesn't care about the outrages that dominate the cable news channels every single day. Some of Trump's supporters see a president who is willing to stand up to China in a way his predecessors in both parties refused to do. Others see a president willing to take a chance on diplomacy with Kim Jong Un. They may laugh off Trump's talk of love letters from a North Korean dictator, but they can rightly ask, did the sober and experienced foreign policy experts who advised Clinton, Bush, and Obama accomplish anything more than Trump? Or did they fail and leave us at the point we now find ourselves: a North Korea with a sizable nuclear arsenal and a missile program that might just be able to deliver an atomic bomb to San Francisco? Trump's gambit may have only a slim chance of success at best, but the approach of his predecessors has already failed in spectacular fashion.

There are Trump supporters all over the country who look at the outrage of the day—the offensive tweet, the rapid-fire untruths—and ask this: Has Donald Trump made a mistake as profoundly damaging as the decision to invade Iraq to rid Saddam Hussein of weapons of mass destruction that he didn't have? Being stubbornly wrong about the trajectory of a hurricane, as Trump was when he said Hurricane Dorian was heading to Alabama, isn't anything like sending thousands of Americans to die in the Middle East because of mistaken intelligence, but judging from the way the hurricane story dominated news coverage during the first week of September 2019, you might legitimately think some in the news media had lost the ability to distinguish a real scandal from a trivial one. And I write this as the first reporter to mention Trump's mistake about Hurricane Dorian and Alabama on a network newscast.

Donald Trump is aggrieved. And arguably he has reason to be aggrieved. But his response is to wage a war on truth that I fear may do as much or more lasting damage to America than any of the mistakes made by the presidents who went before him. I will come back at the end of this book and explain why.

I don't believe there has ever been a more exhausting, exhilarating, dangerous, maddening, frustrating, downright bizarre, or more important time to be a White House reporter. At minimum, I hope this book will convey a sense of what that has been like. Along the way, I will document, as I have seen it, a war on truth waged by the Trump White House and, above all, by the president himself.

I should add here a note on sourcing. When I am talking to a source there are four possible levels of attribution:

On the Record: This simply means I can freely quote anything and use the name of the person I am quoting.

On Background: I can use the information and I can directly quote the source, but I cannot use his or her name. Instead, I characterize the source's position with an identifier such as "Democratic congressional source" or "Pentagon official" or "senior administration official." This allows the source to speak more freely, even if he or she is not authorized to speak to the press.

Deep Background: I can use the information, but I cannot directly quote or characterize the source. Talking to somebody on deep background can help me in the beginning of reporting a story (suggesting leads to pursue) or at the end of my reporting (helping to gauge the veracity of what others have told me).

Off the Record: I cannot use or quote what a source tells me. Off-the-record conversations are of limited or no value in day-to-day reporting, but I still find them an essential part of news gathering. Off-the-record conversations help me get to know and understand the people I am covering, their motivations, and their thinking. In writing this book, I have gone back to some of my sources and asked if I could now, with the passage of time, use information they told me off the record as events were unfolding. A few of those sources have given me permission to do so.

Each of these levels of attribution implies a level of trust between the reporter and the source or subject. In an on-the-record conversation, a source has a right to expect the reporter will quote him or her accurately and not take words out of context. And if the person being interviewed says something that is not true, the reporter, of course, has a right—in fact, a duty—to point that out. When a source tells me something off the record that turns out to be a deliberate lie, I believe it is no longer off the record. As a journalist, my first and most important obligation is to the truth. I've been lied to by people in the Trump White House who asked to be off the record. When a source speaking off the record lies to me, the implicit agreement between reporter and source has been violated. It is no longer off the record.

But the president's war on truth is just one side of the story. While there has been no shortage of great reporting in the Trump era, all too often reporters and news organizations have aided and abetted the effort to undermine the free press by openly displaying how much they detest this president—his policies, his blatant disregard for the truth, or his vilification of the press—and behaving like anti-Trump partisans rather than journalists striving for fairness and objectivity. We are not the opposition party, but that is the way some of us have acted, doing as much to undermine the credibility of the free press as the president's taunts.

How do you report on a president who will look you in the eye and tell you something he knows is not true? How do you maintain standards of fairness and objectivity when reporting on somebody who has branded you a traitor to your own country? I am still trying to figure that out, but this story starts long before anybody thought Donald Trump would ever move into the old mansion at 1600 Pennsylvania Avenue.

CHAPTER ONE

I'D BE SHOCKED

When Donald Trump gave his first political speech in New Hampshire, arriving with fanfare by helicopter, he found a receptive audience. He wasn't yet a declared candidate, but he drew a big crowd—bigger than any of the well-known and experienced Republicans who had already been campaigning for months.

The speech hit what would become familiar Trump themes: He said he was tired of seeing our country "kicked around," especially by our allies who relied on America to bear the financial burden of their military defense but who ripped off the United States through trade practices that had left us with a massive and growing trade deficit. And he darkly warned of impending doom for the United States.

"I'm tired of nice people already in Washington," he told the crowd. "I want someone who is tough and knows how to negotiate. If not, our country faces disaster."

The New York Times covered the visit and gave Trump almost laudatory coverage, possibly the most positive news story the paper has ever published on anything related to Trump's politics. The headline was frame-worthy—"New Hampshire Speech Earns Praise for Trump"—but it was this line in the story that he loved the most: Trump "drew a bigger audience than have any of the Republican candidates."

An ABC News camera crew went along for the ride to New Hampshire, and the network's *20/20* program devoted a half hour of network prime time to Trump's favorite subject: Donald Trump. Even in those early days, Trump coverage seemed more like reality TV than news.

Nobody thought Trump was actually going to run. And in those days, neither did he.

The year was 1987. Trump was just forty-one years old. And as he prepared to visit New Hampshire in the middle of primary season, he insisted he had zero interest in running for office. But the story was irresistible. A flamboyant entrepreneur was taunting the political class and drawing bigger crowds than the professional politicians in first-in-the-nation primary state New Hampshire.

The *20/20* story, which gathered dust in the ABC television archives until Donald Trump became a presidential candidate, is revealing about Trump in ways that could not have been apparent when it ran in 1987 and, as much as anything, explains Trump's serial flirtation with running for president and, ultimately, his decision to finally do it.

Barbara Walters, one of the biggest stars in the history of television news, was the correspondent on the story and devoted half of the show to Trump at a time when TV news magazines in general, and *20/20* in particular, were among the most watched shows on television. The story begins with an introduction from Walters that reads like it was written by Trump himself. Well, all except for the first line.

"He has negotiated with the Soviets to construct a luxury hotel in Moscow," Walters says, referring to Trump's first effort to build a

Trump Tower Moscow, a well-documented one that included a trip to the Soviet capital that Trump boasted at the time was fully paid for by the Kremlin.

"He owns the most sumptuous yacht in the world," she continues. "In New York, building after building bears his name. He gets more publicity these days than almost any movie star. And some people think he should be president."

The language gets even more over the top. From start to finish, this was a celebrity profile.

"Who? Donald Trump, the master builder. The boyish, outspoken, disarming, shrewd winner. The man who seems to have everything. But what makes Donald Trump tick? What does he want? What can he teach us? And where do we find him? Because he's here, he's there, he's everywhere."

It's enough to make just about anyone, except Donald Trump, blush.

Like the *New York Times* story, Walters makes note of the crowd in New Hampshire. "It was a full house," Walters says over images of Trump working his way through a packed meeting of the Portsmouth Rotary Club. "Trump had attracted over nine hundred people, more than three times the audience that turned out for Senator Robert Dole."

Trump would undoubtedly want you to know that *20/20* that night drew a 19.4 rating as more than seventeen million households tuned in to it, winning the time slot and even beating out the popular *Falcon Crest* on CBS. What he would not mention, however, is that *20/20* actually drew slightly higher ratings the week before the Trump segment and the week after too.

The New Hampshire trip and the talk of a "draft Donald Trump" movement gave Trump what he craved—attention, of course, and the chance to look like the richest of the rich, the master entrepreneur.

Walters, like the folks who invited him to the Portsmouth Rotary Club, seems to be almost begging him to run.

She asks him what his ultimate fantasy would be. He says he is already living his dream life.

"Okay, but come on, the next step," she says. "You can't just keep building and building in New York, you own almost everything."

The answer from the forty-one-year-old Trump was a dodge but could also be used to explain the improvisational, governing-by-gut approach Trump would use in the White House.

"The prizefighters had an expression," he says. "You've got to go with the punches. And that's what I want to do. I don't want to predict where I'm going to be or what I'm going to be doing, I go with the punches. I sort of feel my way around. It's a minefield out there."

The interview also features some of Trump's most candid comments on something else that would become a trademark of his presidency: saying things that just aren't true. Trump talks openly about his ability to lie convincingly as a key to his success, like a poker player with a pair of deuces who can convince his opponent he has a full house.

He describes convincing Holiday Inn to invest in his first Atlantic City project by misleading them to believe the project, which hadn't been started, was already well under way.

"Well, a number of years ago, I was trying to convince a company to come in and they thought we were well under construction," Trump tells Walters. "Literally, I told my contractors to get every truck you can get. And let us look like we're building the Grand Coulee Dam."

WALTERS: Even though you're picking up dirt from one side and dropping it on the other side.

TRUMP: And the question was asked, a couple of people said, why are they digging there and filling up over there and I don't know, I just say, boy, I guess we're really busy.

WALTERS: And they put the money in—

TRUMP: Well, they put money in.

To some, that may sound like fraud. To Trump, it was a great story to boast about on national television.

Could Trump do in politics what he did in the private sector? As the conversation turns to the possibility of a Trump presidency, Walters asks, "If you could be appointed president and didn't have to run, would you like to be president?"

TRUMP: Well wouldn't that be an interesting concept. I mean, wouldn't that be nice if you didn't have to run. I mean I think a lot of people would like that.

WALTERS: Would you?

TRUMP: Would I like it?

WALTERS: Yeah—

TRUMP: I don't know, interestingly, you know, part of the, the enjoyment of something and part of the whole, the whole thing is the battle. If you could be appointed, I'm not sure that would be the same ball game—

WALTERS: Wouldn't be the fun of it—

TRUMP: —would be seeking, it's the quest that really I believe— it's the hunt, that I believe that I love.

Three decades later, there's ample evidence Trump still loves the pursuit more than the prize. After getting elected president, he held political rallies before he was sworn in. He filed papers creating his reelection campaign on January 20, 2017, within hours of taking the oath of office.

That New Hampshire trip more than three decades ago began a Trump tradition. He would flirt with a run for the presidency, get lots of attention, promote himself, and then, ultimately, stay on the sidelines. A decade later, in 1999, he actually formed an exploratory committee and said he was considering seeking the nomination of the now-defunct Reform Party. The centerpiece of his platform back then: a onetime wealth tax of 14.25 percent on everything owned by anybody worth more than $10 million. He estimated this would bring in $5.7 trillion, enough to completely pay off the national debt at the time and, in the process, be the biggest tax increase, by far, in the history of mankind. The New York *Daily News* put the Trump tax proposal on page one with a screaming headline: "SOAK THE RICH."

In the lead-up to the elections of 2004 and 2012, Trump would be at it again, following a by-now-familiar script: Talk about all the people telling you to run and find a poll somewhere that shows Trump at the top (at least three polls in 2011, in fact, showed Trump ahead of Mitt Romney in the race for the Republican nomination), do some interviews, and then, ultimately, opt out.

Less than a year after President Obama's reelection, Trump was at it again, announcing another political trip, this time to Iowa. And that's why Jonathan Greenberger, the executive producer of *This Week with George Stephanopoulos,* called me one afternoon while I was working in the tiny ABC News office at the White House.

"Donald Trump is going to Iowa," he said. "Do you want to go out and do an interview with him for us?"

It was August 2013. There wasn't much happening in Washington. And Trump had been invited to speak at an event hosted by Bob Vander Plaats, an evangelical leader who had endorsed the two previous Republican winners of the Iowa caucuses. That alone seemed to make the trip worthwhile: Why did Iowa evangelicals want to hear from Donald Trump, of all people? And beyond all that, I had one specific issue I had wanted to confront Trump about for the last two years. So, I booked my flight to Des Moines.

As I interviewed Trump in Iowa, I leaned in and asked my first question with an air of disbelief: "You're not really thinking about running for president, are you?" It was really more of a statement than a question. Nobody thought he would run, and if there were any who actually did, nobody thought he had any chance of winning.

My NBC News colleague Chuck Todd took a shot at me and ABC News for airing the interview on our Sunday show *This Week with George Stephanopoulos*, telling Politico: "Trump correctly has surmised that political reporters in general are easy marks, and he probably can't believe how easy it is to find folks willing to cover his antics." In the same article, Republican consultant Rick Wilson said, "He's not going to ever, ever, ever pull the trigger on the race." And Sam Stein of the Huffington Post called Trump's interview with me "performance art," getting him a handwritten note from Trump: "Perhaps Sam—But it sure gave them good ratings!"

It turned out to be a compelling interview, but I had to edit it down significantly: We didn't consider Trump a likely candidate either; it was hard to justify putting him on our hour-long Sunday show for more than five minutes. Here's one exchange that *didn't* make the cut:

KARL: If there were a Trump campaign, what would the motto, the tagline, be?

TRUMP: If I had a campaign and I decided to run, I think it would be very simple for me to say, "Make America Great Again."

The issue I had wanted to confront Trump about was the racist nonsense he had been peddling about Barack Obama's citizenship. I genuinely thought he might issue a mea culpa of sorts. Beyond the occasional tweet, he hadn't talked about it much after Obama ridiculed him so mercilessly at the White House Correspondents' Dinner in 2011. He had not mentioned it in the Iowa speech he had given just before my interview. I wanted to know if he was now ready to disavow what he had done and admit he was wrong. After this interview, he rarely talked about his role in promoting the myth that President Obama was not born in the United States. He seemed eager to move on to other subjects, so I started by giving him a chance to admit he had been wrong.

KARL: So I'm going to give you a golden opportunity here to correct the record on this. Will you now acknowledge that you were just plain wrong about the president's birthplace?

At first, he was both defiant and eager to change the subject.

TRUMP: I'm not taking back anything. I think time will tell. At some point I may be wrong and at some point I may be right. There are many people who think at some point, I'll be right. But it's too late for that now. He's president. Jonathan, it's too late for that now. I'd much rather talk about what China's doing to this country, how they're ripping us, how OPEC is ripping us. That's where I am.

KARL: But there's never been any serious question that President Obama was born in the United States.

TRUMP: Oh, really? Well, there's about 49 percent of the public that would disagree.

KARL: You think 49 percent of the public would disagree?

TRUMP: I do. I do. I think a big percentage of the Republican Party absolutely thinks that—you said, though, there was never any question. Of course there's a question. Of course there's a question. There are many questions—and many people are asking those questions and they continue to ask those questions. So again, it's not my issue. But because my real issue is economic and I want to see if this country can again be great. But certainly there are questions, Jonathan.

At this point in the interview I was genuinely surprised that even after Obama's reelection, even after Trump had stopped talking publicly about the birther conspiracy, he was still defending it.

KARL: You don't still question he was born in the United States? Do you?

TRUMP: I have no idea.

KARL: You don't believe him?

TRUMP: I would; I'd love to believe him.

KARL: He put out his birth certificate!

TRUMP: Well, I don't know, was there a birth certificate? You tell me. You know some people say that was not his birth certificate. So maybe it was; maybe it wasn't.

KARL: You don't think it was his birth certificate?

TRUMP: I don't know. I mean, I really don't know. A lot of people say it wasn't. Hey, Jon, you're not a stupid person. You read the same things I read. There are many people that question the validity. And you know what? I hope I'd be wrong. I'm not even saying I'm right or wrong. I'm saying I don't know. Nobody does. And you don't know either, Jonathan. You're a smart guy. You don't know either.

KARL: I'm pretty convinced he was born in the United States.

And now Trump thinks he's got me. I've admitted that I'm only "pretty convinced" that Barack Obama is a natural-born citizen!

TRUMP: Pretty, ah. Pretty. No, no, you said pretty.

KARL: I am convinced totally without question he was born in the United States.

TRUMP: Jonathan, you said you're pretty convinced. Okay? You can't be pretty convinced. That's not convinced. He has to be born in the United States. So let's just see what happens over time, what—it's not my issue, Jonathan. My issue right now is much different.

KARL: Wait a minute.

TRUMP: My issue is economic. Our country is being ripped apart by China and many other countries. That's my issue.

KARL: But isn't it getting harder for people to take you seriously on those issues if you don't acknowledge that you went overboard on this whole birther stuff?

TRUMP: Well, I don't think I went overboard. Actually, I think it made me very popular.

KARL: But on this issue, people think you're out to lunch—

TRUMP: Well, you just said you're pretty sure. You're pretty sure. That's not acceptable because you know, you can't be pretty sure. You have to be one hundred percent sure.

KARL: I'm sure. I'm one hundred percent, for the record.

TRUMP: Jonathan, you're too smart to say you're one hundred percent sure.

After the interview, Sam Nunberg, who was then Trump's sole paid political advisor, called me to say Trump insisted that I include the part of the interview where I "admitted" I was only "pretty sure" Barack Obama was a natural-born citizen. And then, before the interview aired, Trump tweeted about his gotcha moment:

Donald J. Trump
(@realDonaldTrump)

@jonkarl interviews me on This Week during which time he stated that he was "pretty sure" President Obama was born in the U.S. Bad question

8/11/13, 5:59 AM

More than a year later, in December 2014, I learned Trump was coming to Washington to give a speech to a business group and decided I wanted to interview him again. This time I was actually more interested in talking to him about real estate than politics. The Trump Organization had been awarded a contract, and a ninety-nine-year lease, to build a hotel at the site of the Old Post Office building on Pennsylvania Avenue, just five blocks from the White House. The project fascinated me. I had done a series of stories in 2010 on vacant real estate owned by the federal government, and the Old Post Office building was the most outrageous example of the government allowing prized real estate to rot away unused.

The building—truly one of the great architectural gems in Washington—occupied a block of the most valuable real estate in the nation's capital but had been largely vacant for more than a decade. After my first stories on the subject, I covered a congressional hearing on the issue in 2011 that was held right there in the building's run-down atrium. The building was no longer heated—members of the House Committee on Transportation and Infrastructure wore coats as they questioned officials from the General Services Administration.

The Obama administration decided to do something about it and began a process of selling off and leasing vacant federal properties, which is why the Old Post Office was put up for bid by the GSA. And, remarkably, it was Donald Trump who won the bid.

To set up the interview, ABC News producer Jordyn Phelps called up Michael Cohen, who was then Trump's lawyer and fixer. Jordyn, who was then a junior producer just a few years out of college, soon found this was not your ordinary interview booking. Cohen warned her that if the interview didn't go well, he would personally jump in front of the camera. And he'd do more than just jump in front of it. If Cohen didn't like the questions, he told her, he would knock the camera off the tripod. "Do you understand what I am saying?"

Well, there is one thing Jordyn understood completely. After talking to Cohen a couple of times to lock in the interview, she prophetically told a colleague about Cohen's threats and added, "That guy is going to end up in jail."

Sure enough, Michael Cohen ended up in prison. But only after his boss ended up in the White House.

Cohen didn't make any threats to me directly and the interview, which I conducted for an online series I did for ABC and Yahoo! called *Power Players,* took place right where that congressional hearing had been held. The building was then a construction site. He had barely broken ground on the project, but there was already a giant blue sign out front for anybody traveling on Pennsylvania Avenue between the Capitol building and the White House to see: "Coming 2016: TRUMP."

Trump boasted about the project and proclaimed it would be complete before the next presidential inauguration. To his credit, he was right. He managed to win the bid for arguably the most prized piece of commercial real estate in Washington and create a first-rate hotel, completing the project right on time.

With the "Coming 2016: TRUMP" sign out front, I, of course, asked him about politics. Trump was about to make his second trip of the year to Iowa. Looking at the interview now, it seems as if neither one of us is taking the idea of a Trump campaign seriously.

Noting the big sign out front, I asked him if he was disappointed he'd made it to 1100 Pennsylvania, but for all his presidential flirtations, he'd never made it to 1600.

KARL: And I saw outside the huge billboard—you can't miss it—Trump 2016.

TRUMP: It does say Trump 2016, which is an interesting thing.

KARL: Yes it is. So I have to ask you: How does it feel—are you a bit disappointed that you didn't quite make it to the White House five blocks away? You can almost see it.

His answer was classic Trump. His building, he suggested, is better than the one Obama is living in.

"Well in terms of pure real estate this may be better because it's between the both [the White House and Capitol Hill], so it may be better," he told me. "This is where everyone should meet, you know, they should come from the White House and from Congress; they should meet right here and make their deals."

And then, finally, I had to ask:

KARL: But you're not thinking about running for president, are you?

TRUMP: Well I'm looking at it, I'm going to give very serious
  consideration, that I can tell you.
KARL: Are you really?
TRUMP: We're going to see what happens. We may surprise you.
  You would be surprised.
KARL: I would be shocked.

Yes. I would be shocked. But Trump didn't get offended by my flip
dismissal of the idea he would run for president. In fact, he smiled,
not shocked in the least that I said I'd be shocked. In fact, it seemed
as though he might just be shocked too. And for some reason, this
interview would loom large in Trump's mind for years to come. He
brought it up to me and to others more than a half dozen times after
he became president. Each time he mentioned it, he said I deserved
credit for taking him seriously as a presidential candidate, acknowledging that I took heat for the interview, but "You got great ratings."

CHAPTER TWO

THE CANDIDATE

Hope Hicks was a former Ralph Lauren model who just a few months earlier had been doing PR for the Trump Organization's resorts and Ivanka Trump's fashion line. Now, in September 2015, she was the sole spokesperson and press secretary—and the one-and-only communications staffer—for the front-runner for the Republican presidential nomination.

"Mr. Trump is ready to see you now."

That was not what I had expected to hear. I had come to Trump Tower to have coffee with Trump's twenty-six-year-old press secretary and instead was being whisked up the elevator to the twenty-sixth floor to meet with "Mr. Trump." She had kept me waiting in the lobby for nearly forty minutes, and now she was taking me into the elevator and up to meet with her boss.

I had known Donald Trump for years and had already talked to him several times since he'd launched his campaign, but his campaign staff was still a mystery to me. The other candidates had experienced consultants and ad makers, pollsters and state directors, media advisors, press secretaries, opposition research specialists, and communications directors. But as far as I could tell, other than campaign manager Corey Lewandowski, the key players on Trump's campaign were Trump's former caddy, Dan Scavino, who helped out with his Twitter and Instagram accounts, and Hope.

Hope had no previous experience with, nor much interest in, politics before suddenly becoming the sole spokesperson for the Republican front-runner. She was a one-woman communications operation. It was Hope who took all the media calls. It was Hope who booked the interviews. It was Hope who wrote the press releases and sent them out. It was Hope who did it all.

At the campaign headquarters for the Democratic front-runner in Brooklyn, by comparison, there was already a paid communications staff of more than two dozen people that included some of the most experienced people in American politics. Hillary Clinton's campaign employed a former White House communications director (Jen Palmieri), a former communications director for First Lady Michelle Obama (Kristina Schake), a former director of public affairs for the Department of Justice (Brian Fallon), and a former communications director for the Democratic Congressional Campaign Committee (Jesse Ferguson). And each of them had experienced deputies and assistants.

A staff directory of the Hillary Clinton campaign at the time included a lead press secretary, a day-to-day spokesperson, a traveling press secretary, a director of rapid response, a rapid-response spokesperson, a director of media planning, and a regional press team with state press secretaries. Hillary's campaign staff also included a women's press lead, a director of coalitions press, a director of Hispanic media, and a director of African American media. And more. Lots more.

The Trump campaign had only Hope.

So, when I arrived at Trump Tower on September 1, 2015, it was Hope Hicks I really wanted to see. I had talked to her plenty since Trump launched his campaign, but I had not really gotten a chance to get to know her yet. And on this day, I still wouldn't get a chance.

Instead of chatting over coffee, we were on our way to Donald Trump's office.

I hadn't been in Trump's office in years, but it seemed to be almost exactly as it had been when I first talked to him there as a reporter for the *New York Post* more than twenty years earlier. There were the framed magazine covers on the wall from floor to ceiling and, as before, no television set (odd for a guy who watched so much TV news). Trump greeted me with a handshake and invited me to sit down across from his desk.

"Have you seen the latest polls?" he asked. And with that, Trump pulled out a new national poll that showed him with his biggest lead yet.* I actually had not seen it.

"I'm at thirty-seven percent! Nobody else is even close," he said.

And he kept going, saying—correctly and without exaggeration— that he had been way ahead in all the polls since the first Republican debate, hosted by Fox News, a few weeks earlier. Well, all of them except one. There was an Iowa poll, he confessed, that had just come out that morning with Trump and Ben Carson tied with 23 percent.† I hadn't seen that one yet either.

"But I can't go after him," Trump told me, "because he keeps saying the nicest things about me."

As I spoke with Trump about his campaign and his recent sugges- tion that he'd favor raising taxes on "the hedge fund guys" (something that violated what had long been thought to be a cardinal rule of Re- publican primary politics: Thou Shalt Not Raise Taxes), his assistant Rhona Graff walked in and told him Rob O'Neill was on the line.

---

*He was talking about a poll of Republican voters from Morning Consult, and it had Trump at 37 percent with none of the other candidates in double digits. Jeb Bush, the erstwhile front-runner, was tied with Ben Carson at 9 percent.

†A Monmouth University poll of Iowa Republicans released that morning did, in fact, have Trump tied with Carson at 23 percent. The poll had Jeb Bush tied with "Unde- cided" for sixth place.

As Trump reached for the phone, he asked me, "Do you know who Rob O'Neill is?"

No, I said, wondering if he meant the former Yankee right fielder Paul O'Neill. "Who's that?"*

"Rob!" Trump said, answering the phone. "I'm here with the great Jonathan Karl of ABC News and he can't believe you are calling me! He's going wild about it!"

In truth, I was actually sitting there perplexed and a little embarrassed that I had no idea whom Trump was talking to.

I didn't really learn much about Trump's campaign plans during that meeting in Trump Tower, but I did, right there with that phone call, learn that Donald Trump lies for comic effect, he lies to make himself feel good, he lies to make you feel good, he lies because he likes to, he lies because he can.

In his book *Commander in Cheat*, the great sportswriter Rick Reilly recounts playing golf with Trump at the Trump National Golf Club Westchester in Briarcliff Manor, New York. Trump kept on introducing him to people as the publisher of *Sports Illustrated* or, alternatively, the magazine's president. When they were alone, Reilly, who was a columnist and not the publisher or president, asked, "Donald, why are you lying about me?"

"Sounds better," Trump told him.

Trump has no problem lying if the lie sounds better.

After about a half hour, I said goodbye to Trump and asked Hope if I could see the new campaign office downstairs on the fifth floor. She didn't have time to show me around, but she dropped me off and left me to wander about on my own. I couldn't believe what I found. The Trump campaign headquarters, right there on Fifth Avenue in

---

*As I should have known, Rob O'Neill is the retired Navy SEAL who was part of the team that killed Osama bin Laden and later claimed to be the one who fired the bullets that actually killed him.

Trump Tower, looked nothing like anything else in Trump Tower, but it looked exactly like what you would expect a campaign headquarters to look like. Or, more accurately, it looked like a movie set of a campaign headquarters.

This was straight out of central casting.

Here, in the gold and glittering confines of Trump's opulent masterpiece on Fifth Avenue, was a suite of rooms with exposed concrete walls littered with campaign posters. There were card tables—the kind you would expect to see with campaign volunteers sitting around them in folding chairs stuffing envelopes. There was an older woman sitting on a stool at a receptionist desk by the door beside a telephone, ready to answer phone calls. But there were no volunteers stuffing envelopes, just one guy sitting with a laptop at one of the card tables. And the woman by the door smiled and told me how excited she was about Mr. Trump's campaign, but her phone didn't ring once while I was there.

There was a mailroom, where I found a couple of guys going through boxes stuffed with incoming mail—again, central casting. I then saw an earnest and polite young guy who told me his name was Johnny McEntee.

McEntee was twenty-five years old and, I learned, a former University of Connecticut quarterback who had briefly worked for Fox News. He told me he was the campaign's "trip director." He seemed genuinely excited to be part of a presidential campaign and offered to show me around, bringing me up a flight of stairs to the floor immediately above the headquarters. There, he showed me a real movie set. Or, more accurately, a reality TV set. There was a fake bank of elevators opposite an empty seat for a receptionist, just like the one downstairs by the door to the campaign office. And around the corner: a long, imposing conference table and two large doors. It was the set for *The Apprentice*. Trump's hit NBC show had been filmed right there in Trump Tower. The old *Apprentice* set was a little dusty, because it had not been used for the last year or so, but still perfectly intact and just one floor above the campaign headquarters, which also looked just like a TV set.

The campaign was ridiculously understaffed. The campaign headquarters didn't look real. But there was one indisputable reality: Donald Trump was far ahead in the polls and well on his way to winning the Republican nomination. The last people to come to terms with this reality were the people he was running against, especially the guy who had been considered the front-runner.

The day after Trump came down the escalator in the atrium of Trump Tower and declared his candidacy with his infamous attack on Mexico—"They're bringing drugs. They're bringing crime. They're rapists"—Jeb Bush had an interview with ABC News anchor David Muir in Iowa. Minutes before the interview, Tim Miller, one of Bush's top aides, sternly warned ABC News political director Rick Klein that if Bush was asked about Donald Trump, the interview would not go well. Jeb, Miller explained, did "not want to talk about trivialities." Klein did not pass the threat on to Muir.

Trump was a showman with a propensity for insults, exaggerations, and provocations. Jeb Bush portrayed himself as the thoughtful candidate, the former governor with a record of accomplishment and big ideas on everything from immigration to education. He was also the clear front-runner, leading almost all the polls taken before Trump descended down that escalator at Trump Tower. Jeb's wife, Columba, had been born in Mexico, and he had long spoken and written passionately of the benefits of immigration and compassion for those who came to the United States in search of a better life, even if they came illegally. You might think he would have wanted to step forward and condemn Trump's scapegoating of immigrants. Instead, he was determined to ignore him.

Like so many other Republican stalwarts, Bush avoided talking about those Trump "trivialities" until Donald Trump was well on his way to taking over the party.

I traveled to New Hampshire several months later to interview Jeb on his campaign bus. By then, Bush's standing as the Republican front-runner was already a distant memory. A newly released Fox News poll had him in a four-way tie for fifth place with just 4 percent of the vote. I was starting to wonder if he would drop out before the New Hampshire primary. But he still had plenty of money and a sleek campaign bus with "JEB!" emblazoned on the sides.

As we rode around in the bus, I asked him about the news that he had just hired a new consultant to help him prepare for the next round of debates.

"What's he telling you?"

"He's telling me to be me," Bush told me. "To own what I believe."

"You need a consultant to tell you that?" I asked.

"Yeah. It's amazing, eh? Probably not. Probably not."

Amazing, indeed. But what was more amazing was Bush's reaction when I brought up Donald Trump.

"What?" he said to me before I could complete a question. "You want me to talk about Donald Trump? Not going to happen."

"You're not going to talk about Donald Trump?" I asked. "He's the front-runner!"

"I don't need to talk about him."

I also asked him why his campaign and his super PAC were instead unloading on Marco Rubio, whom not long ago Jeb had been touting as a future president. Immediately after the interview was over, Bush campaign manager Danny Diaz was in a rage, denouncing me to others at ABC News and proclaiming I would never get another interview with Jeb Bush. Never.

Bush wasn't alone, of course, in ignoring Trump as he solidified his standing as the undisputed front-runner for the Republican nomination. In the lead-up to the Iowa caucuses and New Hampshire primary, none of the candidates wanted to talk about him. In August, after Trump dominated the first Republican primary debate in Cleveland, John Kasich abruptly ended an interview with me backstage after I started asking him about Trump.

There were exceptions to the thou-shalt-not-talk-about-Trump ethos of most of the Republican field. Scott Walker tried to take on Trump, calling on the Republicans to make a united effort to defeat him. Rick Perry was even harsher, saying Trump's candidacy was "a cancer on conservatism and it must be clearly diagnosed, excised, and discarded." He added: "It cannot be pacified or ignored."

But Perry was so far down in the polls by the time he denounced Trump that barely anybody noticed.* And Walker denounced Trump not as a candidate but as a dropout, waiting until his speech ending his campaign to issue his call for action against Trump.

While the other Republicans were afraid to challenge him, there was one force in Republican circles that was willing to take him on: Fox News.

By the time Donald Trump got to the White House, Fox News, for the most part, had become relentlessly pro-Trump, often sounding more like a Trump mouthpiece than a news channel. There are some very good journalists at Fox News—especially Bret Baier, Chris Wallace, and John Roberts—but the network's morning and prime-time shows spent most of Trump's first years in office relentlessly promoting him and tearing down his critics. In 2018, the network's biggest star, Sean Hannity, actually spoke at a Donald Trump rally.

---

*Rick Perry, who would go on to serve in President Trump's cabinet as secretary of energy, endorsed candidate Trump after it was clear he would win the Republican nomination. "He is not a perfect man. But what I do believe is that he loves this country and he will surround himself with capable, experienced people and he will listen to them," Perry told CNN in May 2016. "He wasn't my first choice, wasn't my second choice, but he is the people's choice."

But as Donald Trump marched toward the Republican nomination, he found Fox News often much tougher on him than his future nemesis, CNN, which was frequently friendly territory for Trump.

In the battle for the Republican nomination, there was no arena more important than Fox News. And Fox News chief Roger Ailes made it clear to the network's top executive that he—and Fox News—had favorites.

"Roger and Rupert [Murdoch] wanted to be kingmakers," one former senior Fox executive told me. "There wasn't a written list, but we all knew the top choice was Jeb, followed by Rubio and Kasich."

Another former Fox News leader confirmed this to me, adding that Chris Christie was sometimes in favor too, but not Donald Trump.

Roger Ailes didn't want to promote Trump, but he also didn't want to be at war with him. After the first debate in Cleveland, that's exactly where he found himself.

Trump, due to his standing already as the leader in the polls, was center stage at the debate on August 6, 2015. But he also found himself a target with the very first question from co-moderator Bret Baier.

BAIER: Is there anyone onstage, and can I see hands, who is unwilling tonight to pledge your support to the eventual nominee of the Republican Party and pledge to not run an independent campaign against that person? Again, we're looking for you to raise your hand now—raise your hand now if you won't make that pledge tonight.

Baier knew exactly what he was doing. He was putting Donald Trump on the spot, highlighting perhaps his biggest vulnerability at that time among Republican voters: He had refused to rule out running as an independent if he lost the nomination.

As Trump stood at center stage raising his hand the crowd in Cleveland booed. Quite a way to start a debate.

That first question enraged Trump, but not as much as the debate's fifth question, which came from Megyn Kelly.

KELLY: Mr. Trump, one of the things people love about you is you speak your mind and you don't use a politician's filter. However, that is not without its downsides, in particular, when it comes to women. You've called women you don't like "fat pigs," "dogs," "slobs," and "disgusting animals." Your Twitter account—

TRUMP: Only Rosie O'Donnell.

(LAUGHTER)

KELLY: No, it wasn't.

(APPLAUSE)

KELLY: Your Twitter account . . .

(APPLAUSE)

TRUMP: Thank you.

KELLY: For the record, it was well beyond Rosie O'Donnell.

TRUMP: Yes, I'm sure it was.

KELLY: Your Twitter account has several disparaging comments about women's looks. You once told a contestant on *Celebrity Apprentice* it would be a pretty picture to see her on her knees. Does that sound to you like the temperament of a man we should elect as president, and how will you answer the charge from Hillary Clinton, who is likely to be the Democratic nominee, that you are part of the war on women?

But perhaps the thing that infuriated Trump most is what happened after the debate.

Shortly after the debate ended, Fox News had pollster Frank Luntz come on air with a focus group of Republican voters. The group trashed Trump, prompting Luntz to declare him the big loser of the debate.

"He just crashed and burned," one focus group participant said of Trump. "He was mean, he was angry, he had no specifics."

Another voter in Luntz's focus group said he was "repulsed" by Trump's refusal to promise to support the eventual Republican nominee.

Trump vented his rage through Twitter, tweeting multiple times about Luntz, calling him a "clown," and also tweeting until three in the morning after the debate, attacking Fox News and the moderators.

Donald J. Trump
(@realDonaldTrump)

@FrankLuntz is a low class slob who came to my office looking for consulting work and I had zero interest. Now he picks anti-Trump panels!

8/7/15, 2:28 AM

The attacks from Trump continued the next day, one after another.

Donald J. Trump
(@realDonaldTrump)

@FoxNews you should be ashamed of yourself. I got you the highest debate ratings in your history & you say nothing but bad . . .

8/7/15, 3:35 PM

The morning after the debate, Fox News executive Bill Shine stayed in Ohio to watch the WGC-Bridgestone Invitational golf tournament at the Firestone Country Club in Akron. There, he got a call from Roger Ailes, who told him Trump was going to war with him and with Fox News.

"Work out a truce," Ailes told him. "This has to stop."

Who do you call when you're ordered to work out a truce with Donald Trump? Shine called Trump lawyer and fixer Michael Cohen.

The Shine/Cohen conversation, filled with shouting and profanities, went on and on and on. Cohen accused Fox of colluding with the Republican National Committee to go after Trump, setting him up with the questions from Baier and Kelly, and attempting a knockout blow by rigging the Frank Luntz focus group.

But eventually Shine and Cohen worked out a truce. The terms were simple: Fox would stop criticizing Trump, and Trump would stop inciting his millions of Twitter followers with attacks on Fox News. Fox couldn't take Megyn Kelly, the network's biggest star, off the air (although she did take the next week off in what Fox described as a long-planned vacation), but they could banish Frank Luntz, who appeared regularly as a commentator in addition to doing his focus groups.

And sure enough, late that afternoon, Luntz got a call from a show producer at Fox. He was scheduled to be on Fox that night, but, the producer told him, he would no longer be needed.

"We're moving in a different direction," the producer explained.

Not long after that, Luntz got calls from other Fox producers saying his scheduled appearances the next day, a Saturday, were also canceled. Each time, the same reason was given: "We're moving in a different direction."

"They took me off the air because Trump demanded they take me off the air," Luntz told me.

But this Fox/Trump truce didn't last more than a couple of hours. And it didn't take much to derail it.

Trump saw Charles Krauthammer appear on one of the Fox shows. Krauthammer, who died in 2018, was a Trump critic who thought Trump lost the debate badly, and he said so right there on Fox News—after the big truce.

An infuriated Trump took to Twitter, declaring: "Dopey @krauthammer should be fired."

Before I go further, a few words about "dopey" Charles Krauthammer. While he was in medical school, he had a diving accident that kept him in the hospital for fourteen months and left him paralyzed from the waist down. He went on to earn an MD from Harvard, study political philosophy at Oxford, and win a Pulitzer Prize for Commentary, and be generally seen as one of the most influential and respected conservative thinkers in America. "Dopey Krauthammer" was not the most inspired Trump nickname.

But it was war once again. Trump booked himself on CNN and went nuclear. He chose CNN's nine P.M. show, anchored by Don Lemon, who would go on to be one of Trump's harshest critics, but with Fox and Trump at war, he was more than happy to play along.

Trump phoned into Lemon's show and stayed on for nearly a half hour. It was in this interview Trump issued his infamous attack on Megyn Kelly.

"She gets out and she starts asking me all sorts of ridiculous questions," Trump tells Lemon, "and you know, you can see there was blood coming out of her eyes, blood coming out of her wherever."

Lemon did not confront Trump about the now-famous "blood

coming out of her wherever" line—words that would be roundly denounced in the coming days as blatantly sexist and misogynist—but
instead asked him about some of the other harsh things he had said
about Kelly on Twitter and posed it as a question of political strategy,
not inappropriateness or morality.

"A lot of people are wondering about this language when it comes
to women. Do you worry that that kind of talk might drive some
women voters away?" Lemon asked Trump.

The entire interview is really something to see. Trump rants
on and on about how unfair Fox had been to him and calls out
debate co-moderators Bret Baier ("I lost all respect, frankly, for
Bret Baier") and Chris Wallace ("He had blood pouring out of his
eyes too").

Lemon tees up one question after another for Trump. And it's
only toward the end of the interview that Lemon says, "Just so you
know, Megyn Kelly is a very respected journalist." Trump: "She's a
lightweight."

And look how Don Lemon—a future Trump nemesis—ended his
interview with Trump the day after the first Fox debate:

LEMON: Donald Trump, you're welcome to come cohost with me
     anytime and we thank you for joining us.
TRUMP: Okay, good. We'll beat everybody. You and I will beat
     everybody.
LEMON: I really do appreciate you coming on.
TRUMP: All right, thank you very much, Don. Thank you
     very much.

A few days later, Ailes himself had to work out a truce.

"Roger Ailes just called," Trump announced with a tweet four days after the debate. "He is a great guy & assures me that 'Trump' will be treated fairly on @FoxNews."

But before long that truce quickly fell apart too, like the first. Tensions between Fox News and Donald Trump would continue to flare up from time to time until once again going nuclear right before the next Fox News debate in January 2016 in Iowa.

Trump announced he would boycott the debate because of Fox's rough and unfair treatment of him.

Fox News responded with a blistering statement, dripping in sarcasm, the first time a major television network went on the attack and mocked a presidential candidate.

"We learned from a secret back channel that the Ayatollah and Putin both intend to treat Donald Trump unfairly when they meet with him if he becomes president," said the Fox News statement. "A nefarious source tells us that Trump has his own secret plan to replace the Cabinet with his Twitter followers to see if he should even go to those meetings."

The statement didn't have a name attached to it, but it didn't need one. It was written by Roger Ailes himself.

The Trump campaign responded with its own statement: "Roger Ailes and Fox News think they can toy with him, but Mr. Trump doesn't play games."

It turned out Donald Trump did not need Fox News as he made his steady march to the Republican nomination, and one of the reasons he did not need Fox is that he was getting so much attention—and free airtime—from CNN and other mainstream news organizations that found his candidacy irresistible for the same reason many of their viewers did: He was unconventional, unpredictable, and far more interesting than the all-too conventional, predictable, and dull candidates he was running against. It's one of the great ironies of Trump's rise as a political candidate. He was fueled by the media organizations he attacks so relentlessly today and thwarted, albeit ineffectively, by the news organization that now often unabashedly supports him. As Fox mocked Trump in those early days and CNN covered virtually his every public utterance, it seemed nobody took his chances of actually winning the Republican nomination seriously until there was no turning back.

CHAPTER THREE

A DARK TURN

Donald Trump was adamant: If he was going to do the interview, it had to be in front of a Christmas tree.

It was just a few days before Christmas 2015, and I suppose it was good to see the Republican front-runner in the Christmas spirit, but the message wasn't exactly delivered in that spirit.

Here's how Trump aide George Gigicos, the person tasked by Trump to get the Christmas tree and place it prominently, put it when ABC's John Santucci talked to him about the logistics for the interview: "You are going to have a fucking Christmas tree in this fucking interview that is going to air during the fucking Christmas season."

Okay, fine, we'd have a Christmas tree, but Santucci wasn't quite ready to agree to it yet. He understood the rhythms of the Trump campaign, and the whims of the candidate, better than just about anybody. John Santucci was the ABC News reporter/producer who traveled everywhere Trump traveled. Television networks have journalists who follow every public move of the major presidential candidates; they're usually young, super-talented, and ambitious recent college grads who are prepared to devote a year (or more) of their lives to a campaign. They are called "embeds" because they spend so much time with the candidates that they are essentially embedded in their campaigns.

As our Trump embed, Santucci went to virtually all of the Trump rallies. He tracked the comings and goings of Trump's unconventional campaign staff. He booked the interviews (by this time, George Stephanopoulos alone had done seventeen interviews—seventeen!—with Trump as a candidate). He made a point of getting to know everybody there was to know on the campaign—the senior staff, the people who set up the rallies, the security staff, the drivers, everybody. He also got to know Trump's family and spoke to Don Jr., Eric, and Ivanka regularly. Santucci is from Queens, New York, which may be why Trump himself also took a liking to him. In fact, his grandfather had been the Queens district attorney and had known Trump's father.

At twenty-six years old, he already had one of the most high-stress and high-stakes jobs in network television. Before becoming an ABC campaign embed, he had been a booker/segment producer for *Good Morning America*, which meant on any given day he could be tasked with getting the big interview for the network morning show, a show that can live or die based on whether someone like John lands the big interview. When a major story hits, one of two things can happen to a *GMA* booker: 1) They book the big guest and be a hero, or 2) They explain to the bosses why *GMA* has just been beaten by the *Today* show.

By the time Trump announced his candidacy, ABC had embeds with more than a dozen Republican presidential candidates. Santucci was assigned to a candidate who was, at that time, believed to be in the top tier, Senator Rand Paul. But Santucci, still playing his booker role, had helped book an interview with Trump for George Stephanopoulos to be taped at Trump Tower immediately after Trump announced he was running for president. That's why Santucci was over there for the famous escalator ride; he had gone along with Stephanopoulos for the interview.

At this point, ABC had not assigned an embed to Trump. I mean, why would we? It didn't seem like Trump was going to put much into the campaign. After all, he was announcing his candidacy downstairs from his office. And this had to be the only presidential candidate to actually pay actors to cheer him on as he made his announcement.* That's right, a company hired by the campaign put out a casting call, offering actors $50 to come over and cheer on Donald Trump as he announced his candidacy. That day, when Trump fixer Michael Cohen brought Stephanopoulos over to the part of the lobby where the announcement was about to be held, he leaned over and said, "Watch this."

"Ladies and gentlemen, George Stephanopoulos!" And with that, the paid actors convincingly applauded as George walked through the atrium—a dress rehearsal of sorts for the supporting cast.

After Trump's announcement, ABC still didn't have an embed assigned to his campaign, but Santucci was told, "You keep an eye on him."

So, as we prepared to do that interview in Grand Rapids six months later, Santucci had two concerns about the Christmas tree. First, he was worried we would arrive in Grand Rapids and find the tree in the middle of the shot; he told Gigicos it had to be in the background. Second, he told Gigicos he didn't want to come there to find the tree decorated with big "Make America Great Again" balls. As Santucci knew better than anybody, you could not take anything for granted with these people.

---

*The *Hollywood Reporter* uncovered the casting call, put out by a company called Extra Mile, which offered actors $50 to attend "an event in support of Donald Trump and an upcoming exciting announcement he will be making." FEC filings later showed the campaign paid $12,000 to the company that hired Extra Mile.

I flew to Grand Rapids with our team, which also included ABC producer John Parkinson and two camera crews, to the DeltaPlex Arena, an old hockey arena built in the 1950s for the Grand Rapids Rockets of the long-defunct International Hockey League. There was a full-blown Trump carnival outside: people hawking MAGA hats, T-shirts, and all kinds of Trump merchandise; a smattering of protestors; and hundreds more Trump supporters than could fit in the arena.

Inside, the arena was loud and packed—easily exceeding its seven-thousand-person capacity. I was ushered to a small room with white cinder-block walls just behind the stage. It was sparse, with nothing inside except for my two camera crews, two black leather love seats, and one big Christmas tree. There were no MAGA ornaments on the tree, but there was an enormous "TRUMP" poster on the wall right behind it.

I had pitched the interview to Hope Hicks as a year-end retrospective on the campaign, on the journey Trump had taken from that first Iowa trip in 2013, when nobody thought he would even get into the race, to being the dominant leader. But there was some current news to get to as well.

That morning PolitiFact, a nonpartisan organization that specializes in fact-checking the statements of politicians, had announced the winner of their "Lie of the Year" award, a dubious annual distinction that had gone to Barack Obama two years earlier for his oft-repeated promise about Obamacare: "If you like your health plan, you can keep it." In 2015 PolitiFact was so overwhelmed by Trump's propensity to say things that are not true that they awarded the Lie of the Year to "the campaign misstatements of Donald Trump." They simply couldn't single one out.

I wanted to ask Trump about that and some of his more recent and flagrant untruths. But I also knew Trump would ask about his favorite subject at the time: polls. He led all of them. None of the other Republican candidates were close anymore. Trump led polls in Iowa. He led polls in New Hampshire. He led polls in South Carolina. He led polls nationally. He led them everywhere. And he loved to talk about how he was trouncing his Republican rivals. But more recently he had been looking ahead to a race against Hillary Clinton and saying he was the only Republican who could beat her, usually adding the admonishment "believe me."

Over the course of the previous several months, there had been more than two dozen polls that included a question on whom voters would prefer in a hypothetical general election race of Donald Trump versus Hillary Clinton. General election polls taken before the first primary voters have even voted are essentially worthless, but Trump loved polls. He talked about them every single day.

I figured that if Trump, in my interview, was going to claim he would trounce Hillary Clinton, I would ask him about those polls. And those general election polls were every bit as one-sided as the GOP primary polls, except instead of showing Trump as the clear front-runner, they projected him to be the clear loser. Every single one of them had Hillary Clinton beating Trump.

Again, so far in advance of the election, those polls aren't worth much, but I wanted to be ready if Trump first brought up the issue. After all, one of the few arguments the rest of the fading Republican candidates would make against Trump is that he would be a loser in a general election. He may have attracted hard-core conservatives, the argument went, but he'd be toxic to the swing voters Republicans needed to win over in a general election, especially independents, suburban women, and Hispanics. And now Trump was claiming exactly the opposite.

With Santucci's help, I found an arena employee who essentially helped us break into a small office upstairs where I could print out a list from the RealClearPolitics website that included some six months of Clinton-Trump polls. As the papers came out of the printer, San-tucci shook his head and told me, "He's not going to like this."

Trump came into the interview clearly energized by the crowd outside, energized by his standing in the race, and fired up about a Barbara Walters special with him and his family that had aired on ABC a month earlier.

"The Barbara Walters special did fantastically," Trump said to me as we took our seats for the interview. "Eleven million people on a Friday night, at ten o'clock on a Friday night!"

And how about that crowd? "There are nine thousand people," he said. "The biggest they ever had was seven thousand. We broke every record."

This was well-placed bravado. And he probably wasn't exaggerating. It may not have been exactly nine thousand, but it was hard to imagine when there had ever been so many people at the DeltaPlex Arena, probably not even when the Rockets took on the Cincinnati Mohawks in the 1953 IHL finals.

As the interview began, I asked Trump if he was surprised by the direction of the campaign, if he had expected to see himself dominating the crowded Republican field so quickly.

"Not to this extent, Jon, and not this quickly," he said. "I mean really it's very quick and we're doing so amazingly well and we have such a big lead and I want to keep the lead because ultimately what difference does it make if you're not going to keep the lead?"

I did not intend to ask about the Hillary Clinton matchup until the end of the interview. After all, this was supposed to be a year-end retrospective on his campaign. But he brought it up first, telling me, as he said so often in his speeches, that he was the only Republican who could beat Clinton.

"The last person that Hillary Clinton and her people want to run against is me," he told me. "And in the recent Fox poll, I'm leading. I'm beating her by five points."

In my hand, I had the list of the polls taken since July. There was no Fox poll, or any other poll, during that entire time that had Trump beating Clinton—but it had dozens of polls showing Clinton beating Trump.

"If you look at every single poll over the six months, they have Hillary beating you," I told him.

I did not know it at that time, but Trump was right. There were, in fact, two recent Fox News polls that showed Trump beating Hillary Clinton by five points. The most recent poll had also shown Marco Rubio and Jeb Bush beating Clinton by even larger margins. But, for whatever reason, they were not, at that time, on the Real-ClearPolitics list of polls. The list I held in my hand was wrong.

"If you are so sure that Hillary Clinton is going to beat me, you shouldn't be interviewing me because you are wasting your time." And with that, Trump reached out his hand and gave me a firm handshake.

"Quote the polls where I win," he said as he got up. "Goodbye."

Alarmed that I had traveled all the way to Grand Rapids and hired two camera crews for an interview that had now lasted less than four minutes, I continued the conversation, getting up and walking with him.

"When you interviewed me in the Old Post Office, people criticized you for interviewing me," he told me, referring to my interview with him in 2014, as the Trump Organization was beginning construction of the new Trump hotel on Pennsylvania Avenue.*

---

*Trump has brought up this interview with me many times, always saying that I was criticized for the interview but got great ratings. It's true that it was one of the early interviews with Trump during the 2016 cycle, but it was not my first with him. And I actually didn't get criticized for this interview. I got criticized for my interview with him in August 2013 in Iowa.

"Yes," I replied, "people said, 'Why are you paying attention to Trump?'"

"So, now I ran, I am beating everybody."

A few steps from the door, he stopped, put the microphone he had been wearing into my hand, and said, "Listen, do you hear that?"

"Trump! Trump! Trump!" The sound of the crowd was booming through the cinder-block walls of our little room.

"You hear those people?" Trump said to me. "I have to go get them."

And with that, he walked out the door. After about a minute, John Santucci followed him, and then I went out. There, in the dark walkway between the wall of the interview room and the black curtain separating us from the massive crowd in the arena, I saw a side of Donald Trump I had never seen before.

About twenty-five or thirty feet away, Trump was about to walk onstage, but seeing me, he started screaming and waving his arms, spewing profanities.

"Fucking bullshit! Fucking nasty guy! That was fucking bullshit!"

As I started to walk toward him, Santucci jumped in front of me and said one word: "Don't."

I noticed that as Trump continued to scream, George Gigicos and Corey Lewandowski were standing between us and Trump, keeping him from coming back to me just as Santucci was keeping me from going forward toward Trump. Gigicos finally got Trump to turn, and he walked through the black curtain and onto the stage to thunderous applause.

And he wasn't done yet.

Onstage, Trump went after me, but he held back from calling me out by name.

"You know, I was just with somebody from ABC, I won't mention who," he told the crowd. "And he said, 'Oh, the Hillary camp said they'd love to run against Trump.' Of course they're gonna say that. . . . Ask Jeb Bush if he enjoys running against me. Seriously. Ask him."

That was actually a good point—Jeb Bush didn't think Trump would be a threat until after Trump had destroyed him.

And Trump kept going, continuing to lash out at ABC.

"I mean, George Stephanopoulos interviewed me the other day, it was terrible," he said as the crowd started booing. And then, in the next sentence, he took that back. "It was one of the great interviews, did anybody see that interview? But you know, he's a big—he's a big Hillary fan. Tonight I was interviewed by another Hillary fan from ABC."

I've been yelled at before by senators and scolded by candidates. I've been threatened by political advisors. But I had never witnessed anything quite like this.

My questions were not hostile or aggressive. I had asked much tougher questions of Trump in virtually every other interview I had done with him, but any suggestion that he was, or could be, a loser enraged him. And although he was enraged, he was also fully aware of the cameras. He didn't show that rage until he was out of the room and out of sight of the cameras.

Later in the speech, he talked about how great it would be if America could have better relations with Russia and attacked those who had said he was too easy on Vladimir Putin.

"They said, he's killed reporters," Trump said. "I don't like that. I'm totally against that."

Then, pointing at the press area in the middle of the arena floor, he turned it up a notch.

"By the way, I hate some of these people over here. But I would never kill them."

And then, pausing for effect and peering out at the press area, he said, "Huh? Let's see, uh . . ."

The crowd laughed as the candidate joked about killing reporters.

And, by the way, an alarming number of journalists have been killed in Putin's Russia. The Committee to Protect Journalists had, by the time of Trump's speech in Grand Rapids, documented the murder of at least twenty-four journalists since Putin came to power in 2000.*

"No, I wouldn't," Trump said. "I would never kill them. But I do hate them. And some of them are lying disgusting people, it's true. It's true. But I would never kill them and anybody that does, I think would be despicable."

While Trump was speaking, I asked campaign manager Corey Lewandowski to get him back to finish the interview. I told Lewandowski I had many things to ask about besides the general election polls—something that came up only because Trump brought it up first. If he came back, he'd have a chance to talk about other things.

And sure enough, Trump came back. The guy who had screamed "Fucking nasty guy" at me just an hour or so earlier was once again all smiles, like nothing had happened.

After the interview, he asked me if I wanted to get a picture taken with him. The true answer was no. Why would I want that? But, not wanting to be rude, I agreed. My facial expression in that photo, right in front of that Christmas tree, captured my mood at the moment—Trump grinning and me staring, without a smile, at the camera.

Trump had insulted and taunted reporters since the early days of his campaign, but there in Grand Rapids, the last rally before Christmas 2015, I sensed he was taking a dark turn. He was no longer complaining about unfair coverage or insulting individual reporters; he was crafting a new role for the press in the Trump Show. We were the villains. His crowds loved the attacks on the press and he was about to give them more of what they wanted.

---

*In this speech, Trump cast doubt on whether Putin had any responsibility for any of those murders. "They say he killed reporters," Trump said. "I said, really? He says he didn't. Other people say he didn't. Who did he kill?"

Trump's first rally of 2016 was on January 2 in Biloxi, Mississippi. Mississippi may seem like a strange place to find a New York real estate developer, but this was, by now, the heart of Trump country. The Mississippi Coast Coliseum—considerably larger than the DeltaPlex Arena in Grand Rapids—was filled with die-hard Trump supporters, well beyond the building's ten-thousand-person capacity. Trump called it the largest political rally in Mississippi history. Maybe or maybe not, but it was bigger than anything Biloxi had seen in a long, long time.

It only took about thirty minutes before this rally got really strange.

"These cameras back here right now, they will never show this crowd," Trump said, pointing to the press area, just as he had done in Grand Rapids, when he said he hated a lot of reporters but would not murder them.

"They'll never show this crowd. No, no, they're never going to show this crowd. They're never going to show it. Turn it. Turn it. Turn it. Spin it. Spin the camera. Spin the camera."

As he pointed to the camera in the middle, the crowd started to pick up Trump's chant: "Turn it! Turn it! Turn it!"

"Ah, look at the guy in the middle," Trump said. "Look at the guy in the middle. Why aren't you turning that camera? Why aren't you turning the camera? Terrible."

The guy behind the camera in the middle that night was a longtime photojournalist named Stuart Clark. And on that night, he was working for all five of the big TV networks—ABC, CBS, CNN, Fox News, and NBC. As the pool camera operator, he had one job that night, and it was a crucial one. He needed to keep the camera focused at all times on the candidate, on Donald Trump. If he failed to do that, he would be letting down all of the television networks.

You see, during the campaign, the networks pool their resources. Everybody needs the head-on camera shot of the candidate, so instead of having five cameras focusing solely on the candidate, there is one. And that camera shares the video feed with all five networks. There's a rotation to determine which network provides the pool camera, and it goes in alphabetical order. After ABC, it's CBS, then CNN, Fox News, and NBC, and then the rotation repeats. The nonpool cameras are free to shoot the crowd or anything else they want, but the pool camera must get the speech and only the speech.

Nobody understands this system better than Donald Trump. If you watch his speeches, he plays to that center camera. He knows it's the pool camera and he knows the pool camera shoots the video that the cable networks use when they broadcast his speeches live.

So, on that night Trump decided to try to bully Stuart Clark into doing something he was not allowed to do.

"It's so terrible," Trump said, staring at Stuart. "Look at him, he doesn't turn the camera. He doesn't turn the camera. It's disgusting— I'll tell you, it's disgusting."

I know Stuart. I've known him for a long time. When I was a reporter at CNN (from 1996 to 2003), Stuart was an Atlanta-based photojournalist, and he was one of the best at the network. If he had any political views, he never expressed them in front of me, and regardless, they were entirely irrelevant to his job. We had worked together during the 1996 campaign, when I was CNN's "Generation X" correspondent, responsible for covering the campaign with an eye toward the issues and concerns of younger voters. In 2000, I alternated between the Bush and Gore campaigns and often found myself on long campaign trips with Stuart.

And now, Donald Trump was inciting ten-thousand-plus supporters. But instead of raging against "the media"—a broad and vague target—he was raging against Stuart Clark.

"I go home all the time, and my wife, she watches on television, it's always live," Trump said. "She watches on television, she always says, like she'll say tonight when I get home like one o'clock in the morning, she'll say, 'Darling, did you have many people there?' she'll say. 'They never take the camera off your face, they don't want to show the crowd.' That's what it is. They don't want to show."

And then, again glaring at Stuart, Trump went on the offensive: "They're really dishonest people. No, they are. No. Look at the guy in the middle. Look at that guy. Turn the camera. Turn it."

Stuart had become a CNN cameraman in 1985, shortly after he graduated from Ohio University. He had seen it all. He'd covered wars, natural disasters, and presidential campaigns. He was a pro, one of the network's go-to videographers for the long, grueling job of covering presidential campaigns, usually spending six to nine months of the year on the road. It's backbreaking work, lugging hundreds of pounds of camera equipment as you follow candidates from city to city, state to state.

But Stuart had never been in a situation where a candidate had singled him out as an object of derision. It took him about a minute to realize Trump was targeting him. The crowd in the coliseum started booing him, making obscene gestures in his direction, and Trump kept going, feeding on the energy of the crowd, now being directed at Stuart Clark. The rant went on for several minutes.

"It's so damn unfair, the press. It's terrible. It's terrible," Trump said, again pointing at Stuart.

"I mean, that guy, that guy right there, who do you shoot for? That guy right there has not moved that camera. It's disgusting. All right, enough. He won't move it. He's instructed by his bosses, do not move the camera."

He knew. Most candidates would not have known, but this was Donald Trump, who knew how this worked better than any of them.

"They'll fire him, I guess," he said. "It's really, it's really terrible."

At that point, the crowd of ten-thousand-plus started chanting: "Fire him! Fire him!"

"Yeah, I'd fire his ass right now," Trump said to thunderous applause, a dramatic moment in the Trump Show, a new villain introduced and called out by the big man.

The crescendo reached, Trump moved on and so did the crowd. But Stuart Clark was shaken. He had stood his ground. He had done his job. But he had just become the most unlikely target of a political smear during the entire campaign.

"I just sucked it up and did my job," Stuart later told me.

As the rally ended and the crowd left, Stuart stayed behind in the fenced-off press area. After that experience, he didn't want to have somebody take a shot at him as he left, lugging all his equipment, heading off to cover the next Trump rally.

The networks recognized the threat, thereafter sending their own security to Trump rallies. But Trump's team did not.

The CNN producer working with Stuart that night went up to campaign manager Corey Lewandowski after the incident and urged him to tell Trump to stop doing that.

"It's dangerous," the CNN producer said.

Lewandowski looked at him and laughed. "Yeah, right."

CHAPTER FOUR

MEXICAN GAMBIT

I t was about ten P.M. on August 30, 2016, when I got the call.

After another long and grueling day on a long and grueling campaign—I had been up nearly eighteen hours—all I wanted to do was go to sleep. But the call was from John Santucci, our frenetic and equally sleep-deprived digital reporter embedded in the Trump campaign. This had to be important.

"Trump is going to Mexico tomorrow."

The guy who wanted to build a wall and force Mexico to pay for it, the guy who launched his campaign by accusing Mexico of sending drugs and criminals and rapists to America—that guy was going to Mexico in the middle of a presidential campaign?

Fascinating.

But what did this have to do with me? Trump was on a western campaign swing and was just about to start speaking at a rally in Everett, Washington. I was not traveling with him. All I was looking forward to at that moment was a full night's sleep for the first time in over a week.

"There's a flight out of Dulles at five forty in the morning."

Good to know. But I still didn't know why he was calling *me* about it.

I rattled off a few questions about the candidate's trip to Mexico. What time is Trump going? Who is he meeting with? Where is the meeting? If I suddenly showed up in Mexico and we knew where the meeting was taking place, would I be allowed in to cover it?

"We don't know."

Santucci had gotten a tip from somebody involved in planning the rather complicated logistics of sneaking one of the most recognizable politicians in the world—one who traveled on a Boeing 757 with his name emblazoned on the sides—into Mexico in the middle of a presidential campaign. Thanks to Santucci, we knew Trump was going to Mexico, but that was all we knew. Now wheels were in motion to send me to Mexico City at the crack of dawn. I wasn't convinced. And I wanted to go to bed.

"What am I supposed to do," I asked, "hail a taxi at the Mexico City airport and say, 'Take me to Donald Trump'?"

As I debated the merits of sending me to Mexico with our political team—or, more accurately, as I was pleading not to go on what I was sure would be a fruitless attempt to run after Trump in a city with about as many people as Donald Trump has Twitter followers—@realDonaldTrump sealed my fate with a tweet:

Donald J. Trump
(@realDonaldTrump)

I have accepted the invitation of President Enrique Pena Nieto, of Mexico, and look very much forward to meeting him tomorrow.

8/30/16, 10:33 PM

We still didn't know the timing of the visit or the exact location, but I had to start packing. And while I was not happy about it at the time, I was about to embark on a reporting adventure unlike any I had ever experienced, in this campaign or any before it. And it would be a trip far more important than I realized at the time. The next twenty-four hours would prove to be a foreshadowing of things to come in the Trump White House.

Trump's son-in-law, Jared Kushner, had been secretly discussing the possibility of a trip with Mexico's foreign minister for about two weeks. He had raised the idea with campaign chairman Steve Bannon, and Bannon had immediately embraced it. Bannon saw the trip not just as a good idea but as a way to turn around a campaign that was struggling badly.

As Kushner had begun working on the trip in mid-August, the RealClearPolitics average of public polls showed Hillary Clinton with a seven-point lead over Trump. And the campaign's internal polling showed Trump had a real problem with working-class voters who were attracted to Trump's economic message but could not imagine him as commander in chief.

"Hillary had such impressive foreign policy credentials," Bannon later told me, "we had to get people to visualize him as commander in chief."

Putting Trump side by side with a foreign leader, Bannon figured, would go a long way toward convincing voters that Trump could play the role of president on the world stage. "We just had to have big presidential visuals," he said. He especially liked the idea of these visuals because Mexican president Enrique Peña Nieto was significantly shorter than Trump; not only would he be sharing a stage with a head of state, he would be sharing the stage with a head of state who would literally have to look up to Trump.

A trip to Mexico might help address that problem, but this was a high-risk gambit. After all, Trump had launched his campaign by accusing Mexico of sending criminals and rapists to the United States. More recently he had declared of Mexico, "They are not our friend, believe me." And then there was the diplomatic challenge of the border wall. Trump, of course, had been promising over and over again that he would force Mexico pay for it. For his part, President Peña Nieto had compared Trump's brand of populism to Hitler's and Mussolini's.

A visit with the president of Mexico could make Trump look presidential. Or it could be a total disaster.

In Kushner's discussions about the trip with the Mexican foreign minister, there were two immutable conditions: 1) There would be no questions from the press, and 2) There would be no discussion in public of the sticky issue of how to pay for the border wall. The two men would appear side by side at podiums as if they were both heads of state. The cameras would roll. They would make carefully scripted statements. They would shake hands. And then they would leave. Mission accomplished.

Back in Everett, Washington, the press corps traveling with the Trump campaign was about to learn they were getting screwed.

At this point in the campaign, Donald Trump was the Republican nominee, which meant there was a press charter plane that went along with the candidate wherever he went, carrying about a hundred or so reporters, photographers, and video camera crews. These were the journalists who were paid to be present for every public move of the candidate, big or small. They worked for news organizations that spent a great deal of time and money and resources traveling around the country with the candidate so they could document and report on everything he did. Day after day, the reporters went from event to event. Press charters are paid for by the news organizations, but they are run by the campaign. This was the case with the

Trump campaign; it has been the case with every campaign I have covered.

Some of these events make a lot of news, some of them don't, but the traveling campaign press has to be there for all of them. Now Trump was about to take off on a hugely news-making, possibly dangerous, and arguably historic trip, and the campaign was going to leave the traveling Trump campaign press stranded hundreds of miles away.

So, in the morning, Donald Trump flew from Washington State to Los Angeles, en route to Mexico City, and the press charter, filled with infuriated reporters, flew to Phoenix, where the campaign said Trump would be giving a speech that evening on immigration. The traveling press was left in the lurch on one of the biggest moments so far in the campaign. Zeke Miller of *Time* magazine summed up the feeling of the reporters left behind, correctly calling it "a troubling departure from precedent."

By reluctantly jumping on a predawn flight to Mexico City, I was gambling that somehow we would find a way to cover the meeting.

By the time I arrived in Mexico City shortly before noon, we'd learned more details about Trump's plans: The event would be at Los Pinos, the residence of the Mexican president, but we still didn't know if any foreign press would be allowed inside to cover the event.

All morning, I had been exchanging text messages with a little-known Trump campaign aide named Aaron Chang. Chang was an advance guy—one of those people that every campaign (and every White House) employs to plan trips. They travel before the candidate— hence "advance"—and run through all the moves a candidate will make ahead of time so everything is in place and tested out by the time the candidate arrives. Chang knew how to handle complicated trips and security issues. He had worked advance for the 2004 Bush-Cheney reelection campaign and worked for a time as operations director for the Washington Nationals baseball team. I had first met him on a trip to Afghanistan with then–Vice President Cheney, a trip that included a suicide bomb attack at the entrance to the base where Cheney, his staff, and those of us in the press traveling with him were staying.

His job wasn't to work with the press, but he made sure that the Mexicans would have my name on the list of people allowed into the presidential palace, along with ABC producer MaryAlice Parks, who was traveling with me and our local camera crew.

When we arrived at the presidential residence, MaryAlice gave me a high five. We were the only American reporters there. The gamble we had taken by jumping on that 5:40 A.M. flight was paying off. The Mexican president's communications staff ushered us into a holding room along with a large contingent of Mexican press. They gave us some food and coffee while we waited, but they also gave us a stern warning: No questions would be permitted. We were there to witness the statements made by Trump and Peña Nieto, not to ask questions. Eventually a few other reporters, including CNN's Jim Acosta, arrived. They had gambled too, ditching the press charter and getting to Mexico City on their own.

When we were escorted into the room for the press statements, both Acosta and I managed to get seats in the front of the press section, right behind the seats set aside for the senior advisors to Trump and Peña Nieto.

The scene was remarkable—two podiums set up before a green marble wall that looked like the backdrop at the United Nations General Assembly. There was a Mexican flag but no American flag— perhaps because Trump was a candidate and not a government official, or perhaps because the Trump team forgot to bring one.

Soon after taking my seat, I spotted Hope Hicks off to the side and gave her a wave. She came over and said, "You made it!" Her enthusiasm struck me as odd; the campaign had done just about everything possible to prevent reporters from making the trip. I told her that after coming all this way, I sure hoped Trump would answer a question or two. She gave me a look that seemed to say, "Yeah, right," and walked back over to the side of the room. Eventually three of Trump's top campaign advisors came in and sat right in front of me: Senator Jeff Sessions, Rudy Giuliani, and Jared Kushner.

Back in New York, Steve Bannon was watching the scene unfold on television as Peña Nieto and Trump came out to make their statements. The visuals were precisely as he wanted them. The statements were perfectly bland and diplomatic. Peña Nieto, speaking through a translator, treated Trump just as he would have the president. Noting that America was in the midst of "vibrant debate" in a presidential election, he said, "I have publicly expressed my respect to both Mrs. Hillary Clinton and Mr. Donald Trump." Perfect! And then: "Just as I have done with my good friend President Barack Obama, the next American president will find in Mexico and its government a neighbor willing to work constructively to further strengthen the relations among our nations."

When it was Trump's turn to speak, he seemed entirely at ease—measured and deliberate as he read remarks that sounded almost like they could have been written by the Obama State Department.

"We had a very substantive, direct, and constructive exchange of ideas," Trump said. "We're united by our support for democracy, a great love for our people, and the contributions of millions of Mexican-Americans to the United States."

There was Donald Trump, in Mexico, praising the contributions of Mexican-Americans to the United States. And he kept going, now adding a little Trumpian flair to his praise for the people he had vilified repeatedly since he launched his campaign a year earlier.

"I happen to have a tremendous feeling for Mexican-Americans, not only in terms of friendships, but in terms of the tremendous numbers that I employ in the United States. And they are amazing people. Amazing people," he said. "First-, second-, and third-generation Mexicans are just beyond reproach. Spectacular, spectacular, hardworking people."*

Trump's statement went on for more than seven minutes. He criticized the NAFTA trade deal and called for a secure border, but he did so in the most diplomatic way. His only mention of a border wall was strikingly vague: "We recognize and respect the right of either country to build a physical barrier or wall on any of its borders." And, of course, there was no mention of who would pay for such a wall.

Bannon got on the phone with Hope Hicks, who was still standing on the side of the room.

"This is fucking great!" he said.

As soon as Trump finished the last line of his remarks—"It has been a tremendous honor, and I call you a friend, thank you"—Jared Kushner jumped up from his chair and so did Jeff Sessions. And so did I. Kushner and Sessions wanted Trump to get out of there. I wanted to ask the great unaddressed question.

From the back of the room somebody bellowed: "Sit down!" and all three of us sat down. It was just one of the camera operators, but he yelled with such authority everybody obeyed.

Acosta yelled a question about how the meeting went and Trump answered with more Trumpian diplomatic talk: "Excellent!" "Tremendous!" "More than an hour!" "Really very good!"

Then he called on me. And as I started to ask my question, Bannon started to flip out back in New York.

---

*Once again, this is the same Donald Trump who said the following on June 16, 2015, when he announced his candidacy for president: "When Mexico sends its people, they're not sending their best. They're not sending you. They're not sending you. They're sending people that have lots of problems, and they're bringing those problems with us. They're bringing drugs. They're bringing crime. They're rapists. And some, I assume, are good people."

"What the fuck are you doing?" he screamed over the phone to Hope Hicks. "Cut it off! We have got to stop it!"

As Bannon later told me: "It was our nightmare. We had it set up so that guys like you could not ask questions."

But as the cable networks carried the event live, Trump wasn't ready to let this moment on the world stage end just yet. He wasn't going anywhere. He looked right at me and waited for my question.

"Mr. Trump, over the course of this campaign, do you regret some of the things you have said about Mexico or Mexicans and do you want to take them back?"

Turning to Peña Nieto, I continued: "And same to you, Mr. President, you've said some very harsh words directed toward Mr. Trump, would you like to take back some of those? And the wall? Is it a non-starter? Is there any chance Mexico pays for the wall?"

"Well, I'll start, there's nothing like an easy question like that," Trump said. "We did discuss the wall, we didn't discuss payment of the wall. That'll be for a later date."

Peña Nieto then responded to my question, but he did not answer it. He had said many times before that Mexico would not pay for the wall, but at that moment, standing beside Donald Trump and asked directly about Trump's oft-repeated promise that Mexico would pay for a wall that Mexico did not want, the president of Mexico said nothing about it.

And with that, the two men shook hands one more time and quickly exited the room. The choreography worked perfectly until that moment at the end. But it was a choreography that defied reality. For these two men to meet and read scripted statements as if the harsh insults had never been said, as if Trump's demand that Mexico pay for his signature campaign promise had never happened, was absurd. I'd had my doubts about making the trip because I did not think I would make it in time and had no guarantee I would be able to get into the meeting. But I didn't make the trip to dutifully transcribe carefully scripted comments.

Despite the repeated warnings, I was going to ask my questions. In a situation like that, it is the reporter's responsibility either to get an answer or to demonstrate that the politicians are ignoring the questions. To Trump's credit, and his campaign's chagrin, he listened to the question and he answered.

But the moment he took the question, the story line for the trip changed. In Mexico, Peña Nieto was eviscerated for failing to stand up to Trump. His approval rating tanked and he was ridiculed brutally in the Mexican press. Former Mexican president Vicente Fox called him a traitor for inviting Trump and failing to stand up to him. Peña Nieto waited until after Trump was back in the United States to answer the question I had asked. Yes, he insisted, despite what Trump had said they did discuss payment for the wall and he had told Trump Mexico would not pay for it under any circumstances. Too little. Too late. The Mexican press pummeled him for not saying that while Trump was standing by his side.

Overall, the trip was a good one for Trump, but the question left him looking weak. With bravado, he had promised countless times that Mexico would pay for the wall, but when given a chance to talk directly with the Mexican president, he'd either failed to bring it up (in Trump's version of events) or he had done so and the Mexican president had rebuffed him (Peña Nieto's version of events). Either way, it didn't look good.

As Trump flew back to the United States, there was growing speculation that he might actually be softening his stance on immigration now that he had secured the Republican nomination and was going into a fall general election campaign where his hard-line positions might not go over so well.

In fact, a week before the Mexico trip, Trump had said he was open to a "softening" of some current immigration laws, and he'd said it in an interview with right-wing talk show host and immigration hard-liner Sean Hannity, of all people.

"Is there any part of the law that you might be able to change that would accommodate those people that contribute to society, have been law-abiding, have kids here?" Hannity asked him during a town hall meeting in Austin, Texas, on August 23, 2016.

"There certainly can be a softening because we're not looking to hurt people," Trump answered. "We want people. We have some great people in this country."

But by the time he returned to the United States after his trip to Mexico City, the old Donald Trump was back. For his speech that night, to a full house at the Phoenix Convention Center, the campaign promised a major policy speech. Trump would be outlining his ten-point immigration plan. Can you guess what point number one was?

"Number one," Trump bellowed. "Are you ready?"

Audience: "YES!"

Again, he said: "Are you ready?"

Audience: "YES!"

"We will build a great wall on the southern border!"

The crowd, of course, went wild. Trump stepped back from the podium and let his supporters take over.

"Build that wall! Build that wall! Build that wall!"

Trump let the chant build for a while and then, staring directly at the network pool camera that was shooting the video being broadcast live on the cable networks, he delivered the message that he had failed to deliver just a few hours earlier when he was meeting with Mexico's president.

"And Mexico will pay for the wall—believe me—one hundred percent."

As the applause died down, he added: "They don't know it yet, but they're going to pay for the wall."

Trump went on for over an hour, introducing parents of children killed by undocumented immigrants. The "amazing," "spectacular," and "hardworking" immigrants he had been talking about just a few hours earlier in Mexico were once again the rapists, drug dealers, and killers he had talked about over and over again on his way to winning the Republican nomination. And now it was rhetoric with specifics. For the first time, Trump outlined in detail his hard-line immigration plan, the plan he would bring with him to the White House.

He said he would repeal President Obama's Deferred Action for Childhood Arrivals (DACA) policy, which allowed those who had illegally come to the United States as children to remain in the country legally. He said he would deny a visa to anybody coming to the United States from a country that didn't have adequate screening (the core of what would become President Trump's travel ban). And he called for a zero-tolerance policy toward illegal immigration, the policy that would lead to the separation of undocumented families at the border.

"Hillary Clinton," Trump said, "talks constantly about her fears that families will be separated. But she's not talking about the American families who have been permanently separated from their loved ones because of a preventable homicide."

And in a rhetorical flourish, he suggested Hillary Clinton herself should be deported.

There would be no more talk of Donald Trump's "softening" on immigration.

CHAPTER FIVE

FOUR HUNDRED FIFTY ROSES

On Friday, October 7, 2016, Vladimir Putin received a massive bouquet of four hundred fifty roses—a gift for his sixty-fourth birthday, one rose from each member of the Duma, the lower house of the Russian parliament.

"Let's send him the bouquet with gratitude for his hard work and with our promise that we will all work with him for the benefit of our great Russia," proclaimed lawmaker Valentina Tereshkova.

Back in the United States, dawn was breaking on the most consequential day yet of the Trump era, a day when just about everybody assumed it was all over, but it was really just beginning.

News coverage that morning was dominated by Hurricane Matthew, a Category 5 storm that had already torn through Haiti and was moving up the east coast of Florida. Several conservative commentators, including radio host Rush Limbaugh, claimed media accounts were exaggerating the storm to scare people about the threat of climate change. In Washington that morning, Secretary of State John Kerry issued a blistering statement accusing Russia of aiding Syrian dictator Bashar al-Assad's attacks on civilians in the city of Aleppo.

"These are acts that beg for an appropriate investigation of war crimes," Kerry said. "And those who commit these would and should be held accountable for these actions."

As for the campaign, it appeared to be a quiet day. With the second of three planned Clinton/Trump debates just two days away, both candidates were taking a break from the campaign trail, huddling with aides and preparing. Hillary Clinton was at the Doral Arrowwood resort, not far from her home in Chappaqua, New York, doing practice debates, complete with a replica of the stage that would be used Sunday night in the town-hall-style debate to be moderated by my ABC colleague Martha Raddatz and CNN's Anderson Cooper. Philippe Reines, Clinton's combative communications advisor with a reputation for browbeating reporters with profanity-laced diatribes, played the part of Donald Trump. There were no mock debates for the Trump campaign, but even the famously practice-averse Donald Trump spent much of the day huddled with his top advisors— including Steve Bannon, Jared Kushner, David Bossie, Kellyanne Conway, Chris Christie, and Reince Priebus—tossing around possible debate questions and answers in a conference room on the twenty-fifth floor of Trump Tower.

Shortly after noon, Hope Hicks received a media inquiry that would throw the presidential race into chaos and dominate news coverage for the final stretch of the campaign—and a story that, in hindsight, was actually only the third-most important development of the day in terms of the lasting impact on the race and the nation.

David Fahrenthold of *The Washington Post,* a quirky and dogged reporter who made a name for himself (and eventually earned a Pulitzer Prize) with his relentless reporting on the Trump Foundation and Trump's dubious claims of charitable giving, told Hicks he had obtained a video outtake from an interview Trump had done with Billy Bush on the TV program *Access Hollywood* in 2005. Hicks had dealt with countless Trump controversies over the course of the campaign, but she knew this one was different. Here was Donald Trump on tape bragging about his ability to sexually assault women because of his fame. The transcript of the tape was horrific.

"You know, I'm automatically attracted to beautiful [women]—I just start kissing them," he is heard telling Billy Bush. "I don't even wait. And when you're a star, they let you do it. You can do anything. Grab 'em by the pussy. You can do anything."

Hicks pulled Conway, Bossie, and Bannon out of the debate prep session and showed them the transcript. Then she called Kushner out. Eventually the only people left with Trump in the conference room were Christie and Priebus.

"Where the hell did everybody go?" Trump asked.

"I don't know," Christie responded, "but whenever all my staff left the room without telling me, it was never good news."

Trump yelled for everybody to come back into the conference room, and as they did, Hicks handed him the transcript.

"This doesn't sound like me," Trump said as he started reading it.

They decided to have the campaign's lawyer, Don McGahn, call *The Washington Post* and demand to see the actual tape. Trump told Kushner to get an audio expert ready to review it and expose it as a fake. Fahrenthold sent over the actual video and Hicks played it for the group on her laptop computer. After listening for less than thirty seconds, Trump looked up: "Oh, yes. It's me."

The campaign now faced an existential crisis.

While Trump and his advisors debated how to respond—and before *The Washington Post* published the story and released the tape for the rest of the world to hear—there was another story developing in Washington.

At three P.M., the Department of Homeland Security and the Office of the Director of National Intelligence released a joint statement placing blame on the Russian government for the recent hacks of the Democratic National Committee's emails and the public release of those emails on WikiLeaks. The release of those emails had been timed to do maximum damage. WikiLeaks had started posting them just as the Democratic National Convention was getting under way. There had been suspicions that Russia was behind the hacks, but this was an official statement by US intelligence placing the blame not just on "Russians" but "the Russian government." And the statement made two other allegations: 1) The theft and public release of these emails was intended to interfere with the presidential election, and 2) "Only Russia's senior-most officials could have authorized these activities." In other words, Putin himself was trying to interfere with the US presidential election.

The statement on Russian interference immediately generated big headlines and breaking-news coverage on the cable news channels. The Obama White House was getting requests from reporters for briefings for more information on these explosive allegations.

But the frenzy of interest subsided an hour later, when David Fahrenthold's story—along with the incriminating video—was posted on WashingtonPost.com.

The story of the *Access Hollywood* video immediately overtook the story about Russian interference. At the White House, Communications Director Jen Psaki and others on her staff watched the *Access Hollywood* story unfold and assumed the presidential race was now over. The idea of putting together briefings for reporters on Russian interference suddenly seemed less urgent. Several members of the White House communications staff went out for drinks—an early Friday happy hour.

As soon as the story hit the *Washington Post* website, Hillary Clinton's mock debate at the Doral Arrowwood resort came to a screeching halt as her top aides gathered around to watch the video on the laptop of Bob Barnett, the Washington superlawyer and longtime friend of the Clintons.

"We thought this was a death blow to Trump," Clinton campaign chairman John Podesta later told me.

But Podesta was about to find out there was more to come. At four thirty P.M.—less than a half hour after *The Washington Post* published the *Access Hollywood* video—Podesta got a call from Clinton campaign headquarters in Brooklyn. It was the campaign's deputy press secretary, Glen Caplin. He had devastating news. WikiLeaks was back at it, Caplin told him. They had just released another cache of Democratic emails: Podesta's emails. This time the Russian hackers had drawn blood from the Clinton campaign and Podesta himself. They had no way to know how many emails had been stolen, so Podesta gave Caplin the green light to look through his entire personal email account. And with that, the team of people at Clinton campaign headquarters started going through the thousands of emails in Podesta's personal email inbox. Any message, no matter how private, could be made public. The campaign needed to know exactly what was there.

The timing of all this is astounding on multiple levels.

Consider all that had just happened in the space of ninety minutes. At three P.M., US intelligence tells the world that the Russian government, at the highest levels, was behind an effort to undermine the presidential election. A few minutes after four P.M., *The Washington Post* publishes the *Access Hollywood* video. Less than thirty minutes after that, WikiLeaks begins publishing the most damaging set of stolen emails yet.

The release of the Podesta emails may have been the most seismic story of all. Their release showed that the brazen attempt of the Russian government to mess with a US presidential election was continuing even as the US government was calling it out.

Conservative outlets, including the Daily Caller and the Drudge Report, were the first to jump on the leaked Podesta emails. ABC News made a decision not to quote the emails in our broadcasts or online. For one thing, we could not confirm their authenticity, and even if they were real, we couldn't guarantee that none of them had been doctored. Furthermore, they were stolen property.

But several other mainstream news organizations charged ahead, publishing stories within hours that quoted liberally from the pilfered emails. The headline in the *New York Times* story that was posted early that evening read, "Leaked Speech Excerpts Show a Hillary Clinton at Ease with Wall Street"—but these weren't "leaked" emails. They were stolen. Stolen by the Russians, no less.

"In lucrative paid speeches that Hillary Clinton delivered to elite financial firms but refused to disclose to the public," the *Times* story began, "she displayed an easy comfort with titans of business, embraced unfettered international trade and praised a budget-balancing plan that would have required cuts to Social Security, according to documents posted online Friday by WikiLeaks."

NBC News ran a story that day quoting the emails, saying, "Their release contains quotes likely to create new headaches for Clinton on both her left and right flanks just ahead of Sunday's second presidential debate."

Neither story made any reference to Russia's campaign to interfere with the election, a campaign that US intelligence had just said featured the theft and distribution of Democratic Party emails.

But at that point, the story dominating news coverage in the United States was the *Access Hollywood* tape. Aside from a few print and online stories about Podesta's emails that were damaging to Hillary Clinton, the political news was wall-to-wall coverage of the tape.

Back in Trump Tower, nearly an hour after the *Access Hollywood* tape was posted, the Trump campaign finally released a written statement. It was short—and defiant:

"This was locker-room banter, a private conversation that took place many years ago. Bill Clinton said far worse to me on the golf course—not even close. I apologize if anyone was offended."

The statement only made matters worse. Republican leaders, who had never liked Trump in the first place, started running from him. Reince Priebus left New York with Senator Jeff Sessions and RNC officials Mike Ambrosini and Alex Angelson aboard the six P.M. Amtrak Acela train to Washington. Throughout the three-hour train ride, Priebus was on the phone taking calls from Republican leaders of all stripes outraged by the *Access Hollywood* tape and what it meant for the campaign.

Priebus heard from Senate Majority Leader Mitch McConnell and several other Republican senators. He heard from top Republican donors. He heard from local Republican leaders and from several of the 168 elected members of the Republican National Committee. In an effort to find some privacy on the crowded train, Priebus got up from his seat as it pulled out of New York and stood outside the bathroom by the doors of the train that open onto the platform. He stayed there for the duration of the trip.

House Speaker Paul Ryan called Priebus several times. So did Wisconsin governor Scott Walker. Trump was scheduled to appear with both of them the following day at an event in Wisconsin. They wanted to disinvite him. Priebus asked them to hold off and give him time to talk Trump into canceling the trip on his own, so it wouldn't look like he was so radioactive that the Speaker of the House refused to share a stage with him, which was, of course, exactly what was happening. Walker also sent Christie a text with a blunt message: The election is over.

Before Priebus could get Trump to cancel the Wisconsin trip on his own, Ryan put out a statement disinviting the Republican presidential nominee from the Wisconsin event: "I am sickened by what I heard today. Women are to be championed and revered, not objectified." Priebus felt blindsided by his old friend and political mentor. The whole situation was spiraling out of control.

Trump's vanquished Republican opponents piled on too. Jeb Bush was among the first to publicly call Trump's behavior inexcusable: "I find that no apology can excuse away Donald Trump's reprehensible comments degrading women." And, a little later, Ted Cruz: "These comments are disturbing and inappropriate, there is simply no excuse for them."

Eventually, even Donald Trump saw how dire his situation was. At about midnight, he put out a video statement that included an actual apology: "I said it, it was wrong, and I apologize."

For candidate Trump it was a first: an unequivocal apology. No parsing, no hedging. He acknowledged the voice on the tape was his, he owned it, and he apologized.

Trump being Trump, he also added a shot at Hillary Clinton and her husband.

"Hillary Clinton, and her kind, have run our country into the ground. I've said some foolish things, but there is a big difference between words and actions. Bill Clinton has actually abused women and Hillary has bullied, attacked, shamed, and intimidated his victims."

And he closed the video statement by telegraphing that not only was he not dropping out of the race, he was ready to go on the attack against the Clintons: "We will discuss this more in the coming days. See you at the debate on Sunday."

On Saturday morning, the top political story on the front pages of *The New York Times* and *The Washington Post* was the *Access*

Hollywood tape. The intelligence community's revelation about Russian election meddling was a secondary story. The *Post* also had a front-page story delving into Podesta's emails—a story that detailed damaging information about private speeches Hillary Clinton had given to groups of bankers before the campaign. The story based on Podesta's stolen emails was given roughly the same prominence as the story on Russian election meddling.

Trump's late-night apology statement wasn't helping. Most of the commentary on it focused either on the strange way the video was shot—the background was a fake nighttime cityscape—or on the fact that the apology also included a personal attack on the Clintons. Christie later said Trump's uncomfortable delivery made it seem like a hostage video.

At seven A.M., Priebus was back on the train, now heading, once again, to New York, because Trump had again summoned his inner circle at Trump Tower. This time they met in Trump's gold-and-marble-adorned apartment on the sixty-eighth floor. As they began discussing what to do next, Trump asked Priebus what he was hearing. Christie and Bannon have both talked about Priebus's response. And now here, for the first time, is what Priebus says happened.

"He asked what I was hearing and I told him," Priebus told me. "I'm hearing that you can either withdraw or you can lose in the biggest landslide that's ever been had."

Others in the room, including Bannon and Christie, took that to mean Priebus was telling Trump he needed to drop out. Priebus insists he was just relaying what he had been hearing from influential Republicans around the country.

But did Priebus agree? Did he think Trump had only two choices: to drop out or to get creamed?

"Yes," he told me long after Trump's election victory had proved him wrong. "I believed it too."

Priebus insists he had also already been telling people that it would be impossible to replace Trump as the nominee even if he did drop out. The party's choice had already been ratified by the Republican convention in Cleveland and there was no practical way of undoing it. Besides, a dozen states had already started voting; absentee ballots had already been sent out in several others.

Regardless, Trump made it clear to everybody in the room he wasn't going anywhere. With that question settled, the discussion turned to how to respond to a story that continued to engulf the campaign.

Melania was on hand for some of this discussion. She didn't think her husband should drop out of the race, and that afternoon she put out a statement saying she had forgiven her husband and hoped voters would too. But she also didn't think he had any chance of actually winning anymore.

According to another member of Trump's inner circle there that day, at one point on Saturday afternoon Melania quipped, "Well, we won't have to worry about moving anymore, will we?"

It was agreed that Trump should do an interview. There was talk of doing it with a friendly interviewer on Fox News. But the idea was rejected. To work, this had to be a serious interview; Trump could not look like he was avoiding tough questions. Someone suggested he do the interview with Jeanine Pirro, a die-hard Trump supporter.

"No, no," said Rudy Giuliani when Pirro's name was mentioned. "That wouldn't be an interview; that would be a lap dance."

And after lots of discussion, it was decided the interview would be that afternoon with my ABC News colleague David Muir.

The team broke for lunch, and Kellyanne Conway reached out to Muir to say Trump was considering doing an interview and if he did, Muir would likely get it. Muir had returned to New York earlier that afternoon on a commercial flight from Florida, where he had broadcast from the hurricane zone; NBC anchor Lester Holt and CBS anchor Scott Pelley happened to be on the same flight. Muir went to ABC News headquarters in Manhattan—located about a ten-minute cab ride from Trump Tower—and waited for the final word on the interview. An ABC News camera crew was in the neighborhood too, ready to set up whenever the Trump team gave the green light.

After the lunch, the Trump inner circle—minus Priebus, who took yet another Amtrak train back to DC began to prepare for the interview by throwing out questions Trump was likely to get.

Conway asked, "How could any woman in America think you are fit for office when you use language like that?" Trump didn't like the question, but he hated one asked by Christie even more.

"You go into great detail on the tape about what it is like to be a celebrity sexually," Christie said to him. "How have you used your celebrity to get sex with women?"

Trump shot back: "You seriously think I have to answer a question like that?"

Trump got more and more agitated and eventually pulled the plug on the interview.

"Fuck it, I'm not doing it."

Conway called Muir and told him the interview was off. In his book *Fear*, Bob Woodward says Muir had helicoptered to New York to do the interview and was already set up with his camera crew in Trump Tower. That's not true. Muir had been working up questions and preparing, but he never left his office at ABC News headquarters. The ABC News crew, however, had arrived at Trump Tower with campaign embed John Santucci. They were about to walk into the elevator to go up to Trump's apartment and set up for the interview when Santucci got a text message from Hope Hicks telling him the interview was not going to happen.

Chris Christie was so demoralized by the way things were

unfolding, he decided he would skip the debate the following day. He told the others he just needed to take a break and that Trump wasn't listening to his advice anyway.

By Sunday morning, the day of the debate, all of the Republican Party's leadership had run from Trump, including Speaker of the House Paul Ryan and Senate Majority Leader Mitch McConnell.

"The cascade of Republicans that have fled Donald Trump includes elected officials from the Northeast, from the South, from the West," I told George Stephanopoulos on ABC's *This Week* that morning. "It includes the establishment, the Tea Party, the full spectrum of the Republican Party."

But Reince Priebus, despite his dramatic admonition that Trump had to either drop out or lose in spectacular fashion, was one Republican who did not jump ship. Stuck between Trump and those who wanted Trump out, he teetered, he wavered, he told Trump he would suffer a historic loss if he remained in the race, but Priebus ultimately stayed with him. On Sunday morning, he was back on yet another train heading to New York again, this time so he could fly with Trump on his plane to St. Louis for the debate.

In this whirlwind, there was one more surprise yet to come. Bannon, Kushner, and Deputy Campaign Manager David Bossie had been quietly cooking up a plan to go on the offensive, opening up a new and ugly front in the war with the Clintons. While the *Access Hollywood* video had Republican leaders everywhere in a state of panic, Bannon had reached out to the women who had accused Bill Clinton of sexual misconduct over the years and asked if they would show up at the debate. Nobody knew their stories better than Bossie. As a conservative activist and an investigator for House Republicans in the 1990s, Bossie had helped lead the Republican crusade to impeach Bill Clinton two decades earlier. Among those contacted by the Trump team were Paula Jones, whose sexual harassment lawsuit against Bill Clinton set off the series of events that led to Clinton's impeachment, and Juanita Broaddrick, who had accused Clinton of raping her back in Arkansas in 1978. They also brought Kathy Shelton, who accused a forty-one-year-old man of raping her when she was twelve years old. Hillary Clinton, then Hillary Rodham, represented her accuser, and Shelton has said Hillary mistreated her by coldly trying to undermine her credibility at trial.

On the campus of Washington University in St. Louis a few hours before the debate, the Trump team was gathered in a private space, continuing to prepare for the debate, when Bannon and Bossie got up and told Priebus they needed to take Trump to meet a group of people who had donated money to the campaign. They told Priebus he did not need to come. Minutes later, Priebus looked up and saw Trump on TV, walking into a room not far from the debate hall with the women who had accused Clinton of sexual misconduct. The move shocked everybody, but nobody more than Reince Priebus.

As the debate was about to begin, I was positioned inside the hall, looking down on the stage. Just minutes before ABC News's coverage began, I noticed the Clinton accusers being escorted to seats right by where I was standing. The Trump team had just tried to have them seated on the debate stage in the seats set aside for the families of the candidates. Here's how I set the scene on live television one minute before the debate moderators, Martha Raddatz and Anderson Cooper, kicked off the debate.

"Those women who accused Bill Clinton are right over my shoulder here," I said, with the women clearly visible over my left shoulder, "but Donald Trump, in terms of his party, comes into this hall a man alone. Party leaders who have not already abandoned him have stopped defending him. Others are watching tonight. A bad performance by Trump and they will leave en masse, taking party resources with them."

In his first question to Trump, Anderson asked about the *Access Hollywood* video. In his answer, Trump both apologized and downplayed the significance of his words:

"This was locker-room talk," he said. "I am not proud of it. I apologize to my family, I apologized to the American people. Certainly, I am not proud of it. But this is locker-room talk."

And then he went on the offensive:

"If you look at Bill Clinton, far worse," Trump said. "Mine are words and his was action. His words, what he has done to women. There's never been anybody in the history of politics in this nation that has been so abusive to women. So you can say it any way you want to say it, but Bill Clinton is abusive to women."

Trump was done apologizing. He was back in the fight. To many of those outraged by what they had heard him say on the tape, the quick pivot to attacking Clinton over decades-old allegations against her husband made the apology seem insincere. Trump's supporters, though, were cheering. After minutes of back-and-forth on the video, the debate turned to other topics. Trump sure didn't seem like a guy ready to give up.

By the time the debate drew to a close, I had received text messages and emails from several Republicans who had been telling me the campaign was over and who now believed he would live to fight another day. Trump was wounded, but his campaign wasn't dead yet.

"I've been in touch with a lot of Republicans during the debate," I told George Stephanopoulos during ABC's live broadcast right after the debate ended, "and my sense is that he has stopped the bleeding. I don't think that he did anything to save himself with Republicans that have already jumped ship, but I think that he will stop the wholesale departure of Republican leaders. He took the case to Hillary Clinton, particularly on issues like Obamacare and her emails and taxes. The Republican base will applaud those attacks."

Trump did recover. And, to a degree, so did Reince Priebus. He had told Trump he was doomed to lose, and after Trump won, he still managed to be named chief of staff. But it wasn't a full recovery. Trump never forgot what Priebus had told him during his darkest hour. He sometimes brought it up during meetings at the White House—sometimes to embarrass his chief of staff, always to remind him that he would never forget.

Perhaps the biggest victor of all during the *Access Hollywood* weekend was Vladimir Putin. He got his four hundred fifty roses. He also received a much more valuable birthday present—one of the greatest political distractions of all time. The blockbuster news that Putin's government had been caught by US intelligence trying to mess with our presidential election was pushed to the background by a scandal so big it convinced just about everyone that the Trump era was over. We were all wrong. It was just beginning.

CHAPTER SIX

BLACK SWAN

Political reporters love making predictions. At least, I love to make predictions. I'm also generally pretty bad at it.

I grew up a New York Mets fan. Year after year, I would predict the Mets would go to the World Series. This habit was locked in when I was in kindergarten and the great Yogi Berra was the team's manager. Yogi actually took the team to the World Series that year, and I thought that was the way it was supposed to be.* After all, the team's slogan was "Ya Gotta Believe." But Yogi had a few sayings of his own, including this one: "It's tough to make predictions, especially about the future." Despite my hopeful prognosticating, the Mets didn't return to the World Series again until I was in college.

On the last Sunday in July 2016, I appeared on *This Week with George Stephanopoulos,* and George asked me for an if-the-race-were-held-today prediction of how many of the 538 Electoral College votes each candidate would get. I had worked through some scenarios and decided to see what would happen if Trump won all of the states we then considered toss-ups.

---

*Alas, the Oakland A's beat the Mets in the 1973 World Series four games to three.

"George, I did the states," I said. "I didn't look at the numbers ahead of time. I got to two hundred sixty-nine to two hundred sixty-nine with Donald Trump—"

And before I could finish my sentence, George interjected: "Wait—how did you do that?"

"I think because Trump holds Florida, he loses Virginia, he takes Ohio, takes Iowa, takes New Hampshire. He gets—"

George again interrupted:

"And what happens to the single delegates in Nebraska and Maine?"

At that point the other guests on the show laughed and George went on with the next prediction. A 269–269 tie would mean a Trump victory because the tie would be broken in the Republican-controlled House of Representatives.

It wasn't a totally insane prediction, but it was far-fetched. An electoral-vote tie hadn't happened since the election of 1800, between Thomas Jefferson and Aaron Burr. At least that tie vote had inspired a great scene in the musical *Hamilton,* where Alexander Hamilton needs to pick whom to support—one nemesis or the other—saying he hadn't ever agreed with Jefferson.

> *But when all is said and all is done*
> *Jefferson has beliefs, Burr has none (ooh!)*

Hamilton aside, the 269–269 possibility was remote. And predictions before the start of a fall campaign aren't worth a damn.

But in a sign of just how bizarre this campaign would be, the very next day my prediction was brought up by a real-life oracle.

At a campaign rally at Omaha North High Magnet School in Omaha, Nebraska, billionaire investor Warren Buffett took the stage with Hillary Clinton.

Warren Buffett had donated to liberal political causes and candidates for years, but now he was kicking up his political activism a notch by actually speaking at a Clinton rally in his hometown. Unlike Trump, the Oracle of Omaha, as Buffett is known, had been a fixture at the top of the Forbes 400 list of America's richest for decades, cracking the top ten every year since 1986.

To see him speaking at a political rally was surprising, but it was downright shocking when the Oracle of Omaha started talking about my goofy prediction on *This Week*.

Apparently, Buffett had been watching the show and he knew exactly what George was alluding to when he mentioned Nebraska and Maine. Those are the only two states in the country that split up their electoral votes, awarding one electoral vote to the winner of each congressional district and two votes to the statewide winner. My 269–269 prediction assumed Trump would win Maine's Second Congressional District and that he would win all three of Nebraska's congressional districts, including the one where Buffett himself lived.*

"Jonathan Karl of ABC News had gone state by state and he came up with his notion of who would carry each state and how that would cause the electoral vote to come out," Buffett told the crowd. "And those of you who watched the show yesterday saw that he came out two sixty-nine to two sixty-nine. He absolutely said that he did not try to come out that way, he just looked state by state—two sixty-nine to two sixty-nine."

Buffett then reminded the crowd that Nebraska's second district could cast its very own electoral vote and, in the scenario I had outlined, change a Trump victory into a Clinton victory.

"I am looking at the people who can change that two sixty-nine to

---

*Nebraska's Second Congressional District, which includes Buffett's home of Omaha, is sometimes referred to as Obamaha because Barack Obama won it in 2008, managing to eke out an Electoral College vote in a state that, overall, is solidly Republican.

two seventy," Buffett declared. And with that he announced he had rented out Ollie the Trolley, Omaha's popular tourist trolley, to transport voters to the polls on Election Day.

This was bizarre. My prediction had gotten a laugh out of the others in the *This Week* roundtable, but it caused Warren Buffett to announce he was renting out Ollie the Trolley.

Once Election Day came, of course, it turned out that Ollie the Trolley wasn't enough to help Hillary Clinton win Nebraska's Second Congressional District, and even if it had been, it would not have been enough to secure a Clinton election victory.

Despite my summertime prediction, I spent most of the fall campaign as convinced as everyone else that Trump had no real shot. With Hillary Clinton a lock to win the big electoral prizes of California and New York and a virtual lock, so it seemed, to win most of the big industrial states in the Midwest, it was hard to see how Trump could get to 269 or 270 electoral votes. And, I figured, Trump had so alienated women, Hispanics, and independents that he was bound to get beaten badly. The polls in battleground states added to the sense of inevitability—Trump seemed to be losing virtually everywhere he needed to win.

On October 24, Eric Trump, Kellyanne Conway, and Brad Parscale of the Trump campaign came by ABC News headquarters in New York to talk to our political team about their plans for the final stretch before Election Day. The timing was unfortunate. We had just started the ABC News/*Washington Post* daily tracking poll of the national vote and the results pointed to a landslide: Clinton with 50 percent of the vote and Trump with 38 percent.

Eric Trump had seen the numbers just before he walked into ABC and it was all he wanted to talk about.

"If you guys think Hillary has a twelve-point lead, you're crazy," he said, shaking his head.

The Trump folks didn't come armed with data to dispute our poll, but Eric had lots of anecdotes. He talked about the big turnout at the rallies. One thing that was true even in the Trump campaign's darkest days is that he generally attracted bigger crowds than Hillary Clinton. And then he started talking at length about his recent trip to Pennsylvania, where, he said, he had seen Trump yard signs everywhere and virtually none for Hillary Clinton.

"Twelve points? Yeah, right."

In other words, it was not a particularly productive briefing. The Trump campaign was still reeling from the repercussions of the *Access Hollywood* tape and the two dozen women who had come out to accuse Trump of sexual misconduct, but I didn't think Clinton was really up by twelve points. Then again, I also didn't think that the number of yard signs in Pennsylvania was a great predictor of who would win. And the size of the crowds at political rallies isn't a great predictor either. During the 1972 presidential election, for example, George McGovern spoke to massive crowds in major cities across the country, often much larger than the crowds turning out for Richard Nixon. McGovern won virtually all of those cities, but Nixon ended up winning forty-nine states.

There was one moment in the campaign's final stretch—five days after Eric Trump and the others visited ABC—when I came to wonder whether Trump actually had a chance. It was October 28, eleven days before the election. On that day, FBI director James Comey sent a letter to Congress saying he had reopened his investigation into Hillary Clinton's use of a private email server. The FBI had learned that Clinton emails had been found on a computer used by disgraced former congressman Anthony Weiner, who was then married to Clinton aide Huma Abedin, and, Comey informed Congress, his investigators were going to take a look. The development dominated the news: Hillary Clinton was once again the focus of a criminal investigation.

I didn't think the Comey letter would be enough to change the course of the race until the Clinton campaign invited me and a bunch of other reporters to join a conference call with Clinton campaign chairman John Podesta to discuss Comey's letter. Podesta's tone made me think the Clinton campaign was terrified about the impact of Comey's letter. He slammed the letter as outrageous and irresponsible. He accused Comey of playing politics and disparaging Hillary Clinton anew after he had already disparaged her several months earlier when he announced he would not be indicting her. It was an extraordinary attack on the head of the FBI by Hillary Clinton's campaign chairman. And remember: Comey, although a career Republican, was Barack Obama's FBI director. If the Clinton campaign was going on the record to attack his integrity, I figured, they had to be worried. I also believed the attacks would backfire; picking a fight with the FBI in the final days of a campaign just seemed like a terrible idea.

And, sure enough, in the coming days the polls tightened. By November 1, the ABC News/*Washington Post* tracking poll, which had already shown the race getting closer, actually showed a one-point Trump lead.

But if I had any reason to believe Trump could actually win, it was erased on November 4, the Friday before the election. On this day, Sean Spicer, who was on the Republican National Committee payroll and splitting his time between the RNC and the Trump campaign, invited reporters to RNC headquarters in Washington for two briefings on the state of the race—one briefing in the morning for TV correspondents and network political directors, and one in the afternoon for print reporters. These were extraordinarily candid briefings that spelled out an unmistakable conclusion: Donald Trump was going to get trounced on Election Day.

Spicer later denied what was said at these briefings, but fortunately I was able to secure an audio recording of the afternoon briefing. All of the quotes that follow, and all of the numbers, come from that audio recording.

Along with about a dozen other reporters, I was brought into a bleak conference room at the RNC headquarters for a presentation by the party's experts on voter turnout, analytics, and ground game. Spicer and RNC chief of staff Katie Walsh were there. So were political director Chris Carr and the party's numbers guru Bill Skelly.

At the start of the briefing Walsh and Spicer spelled out the ground rules: The briefing would be on the record but embargoed until after the election results were in and there was a declared winner. Then, perhaps aware of the widespread speculation that Trump might not accept the results if he lost, they amended the ground rules: It would be embargoed until the loser conceded.

The purpose of the briefing quickly became apparent. The RNC wanted reporters to know that they had done everything possible to set Republicans up for victory and they were confident that Republicans would do well regardless of what was about to happen at the top of the ticket.

"The RNC's ability to correctly project the electorate is really important because Donald Trump is not the only race on Tuesday," Walsh said. "There are Senate races. There are congressional races. There are obviously other races going on down-ballot."

She was laying the groundwork for the national party to claim victory even as they believed Trump was heading for defeat.

"The argument that we don't win elections really isn't true," Walsh told reporters. "We have had a problem winning the White House, and we are very open and honest about it. There's not a lot of getting around it. But we have had great success in other elections."

And on that point she was correct. Republicans had lost four out of the last six presidential elections, but they had dominated Democrats at virtually every other level, in most of those years winning the

House and Senate. During the Obama years, Republicans also won a solid majority of governorships and state legislatures too.

And with that Carr and Skelly described, in detail, the system the RNC had put in place to analyze and reach out to voters in fifteen battleground states. The RNC didn't rely on polls, they explained. They knew exactly who the voters were and had directly contacted millions of them—through phone calls, social media, and volunteers knocking on their doors.

"We are going to show you exactly how many people are going to turn out on Election Day in these states, and we believe these numbers are going to be extremely accurate," Skelly said.

The RNC team said there had been movement in Trump's direction, but as they walked reporters through the fifteen battleground states, the electoral map was downright grim for Donald Trump. The RNC projections had Trump losing must-win Florida (down 2 points) and Iowa (also down 2 points) and barely winning the strongly Republican states of Georgia (up just three-tenths of 1 percent) and Arizona (up four-tenths of 1 percent).

Here are the final numbers the RNC offered to reporters on that Friday before the election on how much they thought Trump was up or down in each of the fifteen battleground states. I have also included the actual results after the votes were counted.

STATE	RNC Projection	Actual Result
AZ	+.4	+3.5
CO	−.5	−4.9
FL	−2.0	+1.2
GA	+.3	+5.1
IN	+10.8	+19
IA	−2.0	+9

STATE	RNC Projection	Actual Result
MI	+.2	+.3
MO	+8.8	+18.5
NV	+.4	−2.4
NH	−2.1	−.3
NC	+2.2	+3.6
OH	+2.4	+8.1
PA	−2.3	+.7
VA	−2.6	−5.4
WI	−3.2	+.7

Two things stand out here. First, the RNC portrayed a race where, barring a catastrophic collapse over the next few days for Clinton, Trump was going to lose. Asked for their projection on the Electoral College, they said it added up to 240 electoral votes for Trump and 298 for Hillary Clinton. In other words: a decisive Hillary Clinton victory.

Reading the reaction of reporters in the room, Walsh said she did not want the main takeaway from the briefing to be that the RNC was predicting a Trump loss, but that is exactly what the numbers they presented were pointing to. A decisive loss.

The second thing that stands out is just how off base the RNC projections were. Despite the bravado about how accurately they could predict the behavior of the electorate, their numbers weren't even close to the actual results in most of the states.

They incorrectly had Trump losing Iowa and Florida. They also, wrongly, had him winning Nevada. And in states they projected correctly, they were way off in predicting their margin of victory. They projected Trump would win Ohio by just 2.4 points—he won by over 8. Trump's actual margins of victory in Missouri and Indiana were almost 10 points higher than the RNC projected. These were numbers way outside the margin of error for a run-of-the-mill poll, let alone for a national party data operation that the RNC had spent tens of millions of dollars building and had insisted would be "extremely accurate."

The RNC projections were actually remarkably accurate in predicting how many people would vote in the battleground states. In Florida, for example, they predicted 9,409,000 people would vote, just 20,000 short of the actual number of voters. They were stunningly accurate about how many people would vote but way off on *how* they would vote. There was only one state where they were spot-on. In Michigan, the RNC projected Trump would win by two-tenths of a percentage point. He won by three-tenths of a percentage point.

Because the RNC briefing was embargoed, I could not report it before the election, but it certainly colored the way I looked at the race in the final days and on election night. I figured if the RNC's own data were showing their candidate losing in Iowa and Florida and barely winning in places like Arizona and Georgia, there was virtually no chance Trump would win.

But on the weekend before the election, I had one more reason to doubt the inevitability of a Clinton victory.

Over the weekend, the ABC political team was testing out our election-night set. As the person responsible for tracking election returns using our so-called magic wall, I needed to be sure I could work the computer system that turned raw numbers into graphics to show where the state-by-state vote stood.

During a break in one of our rehearsals, ABC News political director Rick Klein pulled me aside to show me an experimental analysis done by a researcher at Langer Research Associates, the company that has overseen ABC News polls for years. The researcher, Chad Kiewiet de Jonge, had aggregated more than two weeks' worth of ABC News/*Washington Post* daily tracking polls and crunched the numbers using a method of analysis Rick tried to explain to me but, in truth, neither of us fully understood. It's called "multilevel regression with poststratification." Seriously, that's what it's called. Or, as pollster Gary Langer called it, MRP.

Anyway, using this method, Chad and Gary Langer came up with polling numbers for all fifty states. The numbers seemed odd, because they differed dramatically with where most people thought the race was going. Chad had Trump winning all toss-up states, including Florida, North Carolina, Ohio, and Iowa. That was surprising, but even more surprising, they also had Trump with a narrow lead in Pennsylvania and Wisconsin. And the bottom line was downright shocking: If Trump won every state where MRP analysis showed him ahead, he would win the election with 290 electoral votes compared to 248 electoral votes for Clinton.

The method of analysis was experimental and untested. Rick thought we should consider publishing the numbers in some way even though the results were at odds with what the ABC News political unit's projections were. As Rick and anybody else who has covered elections knows, surprises can happen on Election Day, and publishing this experimental analysis could be a way to remind everybody of that fact. But Gary ultimately did not push to go public with the numbers because the method was new and untested. Gary and Chad eventually published a full explanation of their MRP analysis and its conclusion in *Public Opinion Quarterly* and *The Washington Post* after the election. Next time around, it may be a tool pollsters will use to measure the presidential race. It's still experimental but no longer untested.

That Sunday, two days before the election, George Stephanopoulos again asked for my race projections. I outlined several paths to a Hillary Clinton victory and two much narrower paths to a Trump victory: first, the 269–269 scenario I'd outlined over the summer, and

now a second path, with Trump winning Florida and the other battleground states but also peeling off one of the industrial Midwest
states—Pennsylvania, Michigan, Wisconsin—that a Republican presidential candidate had not won for decades.

Still, with the RNC briefing fresh in my mind, I thought a Trump
victory was far-fetched to say the least.

For political reporters and for candidates, there is actually very
little to do on Election Day. The campaigning is done and nothing
really matters until the results start coming in after polls close in the
evening. Candidates, especially those who make a career of being
politicians, often have Election Day traditions and superstitions.
John McCain would watch a movie while he waited for the votes to
be counted. Obama played basketball, except for the day of the 2008
New Hampshire primary (and he lost that one). Some traditions are
less enjoyable: Former vice president Dan Quayle used to go to the
dentist on his Election Days.

Reporters covering presidential elections often spend the morning
getting one last briefing from the campaigns. On the morning of
Election Day 2016, the first briefing came in the form of a conference
call with the Clinton team. They were organized and convincing,
outlining a state-by-state outlook that included a lot of information
on the early vote in the key states and looked like a slam dunk for
Hillary Clinton.

Then came a conference call with the Trump campaign team.
They too predicted victory. After all, no presidential campaign team
predicts defeat on an election morning. Kellyanne Conway led the
call and said she was confident about Trump's prospects in Florida—
and Pennsylvania, Michigan, and Wisconsin too—but unlike the pes-
simistic RNC briefing, she offered no real specifics beyond talk
about the sizes of the crowds at Trump rallies in those states. I asked

Conway for her county-by-county breakdown of what she thought Trump would need to do to win. She laughed and told me she wouldn't show me anything until after the election.*

After the briefings were over, I bumped into George Stephanopoulos.

"There's really no way he could win, is there?" he asked.

"It would be a black swan event," I told him.[†]

At five P.M. the first wave of network exit polls came in and confirmed all that I thought I knew about the race. Hillary Clinton was up in almost all the battleground states, including North Carolina (+2), Florida (+2), Michigan (+5), and Pennsylvania (+5). Even in Ohio, where Trump had been considered the favorite, they were tied.

It's important to point out this was just the first wave of exit polls.[‡] The numbers could not be reported because the polls were works in progress; they were preliminary because people were still voting in every state and the polls were still being conducted. Even though we don't report the results of the first waves, they do color our thinking.

As I tracked the numbers that night on live television, I was as shocked as anybody to see how they came in. One by one, Trump locked up the battleground states. At 10:39 P.M., he won Ohio, and it wasn't even close. About fifteen minutes later, the big one: Trump took Florida.

During the next commercial break, Rick Klein came out to talk to

---

*By the way, I never did get Conway's list of key-county vote goals.

†The *Oxford English Dictionary* defines a black swan as "an unpredictable or unforeseen event, typically one with extreme consequences."

‡By the end of the night, exit polls, which are conducted jointly by the television networks and other news organizations, are highly accurate because they include many more interviews than a regular poll, and those interviews are done with people as they are leaving the voting booth (you don't have to ask people if they plan to vote; you can see they just voted). The early waves, however, can be wrong, and these sure were, solidifying my impression that Hillary Clinton was poised to win.

me. "This is going to be close!" I told him. The Florida win was huge
for Trump, but even then I assumed Clinton had a good chance to
pull it out by winning most of the remaining states. Rick shook his
head. He told me Ryan Struyk, a twenty-four-year-old numbers sa-
vant who worked for our political unit, had been looking at the returns in Michigan, which was now a must-win state for Clinton, and
was convinced, based primarily on how Democrats were underper-
forming in the Detroit area, that Trump was going to win.

Ryan was one of the most junior people in our political unit, but
he is a bit of a genius and, more important, free of the kind of group-
think that can infect news organizations. Several things made him
unique. He's from the heartland, born and raised in Grand Rapids,
Michigan. He's the son of a pastor and a graduate of Calvin College
(now Calvin University), a Christian school in Grand Rapids. And
there was one thing that really made Ryan stand out among his peers
in our newsroom: He had graduated with a joint degree in political
science and math. Journalists are usually horrifically bad at math.
Not Ryan.

In short, I took Ryan's opinion on these matters more seriously
than just about anybody's. The race in Michigan was a long way from
being called, but on this one, I trusted the young numbers guru from
Grand Rapids. And if Trump was going to win Michigan, the race
was over. And it wasn't just Michigan: Trump had an even larger lead
in Pennsylvania. The race wouldn't be called for another three hours,
but now, I finally saw where it was heading. I said it silently to myself
before we went back on the air: "President-Elect Donald Trump."

ABC News called North Carolina shortly after eleven P.M., and
George Stephanopoulos turned to me to explain where the race
stood. Until I'd heard Ryan's analysis, the idea of Trump's winning
hadn't really sunk in yet. But now I knew our world had been turned
upside down. Hillary Clinton was now the long shot to win.

"She's got to now run the table," I said to George as I turned to our magic wall, "and we've been saying for weeks—Republicans privately have been saying—this is a very narrow path for Donald Trump, but now suddenly here, we see a narrow path for Hillary Clinton."

Now it was Hillary Clinton who had to win Pennsylvania, Michigan, and Wisconsin. She had to win all of them. And she had to win New Hampshire, where votes were still being counted. Of course, Clinton had been expected to win all of those states, but I had all the numbers in my computer on the ABC election set and they showed something amazing: She was in danger of losing all of them.

It turned out Ryan Struyk had been ahead of us all night. The evidence is right there, to this day, on his cell phone. As the returns were coming in and being broadcast live, Ryan was texting his analysis to a friend. At 9:13 P.M., he texted his friend that Hillary Clinton could lose Michigan (keep in mind, the state was not called for Trump until the next morning). At 9:50 P.M., Ryan texted the same friend that the numbers were trending toward a Trump election victory. At 10:16, he texted: "I think he is going to win MI + OH + PA + FL + IA = 275." To emphasize his point, another text a half hour later: "He's gonna win."

The person getting the most timely and accurate read of what was happening on election night was the friend Ryan was texting.

And sure enough, Trump went on to win all those states Kellyanne Conway had told us that morning he could win: Pennsylvania, Michigan, Wisconsin.

At first, I was just stunned. Then reality dawned on me: I was watching the story of a lifetime unfold.

Election nights are always a marathon, but this one was especially exhausting. As we were in our sixth consecutive hour of live broadcasting, the entire ABC political team seemed worn-out and shocked.

It was after one A.M., and we had not yet called the race for Donald Trump, but it was finally clear to everybody he was going to win. During a commercial break, ABC News president James Goldston came out to talk to those of us on the set. I don't remember his exact words, but I remember precisely his message. He wanted us to snap out of it, step up the energy. We were witnessing one of the greatest political upsets ever—maybe the greatest in American history. Whatever anybody thought about the implications of that upset—and already there were signs of global panic, with international markets tanking and the value of the Mexican peso falling—this was one hell of a story.

In the weeks and months following election night, I spent a lot of time trying to understand why I was caught by surprise by Trump's victory. One of the unmistakable conclusions: News organizations, including ABC News, spent a lot of money and time conducting and analyzing polls that didn't tell us a damn thing about who would be elected president. We were measuring the wrong thing.

Our daily national tracking poll actually turned out to be quite accurate. On election eve, the final ABC News/*Washington Post* poll showed Hillary Clinton ahead of Donald Trump 47 to 43, a lead nationally by 4 percentage points. And the final result? Hillary Clinton ended up with 48 percent of the popular vote; Donald Trump had 45.9 percent. In other words, the poll was off by less than 2 points and well within the margin of error. When all the votes were tallied, Hillary Clinton ended up beating Donald Trump by 2.1 points in the national popular vote. And that earned her a ticket back to her home in Chappaqua, New York—not the White House.

I didn't think much about that pre-election RNC briefing until long after Trump settled into the White House. It had been embargoed until after the election was over, but who cared about writing about that as Hurricane Trump was coming to town?

One of the few who did write about the briefing was Ken Vogel, who was then a reporter with Politico. Vogel wrote a straightforward story with the headline "RNC Model Showed Trump Losing."

I frankly didn't see Vogel's story at the time. I didn't notice it until I read the book Sean Spicer wrote after he left the White House, *The Briefing*. I was shocked to see the former White House press secretary claim he and his RNC comrades had known a Trump victory was coming.

"Most of the media refused to believe our data," Spicer wrote, adding that "some outlets actually reported the opposite. Politico, for one, declared, 'RNC Model Showed Trump Losing,' which was absolutely not the case."

Astounding. A brazen lie. Ken Vogel of Politico wrote precisely what had been laid out in a briefing that Spicer himself had set up and supervised, and then Spicer called him a liar. That's chutzpah. Fortunately, I have the tape and the tape does not lie.

CHAPTER SEVEN

THE DAYS AFTER

For many Democrats, and more than a few anti-Trump Republicans, the election of Donald Trump wasn't just disappointing; it was catastrophic. On some college campuses, the election results were treated as the kind of cataclysm that required psychological help for the victims. As the Daily Beast put it, "In the wake of the election, many college students at elite colleges and universities have come down with serious cases of PTSD: President Trump Stress Disorder." Even the University of Pennsylvania, Trump's alma mater, was traumatized to see him, one of its own, elected president.

"Some professors turned Wednesday's classes into 'safe spaces' in which students could freely express their concerns for their futures," UPenn freshman Daniel Tancredi wrote in the *Statesman* campus newspaper after the election. "One of the dorms on campus even set up a 'breathing space' the night after Election Day. Cats, a puppy, coloring pages, and snacks were offered to help students 'decompress in a low-key and low-stress environment.'"

On the day after, there were no coloring pages or puppies in the West Wing of the White House, but few places were hit harder by the election results. The next morning, President Obama's senior White

House advisors gathered together for the daily meeting in Chief of Staff Denis McDonough's office. It was a meeting that happened every weekday at seven thirty A.M. sharp. Because election night was a late one and, for these folks, an emotionally devastating one, McDonough pushed off the meeting until eight thirty A.M. They had an extra hour to sleep, or attempt to begin to come to terms with what had happened.

The chief of staff's office is down the hall from the Oval Office and almost as big. It has a desk, a couple of couches, a large conference table, a fireplace, and a door leading to an outdoor patio. At eight thirty A.M., more than a dozen of the most powerful people in Washington, including public faces of the Obama administration and the behind-the-scenes power players, crowded around McDonough's conference table.

McDonough was as shocked as anybody by the election results, but this was not a time to wallow. The Obama team had an extensive transition plan worked out, but the transition they had been planning was to a Clinton presidency. Now they had to figure out how to transition to a president none of them had thought had any chance of winning and who most of them thought represented a threat to the nation.

McDonough gave the senior staff a pep talk. His message: We have survived terrible things as a country; we will survive Donald Trump. And, in the meantime, he said, the Obama staff needed to show grace during the transition and to be helpful to the incoming Trump staff. He called on them to follow what he called the Bush model. The outgoing George W. Bush team had been gracious and helpful to the incoming Obama staff eight years earlier. Obama was determined to do the same for Donald Trump. As he spoke, several of Obama's top advisors couldn't hold back their emotions; National

Security Advisor Susan Rice, Treasury Secretary Jack Lew, and Communications Director Jen Psaki all had tears in their eyes.

That meeting was emotional, but nothing compared to what happened next.

Psaki and Press Secretary Josh Earnest convened a meeting in Earnest's office of the White House communications staff. These were the true believers, most of them in their twenties, living a dream by working in the Obama White House.

"It was incredibly raw," Psaki told me. She was the most senior staffer in the group and had been working for Obama since the week he announced he was running for president in 2007. "I was crying."

It was like a group therapy session. And it was loud. Word quickly spread throughout the West Wing about the anguish and sobs coming out of the press secretary's office. A knock came on the door before the meeting was over. President Obama wanted all of them to come to the Oval Office. He too offered a pep talk—and some news. He told them he was about to go into the Rose Garden to announce he had spoken to Donald Trump at about three A.M. and he had invited him to the White House the next day. Trump, whom Obama had just two days earlier called "temperamentally unfit" to be president, would be right there in the Oval Office in just twenty-four hours. Obama then went around and offered each of them a hug.

When President Obama went out to the Rose Garden to address the nation for the first time since Trump's victory, the communications staff watched from the White House colonnade, looking grim, several of them with tear-stained faces. Obama started his remarks with a little joke.

"Yesterday, before votes were tallied, I shot a video that some of you may have seen in which I said to the American people, regardless of which side you were on in the election, regardless of whether your candidate won or lost, the sun would come up in the morning," he said. "And that is one bit of prognosticating that actually came true. The sun is up."

With the announcement of Trump's coming visit to the White House, I booked a flight from New York to Washington. The shock of election night was over. I was about to be an eyewitness to the most unlikely meeting of two political figures in my lifetime.

As I flew to Washington, I realized I would be one of a handful of reporters, and the only television correspondent, in the Oval Office for the historic convergence of Obama and Trump. The two men had been bitter enemies since Trump spearheaded a campaign to question whether Obama was truly a natural-born American citizen in 2011. But they had never before met. I would be in the room simply because it was my turn. The Oval Office is too small to accommodate the entire White House press corps, so news organizations take turns. For any given event, there are a handful of still photographers, a newspaper reporter, a reporter for each wire service (the Associated Press, Reuters, Bloomberg, and Agence France-Presse), and a TV correspondent with two camera crews. It's called the White House pool. And for the day of the Trump visit, it happened to be ABC News's turn to be in the pool.

At 11:32 that morning, I was summoned with the rest of the pool to go into the Oval Office. President-Elect Trump had arrived at the White House twenty-seven minutes earlier. The meeting was scheduled to last thirty minutes, with the pool coming in for the last two.

Most first-time visitors to the West Wing are struck by how small the place is. The blue door you see on television over the right shoulder of the press secretary is, literally, twenty-five paces from the Oval Office. Open that blue door and you immediately see another door that opens to a tiny suite of mini cubicles and three small offices collectively known as "lower press." That's where the junior press staff works. There's another door that opens to a little hallway; immediately to the left are the Rose Garden and the iconic colonnade where so many presidents have been photographed walking from the residence of the White House to the West Wing.

With my fellow members of the press pool, I went out the doors, turned left into the colonnade, then made a quick right turn, walked another ten steps or so, and stopped by the door to the Oval Office.

And we waited.

Usually once the pool is called to gather outside the Oval Office, it means we are about to go in. The wait is rarely more than a few minutes. After all, the president doesn't want a gaggle of reporters standing idly right outside his door any longer than necessary.

A few minutes turned into ten minutes.

And we waited.

On the other side of the Rose Garden, I spotted Jared Kushner walking with Denis McDonough, and, behind them, the Trump loyalists: Hope Hicks, Johnny McEntee, Keith Schiller, and Dan Scavino. None of them had ever been here before, but this was the core of Trump's world, the precious few who had been working for Trump since the very beginning of the campaign. Each of them had been there when I visited the empty campaign headquarters that looked like a movie set more than two years earlier. As I waited to go into the Oval Office, I saw them pose for pictures in the colonnade, looking more like tourists than the people who were about to be handed the keys to the West Wing. They smiled for a group photo standing exactly in the place where the tearful Obama staffers had watched President Obama give his Rose Garden speech the day before.

And we waited.

Ten minutes turned into a half hour. Still we waited, right outside the door to the Oval Office. On the other side of that door, Obama and Trump. Meeting one-on-one. No aides present. Just those two men.

As I wondered what was going on, I saw McDonough and Kushner return from a walk around the quarter-mile running track on the perimeter of the South Lawn. They paused for a bit, looked toward the Oval Office, and then set out for another lap.

We waited some more.

The rest of the Trump loyalists were waiting too. Through the windows, I could see them lounging in the Cabinet Room, which is just about twelve feet from the Oval Office. During the first part of the meeting, they had been given a tour of the West Wing. And Hope Hicks had met with Jen Psaki to talk about White House communications. In some ways the two women had much in common. Both were from Connecticut and graduates of Greenwich High School. Their sisters had had their weddings in the very same place in Bermuda. Both were among the first to work on a long-shot presidential campaign: Hope was the first spokesperson for the Trump campaign; Jen was the first spokesperson for the Obama campaign.

But in just about every other way, they were worlds apart.

"How are you feeling? It must all be a shock," said Psaki, who had spent a good part of the last thirty-six hours in tears because of the Trump victory.

"I'm just proud of Mr. Trump," Hicks said. "I am just so proud of him."

That meeting didn't last long.

But the Trump-Obama meeting kept on going. I saw Kushner and McDonough return from their second lap around the South Lawn. We were still waiting. They were still waiting.

Finally, at 12:35 p.m.—more than an hour after I had been called to go into the Oval Office—the door opened and I sent out an email to all five television networks:

"At long last—we are going into the Oval Office."

The two men were seated in chairs in front of the fireplace on the side of the room directly opposite the presidential desk, flanked by busts of Abraham Lincoln and Martin Luther King Jr., a painting of George Washington in his general's uniform on the wall above the fireplace. I positioned myself right next to the coffee table beside Obama's chair, less than five feet from Obama and in direct view of Trump, whose chair was turned in my direction. Trump's small entourage came into the room as well, including Jared Kushner, who stood behind the news photographers and snapped a few pictures of his own with his phone.

As Obama started to speak, I was immediately struck by Trump's body language. I was seeing a side of him I had never seen. He seemed, believe it or not, humbled. Seriously. Hunched over slightly, his hands together between his knees, he looked out at the room and seemed a little dazed. Looking at the video and photos I took with my phone of that moment, even after all that has happened since, Trump still looks to me like somebody both humbled and a little freaked out by what was happening.

I had never witnessed Trump in a situation remotely like this. Virtually any time he walks in a room, he is the center of attention and calling the shots. But not here. Trump was not in charge. Obama was still president, after all. Obama was the one directing the action and setting the tone. And the tone he set was one of reconciliation.

"I just had the opportunity to have an excellent conversation with President-Elect Trump," he said.

As Trump slowly nodded, Obama said he was encouraged by Trump's desire to work with the Obama team.

"Most of all," Obama said, turning to Trump, "I want to emphasize to you, Mr. President-Elect, that we now are going to want to do everything we can to help you succeed—because if you succeed, then the country succeeds."

It all seemed so . . . normal. Except these two weren't just leaders of opposing parties. Each one had defined the other as, essentially, a threat to the republic. That's why there had been so many tears in the West Wing. Three days earlier, Obama had said Trump couldn't be trusted with the nuclear codes, that all he'd accomplished over the previous eight years would go down the drain with a Trump victory.

When it was his turn, Trump spoke softly.

"This was a meeting that was going to last for maybe ten or fifteen minutes," he said, only slightly exaggerating (it had been scheduled to be thirty minutes). "We had never met each other. I have great respect."

In one bit of Trumpian flair, he said Obama had explained "some of the difficulties" he'd be facing but also "some of the high-flying assets." Most amazingly, he said he looked forward to being with Obama "many more times."

"I very much look forward to dealing with the president in the future, including counsel," he said.

When Trump concluded his comments, there was a cacophony of questions from me and the other reporters and Obama offered his first bit of public advice to the president-elect.

"It's a good rule," Obama said, leaning over to Trump. "Don't answer questions when they start yelling at you."

Thankfully, this is one piece of advice Trump ignored completely.

"You'll seek his counsel?" I asked as the Obama press staff tried to escort us out of the room. "You'll seek his counsel?"

Trump nodded when I asked the second time and, looking at me, said this about Barack Obama:

"He's a very, very good man. Very good man."

For their nearly ninety-minute meeting, the only two people in the room were Trump and Obama. Everything we know about their conversation ultimately has to come from one of those two men— either directly from them or from people who spoke with them about the meeting. Trump has said Obama told him North Korea was by far the biggest problem facing the United States.

"I met right there in the Oval Office with President Obama," Trump told reporters during a February 2019 event in the Rose Garden. "And I sat in those beautiful chairs, and we talked, it was supposed to be fifteen minutes, as you know, it ended up being many times longer than that. And I said, what's the biggest problem? He said, by far, North Korea."

On this point, Denis McDonough tells me Trump is correct. Obama did tell Trump that North Korea was the most pressing national security challenge and one that would require his immediate attention. Given Trump's intense focus on North Korea after he took office, perhaps that's one piece of advice he took to heart.

But at that February 2019 Rose Garden event, Trump also claimed Obama told him he was close to going to war with North Korea.

"I don't want to speak for him, but I believe he would've gone to war with North Korea. I think he was ready to go to war. In fact, he told me he was so close to starting a big war with North Korea," Trump said.

That's something President Obama's closest advisors say is simply not true.

"We were not on the brink of war with North Korea in 2016," former Obama deputy national security advisor Ben Rhodes said. "Highlighting the long-standing and widely known threat of North Korea's nuclear program is very different from saying you're about to start a big war."

McDonough also told me Obama warned Trump about the disastrous consequences he would face if he succeeded in dismantling Obamacare, leaving millions without health insurance. McDonough says Obama advised him to make changes and call it his own, but not to completely undo the Affordable Care Act. McDonough says Trump seemed receptive to that idea, but history shows he wasn't. He would work from the very beginning of his presidency to dismantle all of Obamacare.

In his book *The World as It Is,* Ben Rhodes writes that Obama told him that Trump kept bringing up the size of the crowds at his political rallies, apparently in an attempt to bond with Obama as another politician who could draw bigger crowds than Hillary Clinton. Rhodes says Obama also remarked that Trump took pride "in not being attached to a firm position on anything."

As the Trump team left the White House, it was Hope Hicks who ended up in the president-elect's limo, alone with Trump, for the ride back to the airport. Trump said to her in a tone of mild amazement that he had really enjoyed Barack Obama, that he was a nice guy. And after he got to New York that night, he tweeted that message to the rest of the world.

> **Donald J. Trump**
> (@realDonaldTrump)
>
> A fantastic day in D.C. Met with President Obama for first time. Really good meeting, great chemistry. Melania liked Mrs. O a lot!
>
> 11/10/16, 6:10 PM

The happy talk of reconciliation didn't last long.

About an hour after Trump left the White House, the White

House press corps gathered for the daily briefing. I asked press secretary Josh Earnest about what President Obama had said just a few days earlier.

"He said on Monday Donald Trump is 'temperamentally unfit to be commander in chief, uniquely unqualified.' Does he still believe that?"

"The president's views haven't changed," Earnest answered. "He stands by what he said on the campaign trail."

I would never again see Donald Trump in awe of his surroundings the way he appeared that day, or as deferential—to anybody—as he was then to Barack Obama. He would continue to say nice things about the Obamas, but not for long, and he never sought Obama's counsel, as he told me he would.

CHAPTER EIGHT

AMERICAN CARNAGE

n Donald Trump's last full day in New York City before becoming president, I got a call from Rhona Graff, his personal secretary at the Trump Organization. The president-elect, who was just forty-eight hours from being sworn in as the forty-fifth president of the United States, wanted to bring me into a telephone conversation he was having with George Stephanopoulos.

"Jonathan, I have a man named Stephanopoulos on the other line," Trump announced. "How are you, Jonathan?"

"I'm fine. Congratulations, sir. We are excited for Friday," I said, referring to our big coverage plans for the inauguration.

"Thank you," he said to me, and then to George: "He is not a believer, though, George. I watch him in the mornings."

"We are not paid to be believers," Stephanopoulos interjected. "We are paid to have questions."

"No, you're paid to get it right," Trump said.

I didn't know exactly what Donald Trump would be doing in the final hours before becoming president of the United States. Perhaps he would be preparing for his inaugural address, easily the most consequential speech of his life? Or maybe he would be focused on finding the right people to help him lead the executive branch, considering he had not made decisions yet on who would hold some of the most important jobs in the incoming administration. Or maybe he'd be finalizing plans for his first day as president. Or the first hundred days. I wasn't sure, but I figured that on January 18, 2017, President-Elect Donald Trump would have much more important things to do than chat on the phone with George and me.

That's why I was surprised by the call and then doubly surprised when the conversation turned to a breezy reminiscence of the interview I had done with Trump back in 2014 in the Old Post Office building, when construction was just about to start on what would become the Trump International Hotel on Pennsylvania Avenue.

"Jonathan was more of a believer in the Old Post Office, when it was just starting construction. And he interviewed me as though I was going to run for president."

(Side note here: He was talking about the interview where I told him, on camera, "I'd be shocked"—my exact words—if he ran for president.)

"And he took a lot of heat," Trump continued. "But he also got very good ratings."

The president-elect was on a roll and talking like he didn't have a care in the world.

"He was more of a believer then," Trump said, still referring to me. "Somebody got to him. He's not a believer anymore. But that's okay. You know, life, you just continue along and prove yourself."

Now Trump turned to the purpose of the call. Just minutes earlier, he'd had his office email me a copy of a private letter he had received from George Herbert Walker Bush explaining that neither he nor former First Lady Barbara Bush would be attending his inauguration.

He was sharing the letter with me because I had reported on *Good Morning America* just a couple of hours earlier that the ninety-two-year-old President Bush was in the hospital, being treated for complications arising from pneumonia. My report reminded viewers that the elder Bushes had already said they would not be coming to the inauguration. And then, at the conclusion of my report, I said this: "That said, President Bush was certainly no fan of Donald Trump; in fact, he was reportedly seen throwing his shoes at the television set during the Republican primaries because he didn't like Trump's attacks on his son Jeb."

"Did you get the letter, Jonathan, that I got from Bush?" he asked me now.

I said I had, thanked him for sending it, and started to explain that my role as a reporter was to be fair and balanced, not to be a believer. But before I could finish the sentence, Trump interrupted me.

"I sent it because you're saying he hates me, and in the meantime, that letter was hand-delivered yesterday. It was a beautiful letter."

It was a great letter, reflecting the classic graciousness of George H. W. Bush even toward someone who had tormented his son and disparaged the Bush family name. But I hadn't reported that Bush hated Trump; I simply said he wasn't a fan because he didn't like Trump's relentless attacks on Jeb. In fact, Trump still wasn't ready to let up on Jeb, even after trouncing him in the primaries, even after getting elected president, even after receiving the "beautiful letter" from his father.

"Hey, look," Trump said. "I roughed up his son pretty good. His son has not recovered, nor will he recover. He is a very low-energy person. We don't need low-energy people."

As the conversation continued, George pointed out that Trump would have a letter waiting in the Oval Office for him from President Obama.

"I will," Trump said. "And I have to tell you, he has been very nice. We speak to each other all the time. You know, we are on the other side of the spectrum, but he has been very nice.

"So, anyway," he continued, "since you guys knocked the hell out of me this morning on that, and in light of the fact that you said he hates me, I thought I should send you the letter, which you can use if you want."

"You know, Mr. Trump, I was very clear he was upset with your attacks on his son. I did not say he hated you," I said.

"No, I agree with that," Trump said. "I'm not knocking it. You didn't know about the letter. And at the time he was. He used to throw things at the television. Look, it's a father who loves his son—that doesn't make him a bad guy, right?"

It was all good-natured. He was complaining, but mildly, about something I had reported that morning. And he was also giving me a little scoop. I was surprised he'd had time to watch the show that morning, and that he had time to talk to us now, but he was still chatting away.

"How is everything going?" he asked. "Good coverage tomorrow, huh?"

He wanted us to know the Trump Show in Washington would have a blockbuster debut:

"Here's my prediction: You will get the highest ratings you've ever had, by far, for a presidential inauguration."

And he was already talking crowd size, predicting a record but offering up a reason if not as many turned out as he hoped.

"You'll have a massive crowd," he said, "but I am at a big disadvantage because security is so tight, you know, tighter today than it has ever been. And they are only allowing so many people. I tell you what, a half a million people will be turned away."

Before finally saying goodbye, the president-elect recited to us the ratings of his last two major television interviews.

"Did you see *60 Minutes*—thirty-two million people a month ago?" Trump asked, and then, referring to *Fox News Sunday:* "Chris

Wallace on his show two weeks ago got nine point two million people on his, you saw that. On his Sunday morning show. Did you see that?" He added: "That was the highest rating he ever had."

There's no question, especially at this point, that a Trump interview was a big draw and guaranteed to bring a bump in the ratings. No question at all. And Chris Wallace did get his highest rating ever with the interview he did with Trump in December 2016. But there's also no question that the numbers Trump had just told us were wildly exaggerated. The *60 Minutes* interview in November 2016 didn't get thirty-two million viewers. It got twenty million. The Fox News interview didn't draw 9.2 million viewers that Sunday morning as he'd just said. There were 2.3 million viewers watching the broadcast that morning on the Fox broadcast network and another 1.3 million when it was replayed on the Fox News Channel at two P.M.

Of course, Trump didn't need to exaggerate. There's no question he was a ratings draw. There's no question he attracted big crowds wherever he went. And, more important, he was about to be sworn in as president. There was absolutely no need to pad the numbers. Of course, we wanted to interview him and we told him so. Everybody did.

While Trump was, in his unique way, preparing for his inauguration, the White House Correspondents' Association was concerned the incoming Trump communications team would restrict access to the president in the White House. There were reasons to be concerned. On one hand, Trump had been one of the most media-friendly presidential candidates ever. During the primary campaign, he'd held regular press conferences, done lots of interviews, and generally made himself available to reporters. But Trump had also viciously attacked the press, and some of his top advisors had openly mused about throwing the White House press corps out of the White House. And during the general election campaign, access to Trump had been significantly curtailed. In fact, he'd become the first major-party nominee I had ever seen refuse to allow a contingent of reporters to travel on his campaign plane or in his motorcades. Would he attempt to ban reporters from Air Force One? Would he do away with the so-called protective pool, the group of reporters who travel with the president whenever he leaves the White House? To those of us charged with covering the White House, these were existential questions.

On the morning of January 5, 2017, the leadership of the White House Correspondents' Association had boarded an Amtrak train at Washington's Union Station and embarked for New York for a meeting with Sean Spicer, the newly minted Trump press secretary. ABC's Washington Bureau Chief Jonathan Greenberger went along as well, as a representative of the five major television networks. Once in New York, they headed to Trump Tower, got in the elevator, and hit the button to go to the fourteenth floor.

The fourteenth floor of Trump Tower, by the way, is really the sixth floor. Some buildings skip a thirteenth floor, but when Trump built Trump Tower, he skipped floors six through thirteen. This helped him claim the top floor was the sixty-eighth floor, which sounded, apparently, more impressive than calling it the sixtieth floor, which it really is.

So, the fourteenth floor was actually the floor right above the original Trump campaign headquarters I had visited back in the summer of 2015, when it looked more like a movie set for a campaign headquarters than it did a real one. Back then, I had walked up to the floor above to see the shuttered set of *The Apprentice*. As the staff of the Trump campaign had grown and it had become clear *The Apprentice* was not coming back, the old TV set had been dismantled and turned into real offices for the real Trump campaign.

It was in a conference room in those offices—located almost exactly where the famous conference table used in *The Apprentice* had been—where the leadership of the White House Correspondents' Association had its first meeting with Sean Spicer. Hope Hicks was there too, and so was Stephanie Grisham, who would go on to be the communications director for First Lady Melania Trump and eventually President Trump's third press secretary.

Spicer was one of the few players on the Trump transition team who actually had Washington experience. He had served as a press secretary on Capitol Hill for four different Republican congressmen, including Representative Mark Foley of Florida, who would go on to resign amid revelations he sent sexually explicit messages to teenage boys working as congressional pages. Spicer had also worked for several years at the RNC as the party's communications director and, most recently, as its chief strategist. In short, Spicer was an experienced political player and well known by reporters in Washington. But, like just about everybody else on the Trump team, he had no White House experience.

As the meeting got under way, Spicer had some basic questions about how White House press operations worked. How did reporters get White House passes? How did a reporter who didn't have a pass get permission to come into the White House for a press conference or an interview? At one point, *New York Times* photographer Doug Mills suggested Spicer contact an agent in the Secret Service's public affairs office. Spicer asked him for the agent's contact information.

Spicer didn't know much at all about how the White House press operations worked, but he made it clear everything would be under review. He said he was inclined to go along with the idea of a protective pool that would go with the president when he traveled, but he wanted to know why it needed to include so many reporters and

photographers (the total number in the protective pool is thirteen).*
He suggested the number of reporters traveling with the president
would be cut back. Reuters reporter Jeff Mason, then the president of
the White House Correspondents' Association, worried reporters
could lose access to Air Force One. This would have been a severe
blow; White House reporters have been traveling on Air Force One
since Kennedy brought along a group of reporters to a summit meeting in Vienna with Soviet leader Nikita Khrushchev in 1961.†

But after several minutes of Spicer's musing about curtailing access to the incoming president, Hope Hicks interjected. She stated
flatly and with authority that the protective pool would continue in
the Trump White House, and it would continue in its current con-
figuration. It was clear the twenty-eight-year-old Hicks was the one
person at the meeting who could actually speak for the president, not
Spicer.

"And that includes traveling on Air Force One, correct?" Mason asked.

"Yes," Hicks responded.

And it was settled. Thanks to Hope Hicks, the White House Correspondents' Association scored an important victory, ensuring the
White House press corps would continue to have the same degree of
day-to-day access to President Trump that it had had to previous
presidents. Spicer may have wanted to restrict that access (an odd
position for an incoming press secretary to take), but Hicks knew the
one person who would actually want to have reporters around President Trump would be President Trump.

---

*The protective pool that flies on Air Force One includes thirteen people: three wire
reporters, a three-person TV pool (camera operator, sound technician, and correspondent), one radio reporter, two print reporters, and four still photographers.

†Some fascinating details of Kennedy's interactions with reporters on Air Force One are
recounted in the book *Air Force One: A History of the Presidents and Their Planes* by
Kenneth T. Walsh (Hachette Books, 2003).

Six days later, in a practice run of sorts for the White House, Trump held a press conference in the atrium of Trump Tower. It was a chaotic scene. The place was packed with at least twice as many reporters and photographers as would fit in the White House briefing room. There were dozens of Trump supporters there too, acting like an in-house cheering section for the press conference. Anticipation would have been high under any circumstances—he was going to become president in just nine days and this was his first press conference in months—but it was especially high because the night before BuzzFeed had published, in full, the notorious Steele dossier, a document written by former British spy Christopher Steele that included unverified reports of deep Trump ties to Russia and the salacious allegation that the Russians had video of Trump engaged in bizarre sexual activity with Russian prostitutes when he was in Moscow for the Miss Universe competition in 2013.

Sean Spicer opened the presser with a statement condemning BuzzFeed and CNN, which had broken the story that Trump had been briefed on the dossier's contents days earlier by then–FBI director James Comey. After Spicer, Mike Pence briefly took the podium to condemn fake news. And then came the president-elect.

"It's very familiar territory, news conferences, because we used to give them on an almost daily basis," Trump began. "I think we probably maybe won the nomination because of news conferences and it's good to be with you."

And then Trump actually offered words of praise to most of the news organizations in attendance, because nobody had followed BuzzFeed's lead in publishing the Steele dossier and most news organizations didn't report the salacious details about the supposed blackmail video the dossier claimed was possessed by the Russians.

Trump called first on John Roberts of Fox News, who asked if Trump had indeed been briefed on the Steele dossier and if he accepted the findings of the intelligence agencies that Russia was behind the hacking of the Democratic emails during the campaign.

He blasted the salacious allegations in the Steele dossier as fake news, but in response to Roberts's second question, Trump said he accepted at least one of the findings of the intelligence community: "As far as hacking, I think it was Russia," he said. "But I think we also get hacked by other countries and other people."

I jumped in next with a follow-up question.

"On that intelligence report," I asked, "the second part of their conclusion was that Vladimir Putin ordered it because he aspired to help you in the election. Do you accept that part of the finding?"

This was the question that would dog Trump all through the Russia investigation, the Mueller report, and beyond. Did he accept the evidence that the Russians not only meddled in the election, but they did so because they wanted him to win? To answer yes, the president seemed to believe, would be to acknowledge doubts about the legitimacy of his election victory.

"Well, if Putin likes Donald Trump, I consider that an asset, not a liability," he said. "Now, I don't know that I'm going to get along with Vladimir Putin. I hope I do. But there's a good chance I won't. And if I don't, do you honestly believe that Hillary would be tougher on Putin than me? Does anybody in this room really believe that? Give me a break."

He hadn't answered my question, and he never would.

As the press conference went on, the questions got wilder. One question came from a guy holding a microphone adorned with something that looked like a block of Swiss cheese. He identified himself as being with Cheddar TV. A British reporter asked the president, for the first and only time, about the salacious sexual allegations in the Steele dossier.

"During your visits to either Moscow or Saint Petersburg," the reporter asked, "did you engage in conduct that you now regret? Would a reasonable observer say that you are potentially vulnerable to blackmail by Russia or by its intelligence agencies?"

This one, Trump answered with humor.

"Does anyone really believe that story?" he said. "I'm also very much of a germophobe, by the way, believe me."

This was a press conference with more than one hundred reporters present. At most only about ten or fifteen were likely to be called on. But as the press conference was nearing its end, CNN's Jim Acosta grew increasingly agitated that he had not been called on. As Trump called on NPR's Mara Liasson, Acosta jumped up and tried to ask a question instead. Trump wouldn't have it.

"Your organization is terrible," he said, waving him off.

"You are attacking our news organization, can you give us a chance to ask a question, sir?" Acosta responded, standing up and trying to take center stage.

"Quiet," Trump said, motioning for him to sit.

"Mr. President-Elect, can you say—"

"She's asking a question," Trump said, gesturing to Mara Liasson. "Don't be rude. Don't be rude."

Acosta persisted: "Can you give us a question since you're attacking us? Can you give us a question?"

And Acosta kept speaking over the president-elect, as if he had a constitutional right to be called on by the president-elect at that particular moment.

"Don't be rude," Trump said. "No, I'm not going to give you a question. I'm not going to give you a question. You are fake news."

It was an embarrassing start, I thought, for the press corps and for the president-elect. I hated to hear Trump denounce CNN at a press conference. It was decidedly unpresidential. But Acosta was, in fact, rudely interrupting Mara Liasson, a well-respected journalist who wanted to ask a serious question. Acosta was portraying himself as some kind of righteous advocate for the free press, but to most of the reporters in that room, he was just rudely interrupting a colleague as she was trying to ask her question.

All of this would turn out to be a precursor to much more embarrassing, and uglier, interactions with the press that would come after Trump moved to Washington and became the forty-fifth president.

As a reporter, there's no major regularly scheduled event I enjoy covering more than a presidential inauguration. On no other day is history staring you more directly in the eye than on Inauguration Day. It was in FDR's first inaugural address that he said, "The only thing we have to fear is fear itself," and in JFK's that he said, "Ask not what your country can do for you—ask what you can do for your country." The inaugural addresses during my lifetime have been largely unmemorable, but the images and the symbolism, to me, have been unforgettable.

No matter how bitter the election that precedes it, America's top elected leaders come together at the US Capitol to celebrate the crown jewel of American democracy—the peaceful transfer of power. Most of America's state governors are there, seated right above the inaugural platform. The congressional leadership is there. The justices of the Supreme Court. Former presidents, vice presidents, and First Ladies. History looms largest when there is a new president being sworn in and the outgoing president is right there to pass the baton.

The 2001 inauguration of George W. Bush posed a severe test to the endurance of this unifying celebration of democracy. Not only was Bill Clinton by Bush's side when the baton was passed, Al Gore was there too. Not because a majority of Americans had voted for him to be president (although that did happen) or because he'd conceded the election after a narrowly divided Supreme Court stopped a recount in Florida (that happened too), but because he was the out-going vice president.

I had a unique vantage point for the 2001 inauguration. As a CNN correspondent back then, I was positioned on a flatbed truck riding right in front of the presidential limousine as George W. Bush made his way from the Capitol, where he had just been sworn in, to the White House. There were three of these trucks, each shared by two television networks. I happened to be sharing my truck with NBC and its correspondent Maria Shriver, the niece of President Kennedy and the future First Lady of California.

It was bitterly cold and raining on and off. As Bush had taken the oath of office and given his speech, he had looked out over cheering crowds in the reserved seats in front of the inaugural platform. But as we rode with the presidential limo from the Capitol and down Constitution Avenue toward the White House, we were met by throngs of angry protestors. There was no celebration of the peaceful transfer of power here.

The protestors lined the streets beginning just two blocks from the entrance to the Capitol building. They booed. They rhythmically chanted, "Thief! Thief! Thief!" As the limousine approached one group of protestors, I could see them unfurl a sign, about twelve feet long, that said, "THE WHOLE WORLD IS LAUGHING." Other signs along the parade route, easily visible from the vantage point of my post on the flatbed truck and therefore easily visible through the windows of the presidential limo, read "Commander-in-thief," "Re-elect Gore," and "Weasel Dubya." At one point before the limo took the turn onto Pennsylvania Avenue, Bush's limousine was pelted with eggs. There was no way Bush could get out of the limousine for the traditional walk along the parade route until it got in front of the White House, to the most secure zone and an area free of protestors.

My mind raced back to that experience sixteen years later, as I prepared to take the ride once again, this time on a flatbed truck in front of Donald Trump's presidential limousine. Those memories are vivid, and they are a reminder that you don't have to go back all that far to find a time where Americans emerged from a bitter and hard-fought presidential election bitterly divided. In fact, the divide after that election was in many ways deeper. Not only did Bush lose the popular vote, the victory was ratified only after a 5–4 ruling of the Supreme Court where all five of the justices who voted against the recount were appointed by Republican presidents. On January 20, 2001, a significant segment of the population firmly believed the election had been stolen.

As in 2001, for Donald Trump's swearing in, the vanquished opponent was right there with him on the inaugural platform. Hillary Clinton, sitting among the former presidents and First Ladies, was no more than ten feet away from Donald Trump.

But where George W. Bush used his inaugural address to attempt to bridge the divide left by his election victory, Donald Trump exalted the divide. As the former presidents looked on with unease, Trump used the first minutes of his presidency to declare a different kind of transfer of power:

"We are transferring power from Washington, DC, and giving it back to you, the American people."

Trump's inaugural address is remembered, and always will be, for the phrase "American carnage," which he used to describe the state of the nation after eight years of Obama and eight years of Bush. But the part that struck me as the most significant, and the most uncomfortable to those surrounding him, came during those first two minutes of his speech, when he took that visual moment of unity, the image of the new president surrounded by the leaders of both parties past and present, and essentially accused the very people on the stage with him of betraying the American people.

"For too long, a small group in our nation's capital has reaped the rewards of government while the people have borne the cost."

What small group was he talking about if not the group right there on the stage with him?

"Politicians prospered—but the jobs left, and the factories closed."

What politicians was he referring to if not those surrounding him at that moment?

"The establishment protected itself, but not the citizens of our country."

Those words were pitch-perfect to millions of Trump supporters around the country who believed both parties had failed them. But those words were also a direct affront to the human beings on that inaugural platform—the congressional leaders, former presidents, and former vice presidents seated right there with him. They had come to celebrate American democracy and the peaceful transfer of power and ended up getting a verbal kick in the teeth from Donald Trump in his very first act as president of the United States.

Down on the parade route after the speech, there were protestors, but they were not as loud or as intense as during the Bush inaugural. There were no eggs thrown at the presidential limo. There were also sections of enthusiastic Trump supporters. At one point those Trump supporters became protestors too—not protesting the new president but protesting me as I rode down Pennsylvania Avenue in front of the presidential limo.

"You are fake news!" one person yelled as we traveled down Pennsylvania Avenue, his taunt clearly audible on live television. Others started chanting, "CNN sucks! CNN sucks!" The chant, also clearly audible on live TV, lasted for a full minute before being overtaken by chants of "USA! USA!" At Trump rallies during the campaign, "CNN sucks" had become a generic taunt some Trump supporters directed at any reporters who didn't work for Fox News.

As we made it down past the Trump International Hotel on Pennsylvania Avenue, there was something that I had not seen during Bush's inaugural parade or, for that matter, Obama's. There were sections of the parade route with almost no people at all. It was odd.

As we turned onto the two-block section of Pennsylvania Avenue in front of the White House, Trump started to get out of the car to walk and wave, but after taking a few steps, he got right back in. The problem wasn't protestors or security. It was empty bleacher seats. Whole sections of the most prime seats for the parade—right next to the presidential viewing platform directly in front of the White House—were entirely empty.

This had to have been some kind of an organizational snafu. There was certainly no shortage of die-hard Trump supporters who would have loved to have had those seats. But for whatever reason, they were empty. This was embarrassing, especially to a new president who loved nothing more about his winning campaign than the massive size of the crowds who turned out to see him virtually everywhere he went. And now here, right in front of the White House, there was no crowd, just lots of empty seats.

There was nothing Donald Trump obsessed over more during his campaign than the size of his adoring crowds. The sight of those empty bleachers, right there at his moment of ultimate glory, had to enrage him—setting the stage for his bizarre first twenty-four hours as president.

CHAPTER NINE

ALTERNATIVE FACTS

The first weeks of the Trump White House were so filled with drama and chaos that I found myself coming to work every day wondering which of the senior administration officials I was talking to would either be fired, resign, or have a nervous breakdown by the end the day.

On day twenty-one of the Trump presidency I scrawled this note in my journal:

> The speculation—inside Trump world and outside—is which senior staffer leaves or is fired first. Is it Reince Priebus (25% chance)? Is it Sean Spicer (30%)? Michael Flynn, the National Security Advisor (35%) or somebody else—Kellyanne Conway? Steve Bannon? (combined 10%).

This wasn't idle speculation. Flynn would only last another three days. And, amazingly, all of them except for Conway would be gone by August.

While the White House was careening from one self-imposed crisis to another, public fascination with the drama was sky-high. Cable news, network news, and newspapers were filled with all things Trump. Ratings and circulation were up. Suddenly even my daughter Anna's high school friends seemed to know about everything happening at the White House and would pepper me with questions about Trump—and his spokesman too. Sean Spicer at one point during this period told me he was the most well-known press secretary ever. He was probably right, even if his renown was more a case of infamy than fame.

It was quite a change from my experience covering President Obama. The White House briefings of Obama press secretary Josh Earnest, especially during his last year in office, were sparsely attended and watched by a small audience made up of those of us paid to watch and those souls who tune in to C-SPAN in the middle of the day. Now Spicer's briefings were must-see TV, carried by all the cable news networks and inspiring one of the most viewed *SNL* skits in years—Melissa McCarthy's hilarious portrayal of Spicer's combative and tongue-tied disregard for the truth.

At the culmination of the skit, McCarthy, playing Spicer, breaks out a Super Soaker water gun and starts shooting a reporter trying to ask a question: "This is soapy water and I'm trying to wash out that filthy lying mouth!"

Spicer brought an oversized water gun to the White House the following Monday and planned to break it out as a way to show he had a sense of humor too and wasn't bothered by the skit. But when he told the president about his plan, Trump erupted, telling him the skit wasn't funny and it was a terrible idea to acknowledge it at all.

Interest in the Trump White House was off the charts, but the new president's relationship with the press got off to a horrid start.

During his very first speech after the inauguration, it took President Trump all of twenty seconds to start lashing out at what he called "the dishonest media." This was his speech at CIA headquarters in

Langley, Virginia, the day after the inauguration, a speech intended to be a gesture of respect for the intelligence community but remembered primarily for how odd it was.

The audience of CIA employees appreciated the gesture the president made by making his first trip outside the White House a visit to Langley. They gave him a standing ovation when he was introduced by Vice President Pence. But the speech quickly veered off course. He marveled at the number of times he had been on the cover of *Time* magazine (fourteen), wondering aloud if it was an all-time record (Richard Nixon actually holds that distinction with fifty-five covers). Looking at CIA employees, who take pride in being nonpartisan, he proclaimed, "Probably almost everybody in this room voted for me." Touting the credentials of his choice for CIA director (West Point, Harvard) he said, "Trust me, I'm like a smart person." And he complained bitterly about news reports' not giving him full credit for the size of his inauguration crowd, which he said "looked like a million, million and a half people."

Pointing to the journalists in the back of the room he said, "They are among the most dishonest human beings on Earth."

Somehow the words stung a little more than Trump's attacks during the campaign or the transition. This was now the president of the United States vilifying us. It was also proof, as if any was needed, that Donald Trump's tone toward the free press was not going to change now that he was the president.

The president made those remarks in front of a white marble wall in the CIA main lobby, a wall with 117 stars carved into it and an inscription reading, "In honor of those members of the Central Intelligence Agency who gave their lives in the service of their country." To the intelligence community, the CIA's Memorial Wall is sacred ground. Each one of those stars represents a fallen CIA employee. And the poignance of the memorial is magnified by the fact that several of the stars are in remembrance of CIA employees whose names are secret, their sacrifice unknown to the nation they served because they died while serving as undercover operatives.

The president's words that day caused a change in CIA policy, a change that has never been publicly revealed but one that is obvious if you look at how the Memorial Wall has been used ever since. Since that day, there has been no speech or public event before the Memorial Wall except for an annual memorial ceremony, in which the CIA quietly and solemnly pays tribute to the fallen. Outside of that ceremony, the wall is not to be used as the backdrop for anything. The agency's leadership won't ever again allow the Memorial Wall to be used as a backdrop for the kind of speech Donald Trump gave on his first full day as president.

It was almost six P.M. that Saturday evening by the time Sean Spicer made his first appearance behind the podium in the White House briefing room and gave his famous and much-mocked lecture to the White House press corps about the size of the crowd attending Trump's inauguration the day before:

"This was the largest audience to ever witness an inauguration—period—both in person and around the globe," Spicer thundered, managing to lie about both the size of the inaugural crowd and the punctuation of that sentence.

I had traveled to New York that afternoon, so it was my friend and colleague Mary Bruce, ABC's brilliant congressional correspondent, who sat in the front row directly in front of the podium and bore the brunt of Sean's angry harangue. Mary had a perplexed look on her face as Spicer, wearing a suit that didn't fit him quite right and standing at a podium that was a little too tall for him, carried on and on about the "deliberately false reporting" on the size of the inaugural crowd and accused the news media of a "shameful and wrong" effort to downplay the enthusiasm for Trump's inauguration.

Like most of the other reporters in the briefing room being yelled at, Mary had not reported a single word about the size of the president's inaugural crowd. And that wasn't the only perplexing thing about what was happening: Why in the world were the president and his press secretary spending so much of their first day in office obsessing about something as trivial as the size of his inaugural crowd? Trump attracted huge crowds throughout his campaign. His inaugural crowd was massive too. Who cared if it wasn't as big as Obama's? The size of the crowd didn't mean a damn thing.

I counted at least three straight-out falsehoods in Spicer's diatribe. But the thing I found most disturbing about his debut performance in the briefing room was that he did not take a single question. I had never seen anything like it. Answering questions is central to the press secretary's job. You can come into the White House briefing room and yell at reporters, if that is your thing, but you can't walk out without answering questions.

When Spicer came back into that room on Monday, I was sitting front and center and ready to ask the question that would destroy our relationship—although I had no idea at the time.

The whole situation was bizarre. Not just the untruths or the obsession with trivialities or the idea of a press secretary refusing to answer questions in a room created for press secretaries to answer questions. To me, the role of Sean Spicer in this farce was the strangest thing of all. When Donald Trump named him White House press secretary, I thought it was good news. I immediately called to congratulate him and offer any advice he might need in navigating the White House press corps based on my experiences dealing with ten different White House press secretaries since I first walked in the briefing room as a reporter for CNN in 1998.

I figured Trump had picked somebody who was widely known and, for the most part, well liked by reporters in Washington. I had known Spicer for almost twenty years and always thought he was a reasonable guy and a straight shooter. I once even shaved his head on national television. It was Spicer's idea. After the 2012 election, Spicer and the Democratic National Committee press secretary Brad Woodhouse agreed to shave their heads to raise funds for the St. Baldrick's Foundation's effort to help children with cancer. I wielded the razor on a Sunday on ABC's *This Week with George Stephanopoulos*, and they raised more than $12,000 for a good cause. Watching Sean behind the podium four years later, it seemed to me as if he had become an entirely different person after he was named Donald Trump's press secretary.

As Spicer started answering his first questions, he made a point of skipping those of us in the front rows with the largest news organizations. But everything seemed better about Spicer's second appearance in the briefing room. He was calm. He seemed to be more careful with his facts. The podium had been lowered so it didn't look too big for him. And this time, his suit actually fit.

"Before I get to a policy question," I said when Spicer finally called on me, "just a question about the nature of your job."

"Yeah," he said.

"Is it your intention to always tell the truth from that podium, and will you pledge never to knowingly say something that is not factual?"

It seemed to me to be an essential question. Spicer had said several untrue things in his first briefing, and making matters worse, the White House had failed to correct the record. The very next day, on *Meet the Press*, Kellyanne Conway had coined the unforgettable phrase "alternative facts" as she defended Spicer's false statements.

"You're saying it's a falsehood," Conway had told NBC's Chuck Todd. "Our press secretary gave alternative facts."

In light of all that, I believed we needed to establish whether Spicer intended to at least try to tell the truth in his role as the White House spokesman. To his credit, he took the question seriously and with no apparent offense.

"It is," Spicer replied. "It's an honor to do this, and yes, I believe that we have to be honest with the American people. I think sometimes we can disagree with the facts. There are certain things that we may not fully understand when we come out. But our intention is never to lie to you, Jonathan."

The question was an easy one, but this was essentially the answer you want from a White House press secretary. Perhaps the phrase "we can disagree with the facts" was an unfortunate one, but given the events of the past couple of days, I was prepared to take Spicer's assurance at face value: "Our intention is never to lie to you."

What I was not prepared for was Spicer's delayed response. Over the coming hours and days, Spicer came to deeply resent me for asking that question. He believed I had questioned his integrity. How dare I ask him if he intended to tell the truth? He told others that I would never have asked such a question of a press secretary for a Democratic president. Here again, Sean was disagreeing with the facts. I had asked Josh Earnest a variation of the same question when he became Obama's press secretary.

The next day, I went in to see him in his office. He was seething in anger. He didn't mention my question, but he unloaded on me over something that had aired on ABC's *Nightline* program the night before. *Nightline* is an excellent broadcast, but I was sound asleep by the time it aired at 12:35 A.M. Eastern Time and I suspect Sean was too. Still, Sean had learned the show aired an incomplete quote from former White House press secretary Ari Fleischer about Spicer's debut in the briefing room. Fleischer had both criticized and praised Spicer, but the *Nightline* story included only the criticism. Here's the quote as it aired:

FLEISCHER: His briefing made me uncomfortable. It was too truculent, too tough. It looks to me as if the ball dropped on Saturday.

It was a real quote. And it was notable that a former Republican press secretary was so blunt in his criticism. But here is the full quote:

FLEISCHER: His briefing made me uncomfortable. It was too truculent, too tough. It looks to me as if the ball dropped on Saturday. <u>Sean recovered it and ran for a first down on Monday.</u>

The underlined part had been edited out.

I didn't know why Sean was screaming at me about this. I assumed he had more important things to worry about than the editing of a short quote that aired after midnight on his first Monday at the White House. But I also believed the substance of his complaint was not unreasonable. Eager for ABC News to be completely fair and to have a good relationship with the new press secretary, I called *Nightline* and urged them to update the story with the full quote. They did more than that. First, they inserted the full quote in the online version of the story. Then, that evening, the program did an extraordinary on-air correction and apology.

"In our segment about the new administration we interviewed former White House press secretary Ari Fleischer," anchor Juju Chang told viewers. "In editing the piece, his quote was shortened and, as a result, his comments mischaracterized. We corrected the piece online to include his full quote and context. We apologize and regret the error."

Fleischer immediately thanked *Nightline* for the correction and accepted the apology. Spicer never did.

The next day, ABC's David Muir arrived at the White House to interview President Trump, his first network interview as president. ABC News president James Goldston came along as well and found himself accosted by the new press secretary. As the camera crews set up in the Blue Room of the White House, Spicer walked in and went right up to Goldston, loudly lecturing him about the Fleischer quote. Taking heat from a White House official is not unusual for a network news president, but it was odd that Spicer was stuck on something that had happened days earlier. You might think Spicer, seeing a network news president, would have wanted to discuss the exclusive interview that was about to happen, or perhaps the network's plans for covering the administration. But no. Spicer was hung up on the editing of a quote that had aired two days earlier and that ABC had already apologized for and corrected. This was a sign of things to come. Over the next few months, Spicer would spend a lot of time yelling at reporters, but his most passionate complaints were always about things that related to the way he was portrayed, not the president or his policies.

As Spicer vented over and over and over again about that Ari Fleischer quote, it soon became apparent that what really bothered him was that first question I had asked him. At the next briefing, he ignored me completely. This is not easy to do. My seat is right in front of his podium. Spicer made a point of calling on reporters next to me and behind me. He called on people standing in the aisles. He called on a guy with the Russian state-owned website Sputnik—a guy literally on the Russian payroll. But he did not call on me.

There's no constitutional right for a reporter to be called on at a White House press briefing, but I was miffed. I had been in the briefing room with ten different press secretaries for four different presidents while working for two different networks, but I had never been iced out like that. My relationship with Obama press secretary Jay

Carney had been tense—our exchanges were often bitter and sometimes personal both on and off camera—but not even Carney had
gone through an entire briefing without calling on me. But here was
my old friend Sean Spicer, in his first week on the job, trying to keep
me from doing my job.

I was annoyed, but I figured it was a onetime thing.

Then, the next day, the same thing happened. Spicer didn't call on
me. The trend continued the following week. Day after day, I was
going to White House press briefings and Spicer was refusing to call
on me. To make it clear this was personal and not about ABC News,
he repeatedly called on my colleague Cecilia Vega, but he continued
to give me the silent treatment.

During the second week, I went to Spicer's office.

"Sean, what's the problem here?" I asked him. "Why the hell aren't
you calling on me?"

Sean just looked at me in silence. From behind his standing desk
in the press secretary's spacious office, he simply pointed toward
the door.

"You are really throwing me out of your office?" I asked in
disbelief.

He kept pointing to the door. I walked out, marveling at the fact
that the White House press secretary was refusing to talk to me.

This bizarre situation went on for a full three weeks. I eventually
called Hope Hicks to complain and told Chief of Staff Reince Priebus
his handpicked press secretary was out of control. Finally on a Friday
afternoon, the twenty-first day of the Trump presidency, Spicer called
me back to his office. He greeted me with a lecture and a bit of a
threat.

"First of all," he began, "if you have a problem with me, tell me
about it. Don't go calling Hope or Reince, because that will get you
nowhere. It will make matters worse for you."

"Give me a break, Sean. When I came to talk to you, you did this," I said, pointing to the door as he had done when I was last in his office.

And with that we had a heart-to-heart conversation that lasted about ten minutes. He confided in me about the pressures of being Donald Trump's press secretary and acknowledged that my first question had been eating at him. It hadn't really bothered him, he said, until he looked back and watched the coverage of his first few days on the job. The clip had been played over and over again on network after network, often in stories pointing out how Spicer had failed to tell the truth. I told Sean that he would not always like my questions, but I would always treat him fairly.

The next briefing was the following Tuesday, the day after National Security Advisor Michael Flynn was fired for lying to Vice President Pence about his conversations with Russian ambassador Sergey Kislyak. Spicer called on me first. I began by asking if he knew whether Flynn had been in contact with the Russians during the campaign. Then I asked him this:

"Why would the president—if he was notified seventeen days ago that Flynn had misled the vice president and, other officials here, and that he was a potential threat to blackmail by the Russians—why would he be kept on for almost three weeks?"

"Well, that's not—that assumes a lot of things that are not true," Spicer said as he started to respond to my question.

But there was nothing untrue in my question. The president had been notified about Flynn's deception seventeen days earlier by acting attorney general Sally Yates. And he had kept him on as national security advisor.

Spicer was once again responding to me. Now he just wasn't telling the truth.

CHAPTER TEN

FINE-TUNED MACHINE

Mike Dubke was about five minutes into his job interview when the president asked him what seemed like a hypothetical question.

"What do you think?" he asked. "Should I do a press conference?"

Donald Trump had been president for twenty-seven days, and Mike Dubke was in the Oval Office, sitting across from him at the Resolute Desk, interviewing for the job of White House communications director.

"I think that would be a good idea," Dubke answered. "By this time in their presidencies, most presidents have had their first press conferences. Some had already done two."

Dubke continued speaking, explaining where he thought the president should hold the press conference and how he would prepare for it. For the venue, he recommended the East Room of the White House, where Reagan had done his prime-time press conferences, and not the White House briefing room, where Obama sometimes had done his. And he suggested the president hold the press conference the following week—one week before his first address to a joint session of Congress. But he recommended the president first convene meetings with his communications team and senior staff to go over the long list of likely questions they'd face and come up with a strategy for the best way to get his message out.

"No, no—let's do it now," the president said, and as he finished his sentence, he looked over Dubke and toward the back of the Oval Office, where Chief of Staff Reince Priebus and Press Secretary Sean Spicer were lurking by the door and listening in.

At this point, Dubke thought the president was playing a joke on him. But then he turned around and saw the looks on the faces of Priebus and Spicer. The two of them had gone pale. This was no joke. They knew that when the president said "now," he meant now.

Until that moment, the strangest part of the day was that Dubke was there in the Oval Office in the first place. An easygoing and moderate Republican, he had no ties to Trump or the Trump campaign. He didn't even know Priebus or Spicer particularly well. But the White House had been scrambling to find a communications director, one of the most prized jobs in the West Wing and a job that usually goes to a confidant of the president. The guy who was supposed to have the job, Jason Miller, had stepped aside for personal reasons right before Trump took office. Priebus and Spicer thought Dubke would be a suitable alternative. He had built a solid, although low-profile, career advising Republican interest groups on political and communications strategy. And, most important, he was willing to take the job.

"But, Mr. President," Dubke said, reacting to the panicked look on the faces of Priebus and Spicer, "setting up a press conference takes time."

He explained to the president that at this time of day, there could be tourists visiting the White House. They would need to be cleared out. And it takes time to set up the East Room. You need to bring platforms for the cameras, set up the lighting, and put out the chairs for the press corps.

It was too late. Trump's mind was made up. It was time for a press conference. The president hadn't even offered Dubke the job yet.* There was no time for such formalities. The West Wing was now in a mad scramble to set up Donald Trump's first solo press conference as president of the United States on about three hours' notice— something that would usually involve several days of planning.

I wasn't even at the White House when the notice went out to the press about forty-five minutes later. The alert on my phone told me Sean Spicer's daily briefing, which had been scheduled for later that afternoon, would be canceled and the president would be holding a press conference at noon—in less than an hour. I put on my coat and ran the six blocks from the ABC News Washington bureau to the White House.

I am tempted to say this was the craziest day of the Trump presidency up to that point. The press conference that day would be unlike any other ever seen at the White House. But virtually every day so far had followed a similar pattern—White House staff blindsided by an impromptu presidential decision or something else totally unexpected, and White House reporters like me scrambling to keep up. We had already seen a national security advisor fired for misleading the vice president and an acting attorney general fired for refusing to defend the president's policy in court. Leaks were coming out of the West Wing faster than the information could be printed—leaks about infighting among the president's top advisors and leaks about the president's conversations with foreign leaders. And it was still just the first month.

_____

*Dubke did get the job, but his official start date wasn't until March 6, three weeks after that first press conference. He served as White House communications director for three months, resigning on June 2, 2017.

In terms of chaos, the tone had been set earlier in the Trump presidency, on his seventh day in office. Late that Friday afternoon, he visited the Pentagon and, while he was there, signed an executive order that he said would keep radical Islamic terrorists out of the United States.

"We only want to admit those into our country who will support our country and love deeply our people," said the president.

As he spoke, Vice President Pence stood on one side, looking resolute, his head slowly bobbing up and down as he nodded with just about every other word the president said. On the other side of the president was Defense Secretary Jim Mattis, who had nothing to do with the order and seemed uncertain about what exactly the president was talking about.

After signing the order in front of the cameras, President Trump said nothing about what the order actually entailed. Back at the White House, reporters clamored for more information, but the president's own press secretary could not explain the order because he had not seen it—and he couldn't find anybody at the White House with a copy of the order to show him.

By that evening, everybody knew what the executive order was. The so-called travel ban had gone into effect, causing chaos at airports around the United States as travelers with perfectly legal travel documents were told to turn around if they were from any of the seven countries listed in the ban, all of which had majority-Muslim populations. And refugees fleeing the bloodshed in Syria were sent home even if they had already been granted permission and had families in the United States prepared to welcome them. Mattis himself would object to the order, primarily because Iraq was included on the list of banned countries, freezing out Iraqi nationals who had worked with US forces during the Iraq War.

As the COVID-19 pandemic hit the United States, the White House Correspondents' Association had to dramatically limit the number of people in the White House briefing room. This was the coronavirus task force briefing on March 24, 2020, when President Trump predicted life would return to normal by Easter. It didn't happen. *(Doug Mills)*

This is the last remaining invitation to a book party I hosted in 1995. On a whim, I called Trump to ask him to provide a quote for my invitation. He had me write the quote and then approved it. *(Courtesy of the author)*

Donald Trump suddenly stopped our tour of Trump Tower in 1994 to ask if I wanted to get a picture. The photo sat in a box of old photos for more than a decade. I dug it out after he started running for president. *(Francis Specker)*

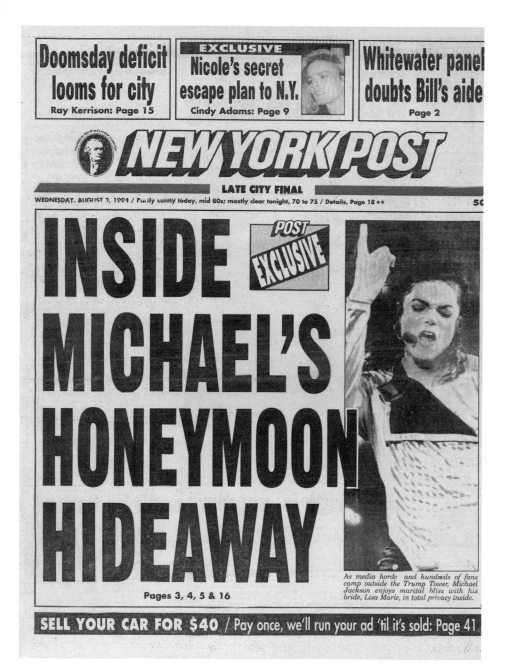

NEW YORK POST

LATE CITY FINAL

WEDNESDAY, AUGUST 3, 1994 / Partly sunny today, mid 80s; mostly clear tonight, 70 to 75 / Details, Page 18 ★★ 50

INSIDE POST EXCLUSIVE MICHAEL'S HONEYMOON HIDEAWAY

Pages 3, 4, 5 & 16

As media horde and hundreds of fans camp outside the Trump Tower, Michael Jackson enjoys marital bliss with his bride, Lisa Marie, in total privacy inside.

SELL YOUR CAR FOR $40 / Pay once, we'll run your ad 'til it's sold: Page 41

My August 1994 cover story in the *New York Post* after Donald Trump gave me a private tour of Trump Tower while newlyweds Michael Jackson and Lisa Marie Presley were staying there. *(Courtesy of the author)*

This photo was taken in the Oval Office on November 10, 2016—just two days after Donald Trump won the presidential election. You can see the intense focus of everybody in the room as Barack Obama offers words of support for the president-elect and Trump says he plans to seek Obama's "counsel." The look on my face is one of amazement. *(Pete Souza, courtesy of the Obama Presidential Library)*

In that Oval Office meeting, I saw a side of Trump I had never seen before. He seemed humbled and a little dazed—as if he was struck by the enormity of what was about to happen. *(Courtesy of the author)*

Campaign flashback: During the 2000 New Hampshire primary, I spent many of my days on John McCain's Straight Talk Express bus. Here I was working my flip phone, flanked by two exhausted colleagues: AP's Scott Lindlaw and John Dickerson, who was then with Slate. *(Todd Harris)*

"Nothing at all on John McCain?" The Monday after John McCain died, I asked President Trump ten times to comment on his legacy, including here in the Oval Office. He ignored me each time. *(Courtesy of ABC News)*

Interviewing Donald Trump in Iowa in August 2013. I was criticized for doing the interview by those who said he was flirting with politics just to get attention. *(Courtesy of ABC News)*

With Trump in December 2014 in the Old Post Office building shortly after he broke ground on the Trump International Hotel on Pennsylvania Avenue. I asked him about his plans for the hotel—and told him "I would be shocked" if he ran for president. *(Courtesy of ABC News)*

The sign outside the Old Post Office in December 2014 as construction began on the Trump International Hotel: COMING 2016: TRUMP. *(Courtesy of the author)*

This is Trump's campaign headquarters on the fifth floor of Trump Tower as it appeared when I stopped by on September 1, 2015. *(Courtesy of the author)*

At the Trump campaign headquarters in September 2015 with Hope Hicks—the most overworked campaign staffer I ever encountered. *(Courtesy of the author)*

Just upstairs from the Trump campaign headquarters was this: the dormant set of *The Apprentice. (Courtesy of the author)*

Backstage before a rally in Grand Rapids, Michigan. The papers in my hand included a list from RealClearPolitics of polls taken over the previous six months on a head-to-head matchup of Trump versus Hillary Clinton. Every single poll showed Trump losing. When I showed him the list, Trump walked out. It turns out the list was wrong: a recent poll had shown him winning by five points. *(John Parkinson)*

After one of the most exhausting and frustrating interview experiences of my life, Donald Trump asked me if I wanted to have a picture taken. As you can see from my expression, I had no desire for a photo, but I did it anyway. *(John Parkinson)*

Front row at the Mexico City Trump show: When candidate Donald Trump made his secretly planned trip to Mexico City on August 31, 2016, the campaign ditched the traveling press. The plan was to answer no questions, but Trump decided to answer my question, creating a big problem—for Trump and for Mexican President Enrique Peña Nieto. *(Courtesy of the author)*

This was my view of Trump's joint appearance with President Enrique Peña Nieto. Future attorney general and Trump nemesis Jeff Sessions took his seat right in front of me. *(Courtesy of the author)*

My friend and former colleague Sam Feist, CNN's Washington bureau chief, sent me this photo on the day of President Trump's inauguration after CNN inadvertently broadcast video of me riding along the parade route, directly in front of the presidential limousine. *(Sam Feist)*

On the South Lawn of the White House shortly after Donald Trump arrived at the White House for the first time as president. *(Courtesy of ABC News)*

Trump emailed me this letter two days before his inauguration and followed up with a memorable phone call. *(Courtesy of the author)*

GEORGE BUSH

January 10, 2017

Dear Donald,

Barbara and I are so sorry we can't be there for your Inauguration on January 20th. My doctor says if I sit outside in January, it likely will put me six feet under. Same for Barbara. So I guess we're stuck in Texas.

But we will be with you and the country in spirit. I want you to know that I wish you the very best as you begin this incredible journey of leading our great country. If I can ever be of help, please let me know.

All the best,

G. Bush

The Honorable Donald J. Trump
President-Elect of the United States

When I walked into the West Wing on January 20, 2017, all signs of Barack Obama were gone. Just a day earlier, these picture frames featured photos of President Obama and his family. *(Courtesy of the author)*

The press secretary's office on January 20, 2017, minutes after Sean Spicer first arrived at the White House as press secretary. *(Courtesy of the author)*

In August 2013, Sam Stein of the Huffington Post called my interview with Trump in Iowa "performance art." Trump printed out the article and wrote a note on it: "Perhaps Sam—but it sure gave them good ratings!"

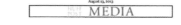

August 13, 2013

MEDIA

'This Week' Criticized For Donald Trump Interview (VIDEO)

Posted: 08/11/2013 12:41 pm EDT | Updated: 08/11/2013 12:57 pm EDT

ABC News' "This Week" took some heat on Sunday over interviewing Donald Trump about whether he wants to run for president in 2016.

Jon Karl, the network's chief White House correspondent, interviewed Trump in Ames, Iowa on Saturday night. He asked Trump whether he "could be taken seriously as a presidential candidate" and to respond to criticism that his talk of running is merely a "publicity stunt." Trump said that he is considering running.

On Sunday, Media Matters blasted ABC News' decision to host Trump on the program. "Trump is unlikely to be an actual candidate in this election or any other, and never has been- why would ABC News allow itself to be used for yet another round of promotional appearances for a charlatan?" the organization wrote.

Other viewers also balked at the interview. The Huffington Post's Sam Stein tweeted:

> **Sam Stein**
> @samsteinhp
>
> I can't tell if this Donald Trump interview on This Week is performance art
> 10:23 AM - 11 Aug 2013
>
> 15 RETWEETS 7 FAVORITES

With President Trump aboard Air Force One on February 3, 2017—his second trip on the presidential airplane. *(Wayne Boyd)*

The founding charter of the White House Correspondents' Association—signed by the eleven original members—disappeared during a renovation of the White House in 2005. It was rediscovered inside this old box somewhere in the White House in 2019. *(Courtesy of the author)*

The only thing on the president's schedule the day after he fired FBI Director James Comey was a meeting with the Russian foreign minister in the Oval Office. No American reporter or photographer was allowed into the meeting, but the Russians had a photographer there and took some remarkable photos, including this one with Russian Ambassador Sergey Kislyak. *(TASS)*

On June 1, 2018, Donald Trump welcomed one of the most intimidating figures in Kim Jong Un's government into the Oval Office. Vice Chairman Kim Yong Chol brought an enormous envelope, which was quickly screened for poisons before it was handed to the president—a letter from Kim Jong Un. About a year later, a senior administration official would show me all of the letters Kim had sent President Trump. *(Shealah Craighead)*

Before the pandemic, the White House briefing room was one of the most crowded and chaotic places in Washington. This is the briefing with then Deputy Press Secretary Sarah Sanders on May 10, 2017—the day after the firing of James Comey. *(Jabin Botsford of The Washington Post)*

During the pandemic, the White House became a COVID-19 hot zone and a dangerous place to work. This was the briefing with Press Secretary Kayleigh McEnany on May 8, 2020. *(Jabin Botsford of The Washington Post)*

After Kanye West proposed replacing Air Force One with a new hydrogen-powered "iPlane One," President Trump turned to me and asked, "Can we get rid of Air Force One? No, you don't like that idea?" *(Courtesy of the author)*

Something I never expected: a surprise hug from Kanye West in the Oval Office. *(Courtesy of ABC News)*

"What you just described is a quid pro quo." My exchange with Acting Chief of Staff Mick Mulvaney in the White House briefing room on October 17, 2019. *(Courtesy of ABC News)*

While the president had yet to do a solo press conference, he had already welcomed a parade of world leaders to the White House— including Theresa May of the United Kingdom, Shinzo Abe of Japan, Justin Trudeau of Canada, King Abdullah of Jordan, and Bibi Netanyahu of Israel—and had appeared before the press with each of them. But in those joint press conferences, the long-established practice is for the president to take only two questions from the US press and two questions from the foreign press. And in those events, the president had called only on conservative news outlets, who'd rewarded him by avoiding any uncomfortable questions.

As I was escorted with the rest of the press corps into the vast East Room, White House employees were still moving quickly about, scrambling to set up the press conference. The presidential podium was already in place up front, but the chairs were still being brought in. Video cameras and lights were still getting set up. At every presidential press conference I had ever attended, there had been assigned seating, name cards on the chairs. There was no time for that. Aside from the first two rows, which were set aside for the president's senior advisors, there were no assigned seats marked here; this would be a free-for-all—for the White House reporters and for the president too. Shortly after suddenly deciding to hold the press conference during Mike Dubke's job interview, the president had gone into a meeting with congressional leaders. He would be coming into the press conference shortly after that. There would be no prep session for the president with his staff, no brainstorming possible questions or refining possible answers. The president would be winging it.

The East Room is much larger, and far more opulent, than the cramped, no-frills confines of the White House briefing room. The biggest room in the White House, the East Room has three enormous crystal-and-gold chandeliers hanging from the twenty-two-foot-high ceiling, gold-colored floor-to-ceiling drapes, and an eight-foot-tall portrait of George Washington looking on—the painting Dolley Madison instructed her fifteen-year-old slave Paul Jennings to remove and save from destruction just hours before the British torched the White House in 1814.

The surroundings may have been more dignified than the cramped and drab White House briefing room, but the cast of characters was the same.

The advent of the Trump era brought about a transformation of the White House press corps. The group of journalists cramming into the White House every day became much larger—and stranger. For Sean Spicer's daily briefings, each one of the forty-nine seats in the briefing room was filled, most of them with reporters working for news organizations who had long covered the White House. During the daily briefings by the press secretaries for Bush and Obama, several of these seats would often be empty. Now not only were they always filled, but people without seats stood elbow-to-elbow along the sides of the room and in the back. Some of those standing were reporters, some photographers, and others people who had somehow managed to get in by claiming they were journalists. There were reporters for major news organizations and reporters for conservative and liberal outlets. There were Trump boosters posing as journalists and Trump haters posing as journalists. There was a large contingent of foreign journalists. And there were often a couple of Americans on the Russian government's payroll, including former MSNBC anchor Ed Schultz, who was working for the Russian TV network RT, and Andrew Feinberg, who worked for Sputnik, a Russian-government website.* Feinberg was a short, stout guy with a booming voice and a permanent look of exasperation on his face. He spent much of his time standing on the driveway outside the briefing room smoking cigarettes.

As President Trump came into the room, we stood up as a customary gesture of respect. He began quietly, almost haltingly, reading from a binder he had brought with him, announcing his nominee to be secretary of labor.

Spicer and Dubke felt it was important for the president to begin his press conference by announcing that little bit of news, but this moment was not about a new labor secretary.

This first press conference was beginning with a declaration of war on the people right there in the room. "I'm making this presentation directly to the American people with the media present," he said, "because many of our nation's reporters and folks will not tell you the truth and will not treat the wonderful people of the country with the respect that they deserve."

This was one hell of a way to start. Here in a room packed with reporters covering his first solo press conference, the president, speaking to the cameras in the back of the room, declared that many reporters in that room didn't tell the truth and didn't respect the American people.

He continued this monologue for a full twenty-four minutes before taking his first question. He lashed out at his predecessors and he lashed out at Democrats in Congress, but mostly he lashed out at the news media.

"The press, honestly, is out of control," he said. "I turn on the TV,

---

*Feinberg eventually decided he didn't want to work for the Russians. He quit his job in May 2017, explaining via Twitter: "Seems @SputnikInt isn't happy with real journalists. They'd rather have ACTUAL propagandists operate anonymously."

open the newspapers, and I see stories of chaos. Chaos! Yet, it is the exact opposite. This administration is running like a fine-tuned machine."

As he went through his litany of complaints about media coverage, he ticked through his accomplishments so far as president and as a candidate, claiming at one point his victory was "the biggest Electoral College win since Ronald Reagan."

When it came time for questions, Trump made it clear he was ready for a fight. He wouldn't be avoiding hard questions this time. One of the first questions went to Peter Alexander of NBC News, who had covered the Trump campaign and never shied away from aggressively asking Trump tough questions. He decided to do some real-time fact-checking, calling the president out for saying something blatantly untrue.

"You said today that you had the biggest electoral margin since Ronald Reagan with three hundred four or three hundred six electoral votes," Alexander said. "In fact, President Obama got three hundred sixty-five in 2008."

"Well, I am talking Republican."

"George H. W. Bush [had] four hundred twenty-six when he won as president. So why should Americans trust—"

"Well, no, I was told," Trump responded. "I was given that information. I don't know. I was just given—we had a very, very big margin."

It was an extraordinary moment. The president of the United States in a nationally televised press conference saying something untrue and then, minutes later, getting called out for it. Alexander then got to the point of his question—a point sure to be an essential one for the duration of the Trump presidency.

"Why should Americans trust you when you have accused the information they receive of being fake when you're providing information that's fake?"

Instead of acknowledging the error and the obvious contradiction of denouncing real stories as "fake news" while at the same time providing his own version of "fake news," the president cast doubt on the facts, which are actually not in doubt at all.

"I was given that information," he told Alexander. "Actually, I've seen that information around. But it was a very substantial victory. Do you agree with that?"

"You're the president," he answered.

As the press conference went on for well over an hour, the president called on seventeen different reporters, personally insulting several of them along the way. At one point he predicted what the news stories would say about the press conference.

"Tomorrow they will say, 'Donald Trump rants and raves at the press,'" he said during a particularly testy exchange with CNN's Jim Acosta. "I'm not ranting and raving. I'm just telling you, you're dishonest people. But I'm not ranting and raving. I love this. I'm having a good time doing it. But tomorrow the headlines are going to be: 'Donald Trump Rants and Raves.'"

And then he said it again: "I am not ranting and raving."

He was right about the headlines. In the *New York Post,* one of the papers the president reads every day, the front-page headline called the press conference an "epic rant."

To be clear: He was ranting and he was raving. But I also got the clear sense he was thoroughly enjoying himself. Press Secretary Sean Spicer had been trying to protect the president from tough questions during his appearances with foreign leaders by giving him the names of conservative journalists to call on. The strategy worked. On the day Michael Flynn was fired earlier that week, the president had held a joint media appearance with Canadian Prime Minister Justin Trudeau and called on two reporters from conservative news outlets, and, amazingly, neither one of them asked about Michael Flynn.

All of that contributed to the tension as the president stood before the press and took questions from reporters he had been avoiding. He was also furious about the press coverage of his first month in office and wanted a chance to fight back. The stories over the previous few days had been particularly brutal. Just two days earlier, *The New York Times* had run a blockbuster front-page story with the headline: "Trump Campaign Aides Had Repeated Contacts with Russian Intelligence."

Citing "four current and former American officials," the *New York Times* story suggested there might be hard evidence that Trump's campaign had colluded with the Russians in their effort to tilt the election in Trump's favor: "Phone records and intercepted calls show that members of Donald J. Trump's 2016 presidential campaign and other Trump associates had repeated contacts with senior Russian intelligence officials in the year before the election."

"Mr. President, I just want to get you to clarify a very important point," I said when he called on me. "Can you say definitively that nobody on your campaign had any contacts with the Russians during the campaign?"

Instead of answering my question about anybody on his campaign, he answered for himself.

"Well, I had nothing to do with it," he said. "I have nothing to do with Russia. I told you, I have no deals there. I have no anything."

I hadn't asked if he had any contacts with the Russians. The *New York Times* story that week was not about Trump himself having contacts. It was about whether people on his campaign and other Trump associates did.

As Trump finished answering my question, I started getting a series of unsolicited text messages from Corey Lewandowski, Trump's first campaign manager.

"Manafort and Gates spoke to Russia," he texted.

He was referring to Paul Manafort, of course, who ran the campaign after Lewandowski was fired, and Manafort's deputy Rick Gates.

Lewandowski didn't have any direct knowledge of this, but while he remained a die-hard Trump loyalist, he sure hated both Manafort and Gates. And while neither man would be found guilty of conspiring with the Russians to interfere with the election, both would become central figures in the special counsel's Russia investigation.

A few minutes after answering my question, the president looked around the room and declared he wanted to find a friendly reporter. There were dozens of people trying to get his attention. He pointed to one of the many, many new faces in the crowd—one of those who had started coming to the White House press room after Trump was elected. The reporter he picked was Jake Turx, a thirty-year-old reporter with *Ami*, an Orthodox Jewish magazine.

Even among this crowd, Turx stood out. He wore a yarmulke with his Twitter handle embroidered on it.

"Are you a friendly reporter?" Trump asked as Turx stood up. "Watch how friendly he is."

Turx began by introducing himself, and gesturing toward the other reporters, he said, "Despite what some of my colleagues may have been reporting, I haven't seen anybody in my community accuse either yourself or anyone on your staff of being anti-Semitic."

Before he got to his question, Turx pointed out Trump has Jewish grandchildren (Jared and Ivanka's kids) and to them, he is their *zayde*—a Yiddish term of affection for "grandfather." Then Turx turned to a serious subject: a recent string of anti-Semitic incidents across the United States.

"What we are concerned about and what we haven't really heard being addressed is an uptick in anti-Semitism and how the government is planning to take care of it," Turx said. "There's been a report out that forty-eight bomb threats have been made against Jewish centers all across the country in the last couple of weeks. There are people who are committing anti-Semitic acts or threatening to—"

President Trump cut him off.

"You see, he said he was going to ask a very simple, easy question," Trump snapped. "And it's not. It's not. Not a simple question, not a fair question."

And with that, Trump ordered Turx to sit down. I have been at White House press conferences of four different presidents. Until this moment I had never seen a president order a reporter to sit down.

"Number one," he said. "I am the least anti-Semitic person that you've ever seen in your entire life. Number two, racism. I am the least racist person."

Turx tried to interject that he wasn't suggesting Trump was racist or anti-Semitic.

"Quiet, quiet, quiet!" Trump commanded. "See, he lied. He was going to get up and ask a very straight, simple question. So, you know, welcome to the world of the media."

I am not sure what was most bizarre about Trump's interaction with this Orthodox Jewish reporter. Was it that he took such volcanic offense to a legitimate question from someone who seemed genuinely friendly toward the president? After all, Turx wasn't suggesting the anti-Semitic events were Trump's fault; he was asking what the government planned to do about them.

Or perhaps more bizarre was Trump's saying "welcome to the world of the media" in response to the perceived slight from Jake Turx, a reporter whose Twitter bio describes him as both a political reporter and a humorist. Turx asked a good question, but he wasn't exactly your typical White House correspondent.

The whole thing was surreal. Turx, by the way, told me later he wasn't offended at all by Trump's outburst. He is hardly a Trump critic. In fact, when he brought his two young children to the White

House a year later for Take Your Daughters and Sons to Work Day, his seven-year-old son, wearing a Make America Great Again hat, participated in a briefing for kids with Press Secretary Sarah Sanders and asked this question: "After President Trump makes America great again, what job will there be for future presidents?"

Even as he called on the next reporter, the president was still stewing about Turx's question.

"See, it just shows you about the press, but that is the way the press is."

As the press conference reached the one-hour mark, Trump called on a reporter named Kyle Mazza who, until recently, had been a high school student.

Mazza was another one of those new faces in the White House press area. Although he was only nineteen, he had a perpetual five-o'clock shadow and dressed like he was fifty. From his parents' house, Mazza had created his own news website called UNF News, which, he explained, stood for "Universal News Forever." Mazza still lived with his parents in New Jersey but somehow found a way to get himself down to the White House several days a week. He had managed to get called on by Sean Spicer, who often liked to avoid questions from the Associated Press and *New York Times* at his briefings, and now he was getting called on by the president of the United States.

Mazza began by noting that First Lady Melania Trump had just announced the reopening of the White House Visitors Office and said, "She does a lot of great work for the country as well."

And then Kyle Mazza came out with his big question.

"Can you tell us a little about what First Lady Melania Trump does for the country?" he asked. "And there is a unique level of interest in your administration, so by opening the White House Visitors Office, what does that mean to you?"

Trump, at last, was thrilled with the question.

"Now, that's what I call a nice question! That is very nice. Who are you with?"

"Universal News Forever."

"Good," Trump said. "I'm going to start watching. Thank you very much."

The president went on to proclaim that the First Lady is "terrific" and "a fabulous woman."

At least there was one question the president could call "nice."

When the press conference was over, he went back to watch how it was covered on the cable news channels. And sure enough, it was just as he'd predicted. On CNN, anchor Jake Tapper called the president's performance "unhinged," and on Fox News, anchor Shep Smith said the press conference was "absolutely crazy" and that Trump kept repeating "ridiculous throwaway lines that are not true."

It was an utterly bizarre press conference, but virtually every reporter in the room that day welcomed it. The president of the United States repeatedly and viciously attacked the press. He said things that weren't true. But he took questions until just about everybody in the room was thoroughly exhausted. Peter Alexander had a chance to challenge his facts in real time. I had the opportunity to ask about Russia and his campaign. Others were finally able to ask about Michael Flynn's firing and about Trump's agenda for urban America. And while he sought out a friendly question at one point, he did not shy from calling on reporters he knew were going to ask tough, even hostile, questions.

As he fought with reporters, the president seemed to truly enjoy the press conference. He was, after all, the center of attention. And more than that, he proved he could command the nation's attention by simply calling in the cameras. He called a press conference, and at his command, the East Room was filled with reporters and television crews in no time. Sure, he got tough questions, but he also got to fight with reporters he saw every day on television. I texted Hope Hicks as soon as it was over and said the president should do more press conferences.

"He will," she answered.

But he didn't. It would be several months before President Trump held another solo press conference. He loved the attention, but he saw that while he could command the nation's attention, he couldn't control the message. If he said things that were untrue, he'd be called out. If he said things that didn't make sense, he'd be called on it. If he ranted and raved, reporters would say he ranted and raved. He loved his ability to call in the press with a snap of his fingers, but he hated his inability to control what we said. As a real estate developer, he had famously suggested all news is good news. Now he was learning that it's not—not when you're president of the United States.

While the president seemed to enjoy doing combat with reporters, the world would soon see, in dramatic fashion, he hated watching the news coverage of his press conference.

CHAPTER ELEVEN

ENEMY OF THE PEOPLE

The very next day after his chaotic and combative first solo press conference, Donald Trump opened a new line of attack against the free press, and it was his harshest, most incendiary attack yet.

> **Donald J. Trump**
> (@realDonaldTrump)
>
> The FAKE NEWS media (failing @nytimes, @CNN, @NBCNews and many more) is not my enemy, it is the enemy of the American people. SICK!
>
> 2/17/17, 4:48 PM

Even by Trump standards, this tweet was shocking. *Enemy of the American people.* As I thought about the significance of those words—and wondered why he had not included ABC in the list of treasonous news organizations—he deleted the tweet.

Did he delete it because he realized how profoundly offensive it was?

Yeah, right.

A few minutes later, he tweeted again, and I, along with my ABC News colleagues, was included as an enemy of the people by the president.

Donald J. Trump
(@realDonaldTrump)

The FAKE NEWS media (failing @nytimes, @NBCNews, @ABC, @CBS, @CNN) is not my enemy, it is the enemy of the American People!

2/17/17, 4:48 PM

There is nothing new or alarming about a president's complaining—even complaining bitterly—about the press. Free-speech advocates often quote Thomas Jefferson's saying, "Were it left to me to decide whether we should have a government without newspapers or newspapers without government, I should not hesitate a moment to prefer the latter." But Jefferson wrote those words in 1787, more than a decade before he was elected president. After he had been president for several years and had endured relentless attacks from newspapers controlled by his political opponents, Jefferson expressed a much darker view of the press. In a private letter written in 1807 to a seventeen-year-old aspiring publisher named John Norvell, Jefferson declared, "Nothing can now be believed which is seen in a newspaper."

"Truth itself becomes suspicious by being put into that polluted vehicle," Jefferson wrote Norvell. "I will add, that the man who never looks into a newspaper is better informed than he who reads them; inasmuch as he who knows nothing is nearer to truth than he whose mind is filled with falsehoods & errors."*

---

*Jefferson actually had a point here. At the time, American newspapers were aligned with political parties. There was no tradition of an independent free press devoted

Enemy of the American People. This wasn't Thomas Jefferson complaining about fake news. Donald Trump was declaring a free press—or at least five of the largest news organizations in America—traitors to our country. And he was using words with a dark and bloody history.

The phrase "enemy of the people" was used to murderous effect by Maximilien Robespierre during the French Revolution and the Reign of Terror. On December 25, 1793, Robespierre addressed France's National Convention with these words:

> *Le gouvernement révolutionnaire doit aux bons citoyens toute la protection nationale, il ne doit aux ennemis du peuple que la mort.**

Translation: "The revolutionary government owes to the good citizens all the national protection, it owes nothing to the enemies of the people but death."

With these words, Robespierre and his fellow revolutionaries embarked on a campaign of mass executions—public beheadings—of anybody they deemed an enemy of the French Revolution as they conceived it. To speed up the trials and executions, the revolutionary government passed a law on June 10, 1794, that eliminated all sentences other than acquittal and death. The infamous 22 Prairial law targeted "enemies of the people" and specifically mentioned "those who have spread false news in order to divide or disturb the people."† Or, you might say, fake news.

---

simply to reporting the news. In his letter, Jefferson suggested to Norvell that the way to run a better newspaper would be "by restraining it to true facts & sound principles only." But Jefferson added, "I fear such a paper would find few subscribers."

*Albert Laponneraye, *Histoire de la révolution française: Depuis 1789 jusqu'en 1814* (1838).

†François-Alphonse Aulard, *Histoire politique de la révolution française: Origines et développement de la démocratie et de la République (1789–1804)* (1901).

As the blood flowed in the streets of Paris, newspaper editors were among those beheaded. Anyone associated with newspapers that supported the monarchy was sent to the guillotine and so were revolutionaries deemed insufficiently loyal to the cause and its campaign of terror. When the pro-revolution newspaper *Le vieux Cordelier* began to editorialize against the campaign of mass murder, Robespierre ordered all available copies of the paper burned. The editor, Camille Desmoulins, who had been an ally of Robespierre's during the early days of the revolution, was sentenced to death and sent to the guillotine.

Donald Trump may not know anything about the French Revolution, but it is striking to hear an American president use a phrase so central to a reign of terror that resulted in the public executions of seventeen thousand people.

And if the president doesn't know his French history, he could have consulted the history of Nazi Germany. The Nazi Party explicitly used the phrase "enemy of the people" to label anybody who opposed the plebiscite that gave Adolf Hitler dictatorial powers. Here's the first paragraph of the story as it appeared in *The New York Times* on August 12, 1934:

> BERLIN, Aug. 11 (AP)—Equipped with blunt accusations that "who votes against Hitler is an enemy of the people," the Nazi propaganda organization will start tomorrow a week of tremendous vote seeking in preparation for the Aug. 19 plebiscite.

The Holocaust itself was justified using the phrase "enemy of the people." Nazi propagandist Joseph Goebbels spelled it out in an essay entitled "The Jews Are Guilty." "Each Jew is a sworn enemy of the German people," Goebbels wrote. "If someone wears the Jewish star, he is an enemy of the people."

And Joseph Stalin, too. To justify purges that sent that millions of people to their deaths or to the gulag in the Soviet Union, Stalin spoke of "enemies of the people."

So, why would an American president use a phrase so closely associated with three of the cruelest and bloodiest periods of modern history? The most generous explanation is ignorance. Perhaps he didn't know about Robespierre's use of the phrase. Or Stalin's. Or Hitler's. But after that first tweet, the murderous connotation of the phrase was widely reported. If he didn't know before, it's impossible to believe he doesn't know now.

The president did not retract the phrase, and he certainly didn't apologize for it. He kept using it. I eventually confronted him directly and in person about it—in a private meeting in the Oval Office that I will describe later in this book—warning him that his words could incite violence.

CHAPTER TWELVE

THE ENEMY WITHIN

As he settled into the White House, Donald Trump actually had good reason to be outraged by what was being reported about his administration.

The biggest issue wasn't the relentlessly negative tone of the news coverage, although it was certainly relentlessly negative. And the central problem wasn't media bias, although there was plenty of that. The real issue was closer to home: Private details of the inner workings of his White House were all over the news. Every president complains about leaks, but the leaks coming from the Trump administration were truly out of control and beyond anything previous presidents had faced.

In his businesses and in his campaign, Donald Trump prized secrecy, requiring his employees to sign nondisclosure agreements that forbade them from talking about anything to do with him. Now, in his early days as president, nothing seemed to be confidential. The president had forced some of his senior advisors to sign new nondisclosure agreements when they started working at the White House, but White House Counsel Don McGahn quietly told them the agreements were meant to mollify the president and would be unenforceable as a matter of law. After all, while White House staff work at the pleasure of the president, they are actually employees of the United States government, not Donald Trump.

One major factor causing the constant flow of unauthorized information coming out of the West Wing was the remarkable ineffectiveness of the White House press office. This wasn't because Press Secretary Sean Spicer or his deputies were leaking. In fact, it was just the opposite. Spicer habitually failed to answer emails and phone calls from reporters. And I found when I could get through to him, he would be just as likely to yell at me for some perceived slight as he would be to answer my questions.

Faced with a situation where an official spokesperson was hostile and not a reliable source of information, reporters naturally looked elsewhere. And, in the Trump White House, there was never a shortage of senior administration officials willing to talk about what was going on—or to trash other senior administration officials.

However, the most alarming leaks coming from the White House were not the many stories about staff infighting or internal deliberations. The most damaging leaks were of the president's conversations with foreign leaders.

At the end of his first full week in office, President Trump had a lengthy telephone conversation with Mexican President Enrique Peña Nieto, one of dozens of calls with foreign leaders he had during his first weeks in office. The call lasted about an hour, and after it was over, the White House issued a bland 150-word statement summarizing the conversation as "a productive and constructive call regarding the bilateral relationship between the two countries."

This is standard operating procedure for the White House—any White House. After the president has a conversation with a foreign leader, the press office routinely releases an announcement that the call took place and offers some vague diplomatic language on what was discussed. These statements are called readouts. The readout of the Peña Nieto call included one sentence on the thorny issues they'd both tried to avoid during Trump's visit to Mexico City during the campaign: Trump's campaign promise that Mexico would pay for his border wall.

"With respect to payment for the border wall," the statement read, "both presidents recognize their clear and very public differences of positions on this issue but have agreed to work these differences out as part of a comprehensive discussion on all aspects of the bilateral relationship."

It turned out that was hardly an accurate description of the call, and before long, the world was able to see exactly what was discussed in intricate detail, the kind of detail that had never before been revealed about a sitting president's private conversation with a foreign leader.

The Associated Press struck first. Five days after the call, it ran a story it says was based on an excerpt from a transcript of the conversation obtained by the AP, which, the article said, was provided "on condition of anonymity because the administration did not make the details of the call public."

Eventually *The Washington Post* obtained and published the complete and entirely unedited transcript of the president's call with Peña Nieto. It's a fascinating read. It was also a profound and unprecedented violation of the president's trust by whoever leaked it.

"On the wall," Trump told Peña Nieto, "you and I have a political problem."

He acknowledged they had both said opposite things. Trump, of course, had promised countless times that Mexico would pay for the wall and Peña Nieto had said countless times that Mexico would never pay for the wall.

"But the fact is, we are both in a little bit of a political bind because I have to have Mexico pay for the wall—I have to. I have been talking about it for a two-year period," Trump said, telling Peña Nieto to stop saying Mexico would not pay and instead say that the two of them would work it out.

"If you are going to say that Mexico is not going to pay for the wall," Trump said, "then I do not want to meet with you guys anymore because I cannot live with that."

In case Peña Nieto did not understand that this was a threat, Trump added another threat he would use again two years later with the next Mexican president:

"I think the most popular thing for me would be just to put a tariff on the border."

"You have a very big mark on our back, Mr. President, regarding who pays for the wall. This is what I suggest, Mr. President—let us stop talking about the wall," Peña Nieto said. "But my position has been and will continue to be very firm saying that Mexico cannot pay for that wall."

"But you cannot say that to the press," Trump shot back. "I cannot live with that. You cannot say that to the press because I cannot negotiate under those circumstances."

Peña Nieto deftly turned the conversation to other areas where there was agreement between the two leaders, getting Trump at one point to say, "It is you and I against the world, Enrique, do not forget."

But it wouldn't matter what Peña Nieto did or didn't say to the press after the call, because the whole conversation would end up on the pages of *The Washington Post*.

The same thing happened with another contentious call the president had the very next day with Australian prime minister Malcolm Turnbull. The official White House readout of the call was even more terse and bland than the readout of the call with Peña Nieto. Here it is, in its entirety:

STATEMENTS & RELEASES

Readout of the President's Call with Australian Prime Minister Malcolm Turnbull

Issued on: January 28, 2017

President Donald J. Trump and Australian Prime Minister Malcolm Turnbull spoke by phone for twenty-five minutes today. Both leaders emphasized the enduring strength and closeness of the U.S.-Australia relationship that is critical for peace, stability, and prosperity in the Asia-Pacific region and globally.

What the readout does not mention is that the call was scheduled to last for an hour but abruptly ended after twenty-five minutes when President Trump hung up on the Australian prime minister.

Like the Mexican call, the transcript of this conversation was eventually leaked to and published in its entirety by *The Washington Post*. The transcript shows something that had never been seen before: the president of the United States losing his temper during a supposedly private conversation with a close American ally.

The conversation started off lightly—Trump began by asking about the great Australian golfer Greg Norman—but it quickly got tense when Turnbull brought up an agreement he had worked out with the Obama administration for the United States to take in 1,250 refugees who had fled South Asia and the Middle East and were being held on two islands off the coast of Australia. Just twenty-four hours earlier, Turnbull told Trump, Vice President Pence had assured him the Trump administration would honor the agreement despite its hard-line position on refugees.

"I am asking you as a very good friend," Turnbull said to Trump. "This is a big deal. It is really, really important to us that we maintain it."

"Malcolm, why is this so important? I do not understand. This is going to kill me."

As the conversation went on, Trump said several times the agreement required the United States to accept 2,000 refugees, and Turnbull kept correcting him by telling him it was 1,250, at one point prompting Trump to say, "I have also heard like five thousand as well."

Turnbull assured him over and over that it was only 1,250 and the United States would not have to take a single refugee who did not pass a background check.

"We are not taking anybody," Trump said. "Those days are over."

After trying, fruitlessly, to convince Trump that the refugees would be fully vetted and not a threat to the United States, he reminded Trump he had a binding agreement with President Obama.

"There is nothing more important in business or politics than a deal is a deal."

That prompted a lecture from Trump about his election victory. He said the Democrats had lost because they had made stupid deals— like the one Turnbull was asking Trump to honor.

"This is a stupid deal. This deal will make me look terrible."

"Mr. President," Turnbull responded, "I think this will make you look like a man who stands by the commitments of the United States."

"I think it is a horrible deal, a disgusting deal that I would never have made," Trump said, getting ready to end the call. "I have had it. I have been making these calls all day and this is the most unpleasant call all day. Putin was a pleasant call. This is ridiculous."

Turnbull tried to steer the conversation to other topics—attempting to bring up the crises in Syria and North Korea. But Trump brought the call to an end.

Turnbull and Trump went on to have much friendlier conversations and developed a seemingly warm relationship. One of those who helped bring the two together was their mutual friend Greg Norman. And the refugees from those Australian detention centers did, by the way, eventually start coming into the United States in late 2017.

But the leaks of the transcripts of these two conversations had ramifications far beyond the immediate political embarrassment and challenges posed to America's relationships with Mexico and Australia. The leaks sparked paranoia throughout the West Wing and an effort to hunt down the leakers.

The concern was shared outside the White House. Senator Mark Warner, the top Democrat on the Intelligence Committee and a frequent Trump critic, called the leaks "disgraceful" and warned they could impair the administration's ability to conduct foreign policy.

The president's top aides believed the culprits were nonpartisan career officials who had also worked in the Obama administration. The majority of employees who work on the National Security Council and at federal agencies like the State Department are career professionals who work under Democratic and Republican administrations. Some of them, likely a very few of them, would have had access to the transcripts.

The leaking put enormous pressure on Press Secretary Sean Spicer, who not only had to answer questions about what was leaked but also had to bear the brunt of the president's outrage over his inability to prevent negative press coverage of his administration.

The truly sensitive and important leaks, such as the transcripts of the calls with foreign leaders, almost certainly did not come from anywhere near the White House press office, but Spicer was fighting his own battles over much more trivial leaks about the inner workings of his press operation. He was outraged, for example, when news got out that Mike Dubke had been hired as the new White House communications director before Spicer was ready to announce it. It was hardly a state secret, but Spicer berated his staff over the leak.

One day in late February, Spicer got word that something said at a press office staff meeting had been leaked to a reporter. This time, Spicer took what he believed was decisive action.

He convened an "emergency meeting" of his staff. As they walked into his office, he demanded everyone put their cell phones—both their work and personal phones—onto the table for what he said would be a phone check.

And right then and there, in the presence of White House lawyers, the phones were all searched to see if any of them had leaked information from the previous meeting via text message. As the search of the phones went on, Spicer warned ominously that there would be more phone checks and that leakers would be caught and punished.

But this phone check came up empty.

And then, a couple of hours later, another leak, this time about what had just happened.

The headline in Politico read: "Sean Spicer Targets Own Staff in Leak Crackdown."*

---

*That would turn out to be the last such phone check. When President Trump saw the stories about what Spicer had done, he told him it was not a smart thing to do.

CHAPTER THIRTEEN

NO RECUSE

A little after ten A.M. on the day Donald Trump would come to see as the worst day of his presidency, Justice Department spokeswoman Sarah Isgur Flores got a call from White House press secretary Sean Spicer and his deputy, Sarah Sanders.

Flores knew Spicer quite well because she had worked as his deputy at the Republican National Committee for nearly three years before the 2016 presidential campaign. In fact, back then, she had viewed him as a mentor. But somewhere over the course of the campaign, Spicer had come to see his former protégée as his enemy and no longer spoke to her.*

So, when Flores picked up the phone, Spicer put the call on speakerphone and had Sanders do the talking.

"We need you to hold a press conference this morning so the attorney general can announce he is not going to recuse himself," Sanders said.

---

*Flores was not the only former Spicer deputy who received the silent treatment. Her predecessor as the deputy communications director at the RNC was Tim Miller, who was also not on speaking terms with Spicer.

Recuse. Merriam-Webster's Collegiate Dictionary defines the word this way:

> to remove (oneself) from participation to avoid a conflict
> of interest

Special Counsel Robert Mueller's report documents the White House's urgent efforts on this day to prevent Attorney General Jeff Sessions from recusing himself from any involvement with Justice Department investigations related to the 2016 presidential campaign. In fact, it's a significant part of the section in the report detailing eleven incidents of possible obstruction of justice by the president. But there's an important element of this effort that Mueller's report omits: The White House press office played a key role in the failed effort to prevent the Sessions recusal.

First, here's what Mueller does include in his report.

On March 2, 2017, Mueller writes, the president called White House Counsel Don McGahn and "urged him to contact Sessions to tell him not to recuse himself from the Russia investigation."

According to Mueller, McGahn did exactly that, but Sessions told him "he intended to follow the rules." As an experienced Washington lawyer, McGahn would have known exactly what Sessions meant by "follow the rules." Justice Department ethics lawyers were unanimous in advising Sessions that he had no choice but to recuse himself. They argued there was a clear conflict of interest: As a top official in the Trump campaign, he could not make decisions on a federal investigation into whether that campaign broke the law. Every single lawyer who weighed in on this question at the Justice Department agreed.

The language of the Mueller report on what happened next is straightforward—and comically understated.

"McGahn reported back to the President about the call with

Sessions," Mueller writes, "and the President reiterated that he did not want Sessions to recuse."*

Right. The president "reiterated that he did not want Sessions to recuse."

It must have been one hell of a reiteration, because, as Mueller documents, McGahn embarked on a frantic effort over the next several hours to prevent Sessions from going through with the recusal despite the broad legal consensus that Sessions needed to recuse himself. He called Sessions's chief of staff. He called his personal lawyer. He called Senator Mitch McConnell, hoping to enlist the majority leader, a friend of Sessions, in the effort as well. And McGahn called Sessions two more times that day.

And, Mueller writes, "Sessions recalled that other White House advisors also called him that day to argue against his recusal."

That's where the White House press office comes in, beginning with the call from Spicer and Sanders to Justice Department spokesperson Sarah Isgur Flores. Flores later described to me in detail what happened next.

Sanders was quite specific when she told Flores to hold the press conference. It had to be done, she said, that morning—specifically before eleven thirty A.M.

Rather than directly respond to the substance of Sanders's request—that she schedule a press conference for the attorney general to announce he was *not* going to recuse himself—Flores focused on the logistics. She explained to Sanders it would be impossible to schedule a press conference on such short notice. Most of the reporters who cover the Justice Department do not work in the building. To hold a press conference, she would need to give the DOJ press corps advance notice of at least a few hours.

---

*Mueller report, vol. 2, p. 49.

"Then put out a written statement saying there will be no recusal," Sanders said.

Flores couldn't do that either, but she also could not tell Sanders and Spicer the real reason: Sessions had already decided to go forward with his recusal. That's what he meant when he told McGahn he would follow the rules. In fact, Flores had already begun working with the attorney general on a plan to announce his decision. She was indeed planning a press conference and writing a press release for later that day—to make the exact opposite of the statement the White House was demanding.

Flores could not tell Spicer and Sanders any of this because Sessions believed the recusal decision and announcement needed to be made in a way that was totally independent—no input or interference from the White House.

"There is no reason for a recusal," Sanders told Flores, saying she had looked at DOJ regulations and it was clear Sessions did not have to recuse himself.*

Flores, herself a graduate of Harvard Law School, found it a little amusing that Sanders, who had no legal background whatsoever, was lecturing her on the finer points of Justice Department regulations and offering an interpretation directly at odds with the collective view of every DOJ lawyer who had looked at the issue. But this was not an issue for them to debate. Sessions had not told the White House about his decision yet and it was not Flores's role to tell the White House about it.

---

*In a footnote on page 50 in the second volume of his final report, Mueller quotes directly from the Justice Department's regulations on recusal. It almost seems like it was written for precisely the circumstances Sessions was now in: "No employee shall participate in a criminal investigation or prosecution if he has a personal or political relationship with . . . [a]ny person or organization substantially involved in the conduct that is the subject of the investigation or prosecution." It defines "political relationship" as "a close identification with an elected official, a candidate (whether or not successful) for elective, public office, a political party, or a campaign organization, arising from service as a principal advisor thereto or a principal official thereof."

"We are getting close to having a discussion that would be inappropriate for us to be having," she told Sanders.

At four P.M. that afternoon, Sessions had his press conference and made the announcement that would doom his relationship with the president forever. And the recusal wasn't limited to the Russia investigation. It was a blanket recusal taking Sessions out of the decision-making process for anything at all dealing with the 2016 presidential campaign.

"Since I had involvement with the campaign," Sessions said, "I should not be involved in any campaign investigation."

And with that, the president learned Sessions would not be able to protect him from any investigation related to the campaign and he would not be able to order an investigation of the president's political opponents. It wasn't until the end of the press conference that Sessions was asked about statements coming out of the White House earlier that day—from the press secretary and the president himself—that he did not need to recuse himself.

"They don't know the rules, the ethics rules. Most people don't, but when you evaluate the rules," Sessions said, "I should not be involved investigating a campaign I had a role in."

The next morning, a Friday, the president was scheduled to fly from Washington to his Mar-a-Lago resort in Palm Beach, Florida, for the weekend.

Any time the president leaves the White House aboard the Marine One helicopter, a contingent of White House reporters is escorted out to the South Lawn to capture the images of the president's departure and to attempt to ask a few questions as he walks out to the chopper and flies away. If the president leaves from the White House residence, he can't be seen until he comes out the door of an area below the Truman Balcony known as the South Portico. But if the president is leaving from the West Wing, he can usually be seen in the Oval Office as he wraps up work or finishes his last meeting before heading out to the helicopter. As the press waits, photographers break out their zoom lenses and can catch glimpses of the president through the windows of the Oval Office. It's like a silent movie: You can see what the president is doing and sometimes make out whom he is talking to, but you cannot hear a word he says.

On this Friday morning, the day after the Sessions recusal, the cameras caught quite a show as they waited for the president to walk to Marine One. As the lenses zoomed toward the windows of the Oval Office, you could see the room packed with the president's senior advisors, including Steve Bannon, Jared Kushner, Reince Priebus, and Sean Spicer. It was anybody's guess what they were talking about, but the conversation certainly looked animated. Bannon was spotted waving his arms around, gesticulating, and then stepping back with his arms crossed and head down. Eventually, the president made his way out of the Oval Office and onto Marine One, accompanied by his daughter Ivanka, Jared, and their children.

A few hours later, I got two separate calls from ABC News colleagues telling me they had heard the president had "gone ballistic" in the Oval Office and ordered Reince Priebus and Steve Bannon to stay in Washington for the weekend. I had asked Sean Spicer about what had happened, but he'd downplayed everything and told me Priebus and Bannon were simply staying behind to work on strategy for passing the Republican bill to repeal Obamacare. Fortunately, I didn't report anything Sean told me, because it was entirely untrue.

With a few more calls, we confirmed Priebus and Bannon had indeed been on the list of travelers cleared to fly on Air Force One to Florida and that their names were scratched at the last minute, apparently on orders from the president. I called Priebus directly to give him a chance to comment before posting my story. My call went straight to voicemail. So, I called Kellyanne Conway, but she wasn't much help because she had not been in the Oval Office for the meeting. While I was on the phone with Conway, I saw Priebus calling me back.

"Jonathan, I have Steve here with me on speakerphone," he said. "I don't know who is telling you this stuff, but we decided together to stay back in Washington. We told the president we wanted to stay. There's just a lot to work on."

And he went on, insisting that everything was just fine. He wasn't fighting with Bannon and the president wasn't fighting with either of them. Although Bannon was on the call too, he said virtually nothing. But Priebus wanted me to know that whoever was telling me that the president kicked them off Air Force One was not telling me the truth.

"But you both were on the manifest," I said.

"Maybe, but we decided it would make more sense for us to stay here and work through the weekend at the White House and the president agreed."

That call took place at 6:14 P.M. on Friday evening. My phone records show that Priebus called a half dozen more times over the weekend. One call came shortly after ten P.M. Friday night. I was having a late dinner at Cafe Milano in Georgetown with United Arab Emirates ambassador Yousef al-Otaiba and retired Navy SEAL Admiral Bob Harward, who, just a couple of weeks earlier, had turned down the president's offer to replace Michael Flynn as national security advisor. It was an important dinner, but when I saw the incoming call was from the White House chief of staff, I excused myself and went outside to talk to him.

As I walked up and down Prospect Street in Georgetown with my phone to my ear, Priebus told me he was distraught over the leak—yet another leak. Usually the reporter is asking the White House official for information. In this case, it was the reverse. Who told me about the blowup in the Oval Office? Who told me he had been taken off the trip to Mar-a-Lago? Who?

"Reince, you know I can't tell you that," I said.

"I know, I know," he said. "But the leaks are out of control. Who is doing this? Is it [top economic advisor] Gary [Cohn]? Is it [Deputy National Security Advisor] Dina [Powell]? I just wish I knew."

Over the course of several more calls on Saturday, I learned the real reason for the president's anger. It turned out it really wasn't directed at Priebus and Bannon. It was directed at White House Counsel Don McGahn, whom the president blamed for not stopping the Sessions recusal.

Two years later, with the release of the Mueller report, we learned the full extent of that anger and the words the president used as he went "ballistic" in the Oval Office during the very meeting that ended with Priebus and Bannon's being ordered to stay behind in Washington.

"On March 3, the day after Sessions's recusal, McGahn was called into the Oval Office," Mueller writes. "Other advisors were there, including Priebus and Bannon. The President opened the conversation by saying, 'I don't have a lawyer.'"

The president, according to Mueller, went on to say he wished Roy Cohn was his attorney, referring to the infamous counsel for Senator Joe McCarthy and, later, lawyer for various controversial New Yorkers, including Mafia boss John Gotti and Trump himself. He demanded that McGahn call Sessions and order him to undo the recusal. McGahn told him that the Justice Department, in light of the recusal, had instructed him not to contact Sessions anymore on any matters related to the campaign. That further enraged the president.

"The President then brought up former Attorneys General Robert Kennedy and Eric Holder and said that they had protected their presidents," Mueller writes. "The President also pushed back on the DOJ contacts policy, and said words to the effect of, 'You're telling me that Bobby and Jack didn't talk about investigations? Or Obama didn't tell Eric Holder who to investigate?'"

And Mueller writes, "Bannon recalled that the President was as mad as Bannon had ever seen him and that he screamed at McGahn about how weak Sessions was."

The extent of Trump's anger with Sessions would not be publicly known until more than four months later, when he told *The New York Times* that the recusal was "unfair to the president."

"How do you take a job and then recuse yourself?" Trump said to the *Times*. "If he would have recused himself before the job, I would have said, 'Thanks, Jeff, but I'm not going to take you.' It's extremely unfair—and that's a mild word—to the president."

This was a dramatic break. Sessions was the very first senator to endorse Trump, an endorsement that helped him secure the Republican presidential nomination. Over the course of the next two years, the president would escalate his public attacks on Sessions, humiliating him repeatedly in interviews, in speeches, and, of course, on Twitter.

Sessions offered to resign multiple times in the months after the recusal, but the president didn't push him out until after the 2018 midterm elections. Months after that, he was still bitter about the recusal, telling NBC News in June 2019 that his biggest regret as president was making Jeff Sessions attorney general.

The recusal—and his inability to get anybody to undo it—enraged the president because it vividly illustrated the limits of his power. He was the president. He believed all instruments of presidential power should be available to promote and protect the president.

CHAPTER FOURTEEN

WITCH HUNT

Late in the evening of May 8, 2017, I got a tip from a trusted source: President Trump would be firing FBI director James Comey the following day. I was in New York at the time and had several meetings planned for the next day at ABC News headquarters on West Sixty-Sixth Street.

"You'll need to be in Washington by midday," my source told me.

Because of the explosive nature of this information and the fact that only a handful of people knew it was coming, my source swore me to secrecy. I could not tell a soul, but I could get prepared for what would be the biggest story yet of the Trump presidency. I canceled my meetings and got on an early-morning flight to Washington.

When I got to the northwest gate of the White House, I ran into George Stephanopoulos, who, it turned out, had a meeting with the president. I could not tell George what I knew, but I said cryptically, "You should ask him about Comey. I don't think things are going well with him." Unfortunately, Comey did not come up during their conversation and the president gave absolutely no indication of the deeply consequential move he would be making within a few hours.

As I walked into the White House briefing room, Deputy Attorney General Rod Rosenstein was putting the final touches on a three-page letter criticizing Comey's handling of the Hillary Clinton email investigation—a letter that would be used by the White House to justify Comey's firing.

At the White House press briefing that afternoon, I asked Sean Spicer what seemed like an innocuous question.

"Does the president still have confidence, full confidence, in FBI director James Comey?"

Spicer stumbled over his words as he answered me.

"I have no reason to believe . . ." he began, without finishing the thought. "I haven't asked him, so I don't, I have not asked the president since the last time we spoke about this."

"And the last time you spoke about it, you said he did have confidence, but you're not saying that again now," I said.

"I don't want to start speaking on behalf of the president without speaking to him first," he replied.

After the briefing, I went up to Spicer's office to see if he would tell me anything more. Based on what my source had told me, I knew Comey was about to be fired, but I couldn't tell that to Spicer. He insisted he knew nothing but said he would check. As it turned out, Spicer had not yet been told the firing was coming, but he had seen and heard enough to get the sense that something was up.

Later that afternoon, the letter from Rosenstein arrived at the White House, along with a shorter letter from Attorney General Sessions. The president quickly dispatched one of his most trusted aides, longtime personal bodyguard Keith Schiller, to deliver his own letter to Comey at FBI headquarters. It read:

I have received the attached letters from the Attorney General and Deputy Attorney General of the United

States recommending your dismissal as Director of the Federal Bureau of Investigation. I have accepted their recommendation and you are hereby terminated and removed from office, effective immediately.

It has been well documented that the president wasn't actually accepting Rosenstein's recommendation. He had already decided to fire Comey and had asked Rosenstein to write the letter to be used to justify the firing. In fact, the Rosenstein letter, while harshly critical of Comey, does not actually recommend that he be fired. Rosenstein felt that decision was up to the president.

Once Schiller dropped off the letter, the White House made the announcement. I was waiting outside the press office door when Sean Spicer came out and told the handful of reporters who were there with me in the briefing room to look for an email he had just sent out.

"It's your question," Spicer said, pointing to me.

It was six P.M. But thanks to the warning I'd gotten, I had already written most of my story for the six thirty P.M. *World News Tonight* broadcast. I had also quietly warned senior producer Claire Brinberg that there might be late-breaking news on Comey and we would need to be prepared to move quickly if it happened before showtime. So, while I was not able to break the story before the White House announced it, ABC was the only network to have a story edited and produced on the Comey firing for the evening's six thirty network newscast.

For his part, Comey found out he had been fired when he saw the news on television at the FBI office in Los Angeles. If the White House had bothered to check his schedule, they would have known he was out of town, speaking to FBI employees on the West Coast, when Schiller dropped off the president's letter.

In one of the oddest twists in the entire Russia investigation saga, the only thing on the president's public schedule the day after he fired Comey was a meeting with the Russian foreign minister in the Oval Office.

The meeting was listed on the schedule as "closed press," which meant no reporters and no photographers would be allowed in. Or, as it turned out, no American photographers. The White House press corps was excluded, but a photographer for Russia's state news agency TASS was allowed to attend and later released several remarkable photos of the president enjoying a laugh with Russian foreign minister Sergey Lavrov and Russian ambassador Sergey Kislyak.

But ten days later, *The New York Times* got much more than a photo op for the president's Oval Office meeting with the Russians. In yet another extraordinary leak of sensitive national security information, the *Times* gained access to a secret White House document summarizing, in detail, the president's conversation with the Russians. The quotes were damning.

Here's what the *Times* reported about what the president told the Russians in the Oval Office:

> "I just fired the head of the F.B.I. He was crazy, a real nut job," Mr. Trump said, according to the document, which was read to *The New York Times* by an American official. "I faced great pressure because of Russia. That's taken off."*

---

*Matt Apuzzo, Maggie Haberman, and Matthew Rosenberg, "Trump Told Russians That Firing 'Nut Job' Comey Eased Pressure from Investigation," *The New York Times*, May 19, 2017.

And, the *Times* reported, the president also told the Russians: "I'm not under investigation."

The leak was an extraordinary breach. Summaries of the president's private meetings with world leaders are shared with a small circle of aides. Releasing them is a remarkable violation of a president's expectation of confidentiality. This was clearly leaked by a senior advisor horrified to see the president boasting to the Russians about firing his FBI director and telling them he was now not under investigation.

The White House did not deny the accuracy of this account of the meeting. In fact, when Hope Hicks told the president what the *Times* had reported he'd told the Russians about Comey, he expressed no concern, telling her, "He *is* crazy."*

The meeting with the Russians added fuel to the demands for an appointment of a special counsel after the firing of Comey. Thanks to Sessions's recusal, the decision on whether to do that rested with the deputy attorney general, Rod Rosenstein.

On May 17, just over a week after Comey's firing, Rosenstein appointed Robert Mueller as the special counsel. Mueller was given authority to investigate Russian interference in the 2016 election and whether the Trump campaign was involved. The initial public response from the White House was uncharacteristically restrained. The press office released a statement from the president that almost seemed to welcome the investigation as an opportunity to absolve the president's campaign. Here it is in its entirety:

> As I have stated many times, a thorough investigation will confirm what we already know—there was no collusion between my campaign and any foreign entity. I look forward to this matter concluding quickly. In the meantime,

---

*Mueller report, vol. 2, p. 71.

I will never stop fighting for the people and the issues that
matter most to the future of our country.

That was the official statement at least. In reality, the Mueller appointment blindsided the White House and enraged the president.
The president learned of the Mueller appointment only thirty minutes
before Rosenstein told the world about it. He was in the Oval Office at
the time with Attorney General Sessions, of all people. They had been
interviewing candidates to replace Comey as the head of the FBI.

Rosenstein first called Sessions to tell him about his decision, unaware Sessions was with the president. He stepped out of the Oval
Office to take the call. When he came back, Sessions broke the news
to the president. The Mueller report dramatically detailed what happened next, based on notes from the meeting taken by Jody Hunt,
Sessions's chief of staff.

"The President slumped back in his chair and said, 'Oh my God.
This is terrible. This is the end of my Presidency. I'm fucked,'" Muel-
ler writes. "The President became angry and lambasted the Attorney
General for his decision to recuse from the investigation, stating,
'How could you let this happen, Jeff?'"*

According to Hunt's notes of the meeting, the president was distraught about what the special counsel appointment would do to his
presidency.

"Everyone tells me if you get one of these independent counsels it
ruins your presidency," the president said. "It takes years and years
and I won't be able to do anything. This is the worst thing that ever
happened to me." The president then told Sessions to submit his letter
of resignation and Sessions walked out of the Oval Office. Sessions left
to return to his office at the Justice Department and write the letter.

---

*Mueller report, vol. 2, p. 78.

In yet another dramatic turn, White House Counsel Don Mc-Gahn rushed down the hallway to tell Chief of Staff Reince Priebus what had happened, prompting Priebus to run out to the White House driveway, where he found Sessions in the back of his SUV about to be driven back to the Justice Department. Priebus got in the vehicle with Sessions and pleaded with him not to resign.

Early the next morning, the first public hint of the president's rage over the Mueller appointment came in the form of a one-sentence tweet: "This is the single greatest witch hunt of a politician in American history!"

Later that day, I went into the East Room of the White House for a joint press conference with President Trump and Colombian president Juan Manuel Santos. I had zero expectation I would be called on to ask a question. Joint press conferences like these include only two questions from the US press. And lately, I had been essentially shut out by the White House. Sean Spicer had stopped calling on me again at his briefings, and the president, for the past couple of months, had been calling almost exclusively on reporters for Fox News or smaller conservative outlets.

So, for the first time in my life, I went into a presidential news conference without a list of questions for the president. After all, there was no way he would call on me. If recent precedent held, he'd call on friendly reporters who wouldn't even ask about the investigation. I figured the only thing I'd be able to do would be to yell out a question as the president walked out at the end of the press conference.

To my shock, he did call on me. For the first question. I asked him to clarify his view of Robert Mueller's appointment. In the statement put out by the White House press office, he'd seemed to welcome the appointment as a chance for vindication. But then there was the early-morning "witch hunt" tweet. That tweet didn't mention Mueller by name. Could he possibly have been suggesting the widely respected former FBI director, a lifelong Republican, was part of a witch hunt?

"Mr. President, I'd like to get your reaction to Deputy Attorney General Rod Rosenstein's decision to appoint a special counsel to investigate the Russian interference in the campaign. Was this the right move, or is this part of a 'witch hunt'?"

The president's answer to me may have been the last measured thing he said about Mueller before the special counsel finished his final report.

"Well, I respect the move," he said, "but the entire thing has been a witch hunt. And there is no collusion between certainly myself and my campaign, but I can always speak for myself—and the Russians, zero."

President Santos next called on a reporter from Colombia. That reporter first asked President Trump a question. As the president finished answering, he looked at me.

"And, Jon, I think you also had a question for the president."

I nodded and said, "Of course."

Translation: *I will come up with one quickly.* I had been so consumed with the breaking news surrounding the fallout of the Comey firing and the Mueller appointment, the last thing I had been thinking about was a question for the Colombian president. After all, I truly did not think I would be called on. I quickly decided to seize on something President Trump had said in his opening remarks—that the wall he was going to build on the Mexican border would stop the flow of drugs from South America into the United States. To this day, I don't know if the president was genuinely concerned that I had missed my chance to ask the Colombian president a question or if he had sensed that I didn't have a question and wanted to embarrass me. Either way, I got an extra question.

Meanwhile, Attorney General Sessions totally disregarded the pleadings of Reince Priebus. He wrote a lengthy letter of resignation and, without telling Priebus, handed it to the president. The letter has never been made public, but a former official who has read it tells me Sessions made it clear this was not a voluntary resignation. Sessions would not be pretending he was resigning for innocuous reasons like spending more time with his family. He was making it clear he was resigning under duress. Sessions knew that writing it this way would make it harder for the president to accept, because actively firing Sessions—forcing him to resign—would raise questions about the president's motives and whether he was doing it solely to get a new attorney general who would bring the Russia investigation to an end.

The president took the resignation letter from his attorney general and put it in his jacket pocket. He took the letter with him when he left the next day for Saudi Arabia, the beginning of his first foreign trip as president.

Reince Priebus couldn't believe it when he found out about the letter.

"Jeff, what did you do?" Priebus asked. "That letter is going to be a shock collar he can use whenever he wants." Any time the president didn't like something, he could wave the letter around and threaten to remove Sessions in an instant. As Priebus later told the special counsel, the president now had "DOJ by the throat."

Priebus, with help from Steve Bannon, eventually convinced Trump to return the resignation letter. According to the Mueller report, he returned the letter to Sessions with a notation saying, "Not Accepted." But that is not all the president wrote on Sessions's resignation letter. He also scrawled the words "Make America Great Again" across it. To this day, Sessions has saved that letter with the presidential inscription, an artifact of his incredibly strange tenure as the attorney general for a president who grew to despise him and repeatedly disparage him in public and in private.

With Mueller now in charge of a wide-ranging investigation, and Deputy Attorney General Rosenstein promising him the resources and independence to do his work, there was one particularly pressing question: Would the president cooperate?

Over the course of the next year, the answer was an emphatic yes. The president's complaints about the investigation grew louder and louder, but the White House turned over more than a million pages of documents, and virtually all the president's top advisors testified under oath. The president could have tried to fight to prevent that testimony by exerting the right of executive privilege—the right of a president to get confidential advice from his aides—but he did not. But what about President Trump himself? Would he agree to answer questions from the special counsel?

Three weeks after Mueller's appointment, I got the chance to ask the president myself. There was another joint press conference at the White House, this time with the president of Romania. James Comey had just testified before the Senate Intelligence Committee and described, in vivid detail, the ways he believed the president had tried to interfere with the Russia investigation. Comey had testified that Trump had asked him for a vow of loyalty. The testimony had been carried live on all the major television networks and dominated the front pages of newspapers around the country.

Once again the president called on me first.

"Go ahead, Jon," he said. "Be fair, Jon."

"Oh, absolutely."

"Remember how nice you used to be before I ran? Such a nice man."

Nobody else would have picked up on it, but here, once again, with the former FBI director essentially accusing him of attempting to obstruct justice and a special counsel investigation looming, the president was making a veiled reference to the interview I did with him at the Old Post Office building in 2014, before it was transformed into the Trump International Hotel and before he decided to run for president.

"Always fair," I said, and turned to my questions. "Mr. President, I want to get back to James Comey's testimony. You suggested he didn't tell the truth in everything he said."

I pointed out that Comey had said, under oath, that Trump had told him he hoped he would drop the investigation into fired national security advisor Michael Flynn.

"I didn't say that," the president responded.

"So he lied about that?" I asked.

"Well, I didn't say that. I mean, I will tell you, I didn't say that."

I then asked about Comey's assertion that the president had demanded a pledge of loyalty, and, finally, I turned to the big question.

"Would you be willing to speak under oath to give your version of those events?"

"One hundred percent," the president said. "I hardly know the man, I'm not going to say, 'I want you to pledge allegiance.' Who would do that? Who would ask a man to pledge allegiance under oath? I mean, think of it, I hardly know the man. It doesn't make sense. No, I didn't say that and I didn't say the other."

The president was flatly denying that he had ever asked Comey for a pledge of loyalty.

"So, if Robert Mueller wanted to speak with you about that, you—" And before I could finish, he completed the answer that would haunt him for the next year.

"I would be glad to tell him exactly what I just told you, Jon."

And with that, the president publicly committed to being interviewed by Robert Mueller. The video clip of his answering my question would be replayed again and again over the next several months, a constant reminder that, whatever the president's lawyers would say, he had already vowed to be interviewed by the special counsel.

And yet, seven months later, the president had still not been interviewed by the special counsel. His legal team, in fact, was doing everything they could to avoid it. One morning in late January 2018, I met with a former top White House official who told me that an interview with the special counsel would be a disaster for Trump. This former Trump advisor had himself been interviewed under oath for hours and knew exactly what it was like. He also knew the president well. It is one thing for the president to lie in public, he told me, but a lie to the special counsel would be a crime and could ultimately spell the end of his presidency.

Not long after leaving that meeting, I got a message from the White House. John Kelly, who had replaced Reince Priebus as chief of staff, wanted to have an off-the-record meeting in his office with a group of White House reporters. It was four fifteen P.M. He wanted to do the meeting at five P.M. Could I make it?

Fortunately, I wasn't far from the White House and was able to make it on such short notice. It was a good thing I did. After Kelly spoke off the record with the group of about twenty reporters, the president stopped by. And with that, this off-the-record meeting with the chief of staff turned into a meeting with the president himself. I asked him the same question I had asked him in the Rose Garden seven months earlier.

"Are you going to talk to Mueller?"

"I'm looking forward to it, actually," he told me after a short pause. "There's been no collusion. There's been no obstruction. I am looking forward to it."

Remember: At this point, his legal team was doing everything they could to prevent a special counsel interview from happening. And I had just been with one of the president's former top White House officials, who had told me such an interview could lead to the end of the Trump presidency.

From the corner of the room, Maggie Haberman of *The New York Times* asked a follow-up question.

"Would you do it under oath, sir?"

"Did Hillary do it under oath?" the president shot back.

"I have no idea," Haberman answered. "But I am not asking about her."

"She didn't do it under oath. And you know that. I would do it under oath," he said, adding, "Oh, absolutely I would do it under oath."

You could see the unease on the faces of the White House aides in the room. The president was once again committing to do something his legal team was specifically trying to prevent. But at least this whole meeting was off the record. Or was it?

As the president turned to leave, Kristen Welker of NBC had another question.

"Can we use this?" Welker asked, pointing to the recording of the conversation on her phone. "Can we use the audio?"

If Welker had asked the White House press office, the answer would have been an emphatic no.

But she asked the president and he said yes. And within minutes the audio was playing on television. It was another headache for his legal team, but ultimately the president took their advice, perhaps agreeing that an interview under oath would be a disaster.

It was a quintessential Trump moment: The president talking to the press against the counsel of advisors who were trying to protect him from himself, saying things that directly contradicted those advisors and ultimately doing the opposite of what he said he would do.

CHAPTER FIFTEEN

TWO DOOR SLAMS

By the summer of 2017, covering the Trump Show had become something of a family affair. My older daughter, Emily, was working for CNN as an intern, spending most of her time on Capitol Hill. My younger daughter, Anna, still in high school, spent the month of July helping me out at work. Both of them already knew journalism requires a willingness to work long, unpredictable hours and a thick skin, but none of us could have predicted the events we would witness during the summer ahead.

I congratulated Emily on Twitter when she wrote her first story for CNN. I was incredibly proud, but one troll seized the opportunity to attack both of us.

"Father crooked = Daughter crooked," said the tweet by a self-described supporter of the president, "double the lies = double the sedition."

You expect that kind of thing from anonymous trolls on Twitter, but Anna quickly saw firsthand that the nastiness extended straight into the West Wing of the White House.

Early on the morning of July 21, 2017, I spoke to both Sean Spicer and Reince Priebus over the phone. There had been reports that

Anthony Scaramucci, a brash and fast-talking investment banker from Long Island, was about to be hired as the White House communications director. Both Spicer and Priebus assured me the reports were wrong. Priebus acknowledged there were some in the West Wing who were encouraging the president to hire Scaramucci, but he said if Trump decided to bring him onto the White House staff, it would almost certainly be in another role. After all, he told me, Scaramucci had no experience in either government or communications. Why, Priebus asked me, would the president hire him to be communications director? Spicer gave me a more definitive denial.

"It's not going to happen," he told me.

A couple of hours later, I got word Scaramucci had just been offered the job.

So, at 11:20 A.M., I hustled up to Spicer's office to try to find out what was going on. Anna grabbed a notepad and pen and followed me through the briefing room and up the ramp to the suite of offices known as "upper press." As we turned down the narrow hallway leading to the press secretary's office, we saw Spicer and Deputy Press Secretary Sarah Sanders walking into his office from the other direction. Anna and I arrived at the door to his office at almost exactly the same time Sean did.

"Hey, Sean," I asked. "So, this *is* happening?"

Spicer looked at me with a smirk, and before I could say another word, he slammed the door in my face. If I had been six inches closer, I might have had a broken nose. As it was, both Anna and I felt the breeze from the door slamming shut.

Twenty minutes later, the White House announced that Sean Spicer had resigned. I would later learn that just minutes before slamming the door in my face, Spicer had turned in his letter of resignation to the president. And yes, Scaramucci would be the new communications director, Sarah Sanders the new press secretary.

The press release announcing Scaramucci's appointment said he would be reporting directly to the president, not to the chief of staff, which would have been customary for a communications director. Before it was sent out, Priebus went into Scaramucci's new office.

"We need to take this out," Priebus told him, pointing to the line in the press release that said Scaramucci would be reporting directly to the president.

"It's staying in, Reince," Scaramucci said. "That's the way it is. Don't worry about it."

And with that, Priebus slowly walked out, powerless and humiliated. Priebus had the title chief of staff, but that moment made it clear who held the power. Scaramucci was calling the shots and Priebus couldn't do anything about it.

As it turned out, this was not only the end of Spicer's brief and troubled tenure as White House press secretary. This would also be the beginning of the end of phase one of the Trump presidency. Within a month, Priebus and chief strategist Bannon would be gone, and a retired marine general, John Kelly, would be the new chief of staff. Kelly would make a valiant effort to impose order in the West Wing.

But between phase one and phase two, there was Scaramucci. He would go out in an inglorious blaze just ten days later, but what a ten days it was.

Scaramucci spoke a little like Trump—almost always off the cuff, making grand pronouncements and loving every minute of the spotlight. That first day—and he had still not officially taken over as communications director—he came into the White House briefing room and gave a wonderfully absurd performance. Spicer had not held a televised briefing in nearly a month; as Scaramucci went on, it seemed like he might never stop.

He was full of love, really full of love, and he made sure everyone knew it, using the word twenty-one times—professing his love for the president, his love for Sarah Sanders, his love for the people who loved the president, and even his love for Sean Spicer and Reince Priebus, who had both done everything they could to prevent Scaramucci from getting his job ("I love these guys").

When he called on me, I asked a variation of the same question that had offended Spicer so greatly.

"Is it your commitment to the best of your ability to give accurate information, the truth, from that podium?"

He seemed to love that question too: "I am going to do the best I can."

I also asked if he and Sarah Sanders would commit to holding regular on-camera press briefings, something Spicer had slowly done away with.

"If she supplies hair and makeup, I will consider it, okay?" Scaramucci said, provoking laughter, something we had not heard in the briefing room for a long time. "But I need a lot of hair and makeup, Jon. I don't know. Maybe."

And then I snuck in one more:

"I know you've been one of the president's strongest supporters for a while now. But does he know what you said about him back in 2015, when you said he was a hack politician?"

"Yes, he brings it up—he brings it up every fifteen seconds, all right?" Scaramucci said, provoking more laughter. "I should have never said that about him. So, Mr. President, if you're listening, I personally apologize for the fiftieth time for saying that."

Compared to our last six months with Spicer, "the Mooch" was a breath of fresh air in the press room. But he was a terror to the press office. It began at his first meeting with the roughly forty people who worked on the White House communications staff.

He walked into the meeting, which was held in the Roosevelt

Room of the White House, with a junior press aide named Cliff Sims. Scaramucci decided he trusted Sims, apparently because Spicer had not. Sims, who was by Scaramucci's side for his entire ten and a half days on the job, describes the scene vividly in his own book, *Team of Vipers*.

"There are some people in this room who are leakers," Scaramucci began. "And guess what? I know who you are."

When word of that meeting leaked out, Scaramucci convened another one the following day and said the firings would start right away and continue until the leaks stopped.

To illustrate his plan to crack down on leaks, he started drawing an organizational chart that had Scaramucci at the top and then Sarah Sanders and then others down the line. As Scaramucci drew an elongated oval around the names, one person in the meeting later told me he and others in the room had struggled to keep from laughing because Scaramucci's diagram looked just like a penis. Not a propitious start for the new communications director.

According to Sims, during the second meeting, Deputy Communications Director Jessica Ditto broke down in tears, telling Scaramucci "there [were] some really good people" on the communications team. The tears prompted Scaramucci to soften his tone, telling a story about how he had once fired a manager of an ice-cream shop he used to own because he caught the manager stealing from him. But the guy was married to somebody in his family, so he forgave him and helped him find another job. The point: The Mooch is tough but compassionate.

"You see, guys, I've got a big heart, just like our president," Scaramucci said, according to Sims. "I may end up firing all of you, but I'll help you find the best job you've ever had somewhere else."

In the end, there was only one person Scaramucci ended up forcing out: a junior staffer named Michael Short, who had worked at the

Republican National Committee during the campaign. I never knew Short to leak anything and doubt he ever did. He was forced to resign but the steady stream of leaks at the White House didn't stop.

While Scaramucci was terrorizing the White House press staff, he was waging an all-out charm offensive with the news media. On one of his first days on the job, he met over breakfast with leaders of the White House Correspondents' Association and the bureau chiefs of the five major television networks.

Meetings between Spicer and this group had often devolved into shouting sessions with Spicer complaining, usually about some perceived slight against him. This breakfast meeting was a few blocks from the White House at a large table in the back of the restaurant at the St. Regis hotel. Scaramucci walked in smiling with big handshakes for everybody around the table. He sat down and proclaimed he was going to repair the president's relationship with the press.

CNN bureau chief Sam Feist wanted to clear up one thing first: What did the new communications director want to be called?

"Do you want to be called 'Mooch'?" he asked. "Or is that too informal?"

"Shouldn't it be 'Mr. Scaramucci, sir'?" I joked.

And with that, he jumped out of his chair, leaned across the table, reached out his right arm, and gave me the middle finger. For a nanosecond, it seemed he might have actually taken offense, but then he let out a big laugh, and so did everyone else.

Without being asked, he declared: "I'm bringing the president to your dinner next year!" President Trump, just a couple of months earlier, had skipped the annual White House Correspondents' Dinner, ordered everybody in his administration to skip it too, and held a rally in Harrisburg, Pennsylvania, on the same night. Trump was the first president to skip the dinner since Ronald Reagan in 1981. And even Reagan, who couldn't attend because he had recently been shot, called in and addressed the dinner over the phone.

Trump seemed to love the Scaramucci sideshow at first, but by about day four or five, I began to sense the new communications director was communicating a little too much for a president who likes to do the communicating himself.

His fate was sealed during a late-night, profanity-laced phone call to Ryan Lizza of *The New Yorker* that Scaramucci failed to specify was off the record. And like so much else in this presidency, it all started with a tweet.

Earlier that evening, Lizza had tweeted what appeared to be a minor scoop. It was interesting but hardly a state secret:

> **Ryan Lizza**
> (@RyanLizza)
>
> Scoop: Trump is dining tonight w/Sean Hannity, Bill Shine (former Fox News executive), & Anthony Scaramucci, per 2 knowledgeable sources
>
> 7/26/17, 7:36 PM

Scaramucci called him to ask who had told him about the dinner. He wanted to find—and punish—the leaker, looking to make good on his zero-tolerance promise.

The Scaramucci/Lizza conversation was one of a kind, even by the standards of the Trump White House, where outrageous statements, infighting, sniping, and recriminations were a daily reality. It was a White House interview for the ages. And Lizza not only wrote the whole thing up, he recorded it and put out the audio, which ran over and over again (with lots of profanities bleeped out) on CNN and MSNBC.

The quotes are unlike any ever uttered by a White House communications director to a reporter and they spelled the end of his brief tenure as communications director.

"Reince is a fucking paranoid schizophrenic, a paranoiac," he said of the White House chief of staff.

He said Reince would be fired. And that he had called the FBI and Department of Justice to ask them to investigate Priebus for leaking information contained in his financial disclosure, a document that, incidentally, was publicly available.

Then he went after Chief Strategist Steve Bannon.

"I'm not Steve Bannon, I'm not trying to suck my own cock," Scaramucci told Lizza. "I'm not trying to build my own brand off the fucking strength of the president. I'm here to serve the country."

There was no recovering. Though it took a few days, Scaramucci was done. The "Mooch" era was over. And though he didn't last, he was able to enjoy watching the collateral damage from afar. Within weeks, Bannon and Priebus would be gone too.

A few days earlier, on the evening of Spicer's resignation, I had gone up to his office to see him one last time before he left. This wasn't a news call. I wanted to wish him well and, just maybe, let bygones be bygones. I wanted to let him know that I knew he had been under enormous pressure. I thought there was even a chance he might apologize for slamming the door in my face that morning. I would tell him that I understood. After all, he had just been put in a situation so bad that he was forced to quit. Once again, I brought my daughter Anna with me.

Anna and I ran into Priebus in the hallway outside Sean's office. As we talked for a few minutes, Priebus assured me that he and Scaramucci were actually friends. He told me a story about how Scaramucci had offered him a job, after the 2012 election, running his company SkyBridge Capital. After Priebus walked away, I saw Spicer coming out of his office. He looked my way and scowled. And then he saw NBC News correspondent Hallie Jackson, who had just walked up from the briefing room, and smiled.

"Do you have sixty seconds for me?" Jackson asked.

"Sure," Spicer replied.

"Sixty seconds for me, Sean?" I asked, walking with Anna up to the door of his office.

"Not for you," came the reply, and for the second time that day, he slammed the door in my face, my daughter Anna again by my side.

Spicer was able to watch all of Scaramucci's rise and fall from right there in the White House complex. He moved out of the press secretary's office and into an office next door in the Eisenhower Executive Office Building. He didn't seem to have much work to do, but he remained on the government payroll for another month. Of course, everybody asked him about his plans. He told people he was being courted by ABC's hit show *Dancing with the Stars*, but that he was likely to turn them down.*

Spicer had lofty ambitions for turning his fame into a big post–White House career. As soon as he left, he hired Washington super-lawyer Bob Barnett to help him make his next move. Barnett is the friend of the Clintons who, as described in chapter 5 of this book, was helping Hillary Clinton prepare to debate Donald Trump when news of the *Access Hollywood* video broke. It was Barnett who, on his laptop computer, first played the video for Hillary Clinton that so many people thought would doom Trump's campaign. With Barnett's help, Spicer met with executives at the major TV networks, hoping to land a high-profile job as a network analyst. It didn't happen. As an

---

*Two years later, Spicer did end up on *Dancing with the Stars*, competing in the fall 2019 season. He endured quite a bit of ridicule for his dancing and his costume choices, but he did get tweets from the president of the United States urging viewers to vote for his former press secretary.

executive for one broadcast network (not ABC) told me at the time, they agreed to meet with Spicer out of curiosity more than anything else; they wanted to see what the angry man behind the podium was like in person but had no desire whatsoever to hire him.

The week after his resignation, while he was still at the White House, Spicer ran into my daughter Anna but clearly did not recognize her from the door slams just four days earlier. Or maybe he hadn't noticed she had been there in the first place. Spicer said hello to her, and my ABC News colleague Gary Rosenberg snapped a photo.

Just after taking that photo, Gary told Spicer that Anna was my daughter. He just shook his head, laughed, and walked away.

With his history in Washington, Spicer had come into the job as one of the most experienced and seemingly well-qualified members of President Trump's senior staff. But he turned out to be comically unfit for the job. To the public, he'll be remembered for the unforgettable skits on *Saturday Night Live*. To White House reporters, he'll be remembered as the press secretary who killed the televised daily White House briefing and tried to move the press corps out of the White House.

To be sure, Spicer had an impossibly difficult job. Every press secretary makes mistakes, but because of the public fascination with Trump, Spicer's mistakes were magnified many times over. Day in and day out, his briefings were carried live by the cable news channels, something that only occasionally happened with his predecessors. So, when Spicer walked out to the podium one Friday in May 2017 wearing an upside-down flag pin, it was headline news. After all, according to the US Code, the flag should be displayed upside down only "as a signal of dire distress." Jennifer Bendery of the Huffington Post tweeted the question on many minds: "Spicer's USA flag pin is upside down. A silent scream for help?"

Any time Spicer misspoke, he faced instant ridicule on Twitter and provided material likely to be used by late-night comedians. Some of the mistakes were trivial. He had a famously hard time pronouncing names and he seemed unable to say more than two or three complete sentences without messing up the grammar.

In one briefing that Spicer gave, he made mistakes from which he would never recover. On April 11, 2017, Spicer addressed the press shortly after President Trump ordered air strikes on Syria in retaliation for a poison gas attack blamed on Syrian dictator Bashar al-Assad. The transcript of the briefing is a challenge to read because Spicer continually misspeaks and cannot seem to pronounce Assad's name. He was trying to make a point that should have been an easy one to make: What Assad had done was bad, really bad.

"Look—we didn't use chemical weapons in World War II," he said.

Fair enough. And that much was accurate.

"You know, you had someone as despicable as Hitler who didn't even sink to using chemical weapons."

Uh-oh. Hitler didn't use chemical weapons? Could the White House press secretary really not know that millions of Jews were gassed to death during the Holocaust?

This was a catastrophically bad thing for a White House press secretary to say. Was he denying the Holocaust? Or, alternatively, had he really never learned about the gas chambers?

Spicer continued to talk, totally unaware that he had just made a disastrous mistake. And amazingly, at first nobody in the briefing room called him on it.

The next reporter he called on asked him if the White House planned to release the president's tax returns on April 15 (that was a no) and how many people would be at the White House Easter Egg Roll (seriously). Several more questions followed. One reporter asked about Ivanka Trump's role in the president's decision to attack Syria. There were questions on North Korea and on health care.

Finally, Spicer called on my ABC News colleague Cecilia Vega.

"I just want to give you an opportunity to clarify something you said," Vega said, reading back his words. "'Hitler didn't even sink to the level of using chemical weapons.' What did you mean by that?"

You could almost see Spicer searching through his brain to find the answer. Again, the transcript here is difficult to read, but only because it is exactly what Spicer said.

> SPICER: I think when you come to sarin gas, there was no—he was not using the gas on his own people the same way that Assad is doing, I mean, there was clearly—I understand your point, thank you.
>
> VEGA: I'm just getting—
>
> SPICER: Thank you, I appreciate that. There was not—he brought them into the Holocaust center, I understand that. But I'm saying in the way that Assad used them, where he went into towns, dropped them down to innocent—into the middle of towns. It was brought—so the use of it—I appreciate the clarification there. That was not the intent.

And there were the words Spicer will never live down: "Holocaust center."

To his credit, Spicer completely owned his mistake.

"This may have been the lowest moment I had in the White House," Spicer later said. "I alone had fumbled; no one else made me do it."

Not long before he quit, a White House colleague of mine told Spicer he would be able to write quite a book, given all that he had witnessed behind the scenes at the White House. He looked at the two of us and smiled.

"No, no," he told us. "Two books."

The first book, he said, would be written for the Trump faithful. He would write about the brilliance of Donald Trump and it would be bought by all those people at Trump rallies wearing "Make America Great Again" hats and clamoring to take selfies with the president.

The true tell-all, where he would reveal all the chaos he had witnessed behind the scenes, would come later, presumably when he wouldn't mind offending Trump or his supporters.

A couple of months after Spicer resigned, Mike Allen of Axios emailed him for comment on a story he was writing that involved Spicer.

"Mike, please stop texting/emailing me unsolicited anymore," Spicer wrote back.

Allen wrote back with a question mark.

"I'm not sure what that means," Spicer answered. "From a legal standpoint I want to be clear: Do not email or text me again. Should you do again I will report to the appropriate authorities."

The incident was bizarre but a perfect capstone to Spicer's career as a White House press secretary—thin-skinned, grammatically incorrect, and wrong on the facts. What law did he think Mike Allen had violated by asking a question of a former White House press secretary?

Despite Mike's experience, I reached out to Spicer in writing this book and he agreed to meet with me. We spoke for about an hour in a small conference room in the basement of the Willard Hotel in Washington. About twenty minutes into our conversation, I asked Sean about slamming the door in my face. After a long pause, he said something that surprised me.

"Sorry about that," he said.

I didn't say anything at first, waiting for him to speak again. After another pause, he told me I had seen him right after the most difficult and painful moment of his life. He had resigned from what he thought was his dream job. And he felt let down by people close to him. Priebus had assured him he would not let the president hire Scaramucci as communications director. And then when the president said he was doing just that, Priebus did not speak up or do anything to convince the president not to do it. From Spicer it was a rare moment of self-reflection. And although the apology came two years later and only after I asked about what he did, it seemed genuine.

"And I don't know if you knew this," I told him. "But that was my daughter who was with me."

"I know," he said. And after another pause, "Tell her I said sorry."

In my career as a journalist, I have interacted with thirteen different press secretaries (so far) under four different presidents. Those interactions can be challenging. They can be adversarial. It's the nature of the job. I had a particularly tense relationship at times with Obama's press secretary Jay Carney. In fact, when Spicer was the communications director for the RNC, he would often gleefully send out press releases with video clips of my aggressively questioning Carney during White House briefings. But even in the most heated moments, Jay Carney did not take it personally. He was never afraid to call on me in briefings and I don't believe he ever intentionally lied to me. Spicer was the first White House press secretary I encountered who habitually said things that were simply untrue.

I don't know if he will ever write a second book, but Spicer wrote the first one. In the book, he suggested that I had branded him a liar by asking him during his first briefing if he intended to tell the truth from the White House podium.

"Rarely do reporters have their integrity questioned the way Jonathan questioned mine," he wrote.

That's quite a statement coming from the former spokesman for a president who routinely accuses reporters of making things up and betraying their country.

I wrote a scathing review of Spicer's book in *The Wall Street Journal*. In a measure of how many people Spicer had alienated during his brief White House tenure, I heard from several of Spicer's former White House colleagues, who praised the review. The first response came in a text message from the person who precipitated Spicer's abrupt departure.

"Jonathan, it's Anthony Scaramucci," the text read. "Rough review in WSJ. You left two things out: he was a bag carrying congenital liar for Reince and if he was born 100 years ago, the movies would have been called 'The Four Stooges'. My nickname for him was Liar Spice. Every Spice Girl has a nickname—that's his!"

Years from now, the veterans of the Trump White House will have one hell of a reunion.

CHAPTER SIXTEEN

CHARLOTTESVILLE

Nearly two weeks after replacing Reince Priebus as Donald Trump's chief of staff, John Kelly had a major crisis on his hands. A protest in Charlottesville, Virginia, led by white nationalists had turned into an ugly and deadly display of racial hatred.

Kelly summoned newly installed FBI Director Christopher Wray, Attorney General Jeff Sessions, and Homeland Security Advisor Tom Bossert to the White House residence to meet with the president. The official reason for the meeting was to update the president on plans to open a federal investigation into the murder of Heather Heyer, a thirty-two-year-old woman who was killed following the so-called Unite the Right rally, which included neo-Nazis and Ku Klux Klansmen. Heyer had been killed two days earlier when one of the white nationalists drove his Dodge Challenger into a group staging a counterprotest.

Attorney General Sessions and FBI Director Wray came prepared to brief the president on the investigation, but Kelly had another reason for calling the meeting. The president was about to make a public statement on the violence in Charlottesville, and the president's senior aides wanted to make sure it was a clear and unequivocal condemnation of the hateful violence perpetrated by the white supremacists who had organized the rally in the first place.

This meeting, the details of which have never been reported before, set the stage for the low point of Trump's first year in office, and one of the lowest points of his presidency.

You wouldn't think the president would need to be convinced to make a statement condemning the hate groups behind the violence in Charlottesville. The protests looked like a scene out of Nazi Germany in the 1930s. They had begun the night before Heyer's murder with an unannounced late-night parade of white supremacists carrying tiki torches and chanting, "Jews will not replace us." The rally the following day was billed as a protest against plans to remove a statue of Confederate general Robert E. Lee from Charlottesville's Lee Park, but it was organized by white nationalists Richard Spencer and Jason Kessler. Some of the protestors arrived carrying semiautomatic weapons and flags with swastikas and other Nazi symbols.

President Trump had already made one statement on the violence in Charlottesville, but he had been criticized for not specifically condemning the racist groups who had organized the protest. This first statement came a couple of hours after the killing of Heather Heyer. He made the comments at his golf resort in Bedminster, New Jersey, where he was spending a seventeen-day working vacation. It was Saturday, August 12, 2017.

This was not a forceful address to the nation. He spoke at the beginning of a previously scheduled event where he was signing a veterans' employment bill he had previewed with a remarkably tone-deaf tweet:

> **Donald J. Trump**
> (@realDonaldTrump)
>
> Am in Bedminster for meetings & press conference on
> V.A. & all that we have done, and are doing, to make it
> better-but Charlottesville sad!
>
> 8/12/17, 2:00 PM

And as he came before the cameras, he presented his words on Charlottesville as an afterthought, just as he had in that tweet.

"I thought I should put out a comment as to what's going on in Charlottesville," he said, pausing first to shake hands with the veterans who were there for the bill signing before starting his written statement on Charlottesville.

"We condemn in the strongest possible terms this egregious display of hatred, bigotry, and violence. . . ." But then, looking up from the paper he had been reading from, he added, "On many sides, on many sides."

Continuing to speak off the cuff, he wanted everybody to know it wasn't his fault.

"It's been going on for a long time in our country," he said. "Not Donald Trump, not Barack Obama. This has been going on for a long, long time."

These comments set off a torrent of criticism.

Republican Senator Cory Gardner was among those criticizing the president, calling him out directly on Twitter: "Mr. President—we must call evil by its name. These were white supremacists and this was domestic terrorism."

The next morning, a Sunday, the White House put out an unsigned statement aimed at addressing that criticism:

> The President said very strongly in his statement yester-
> day that he condemns all forms of violence, bigotry and
> hatred and of course that includes white supremacists,
> KKK, neo-Nazi and all extremist groups.

But even the president's senior advisors knew an unattributed written statement put out by the White House press office was not enough. The president needed to make it clear he was condemning the white nationalists behind the violence. Staff Secretary Rob Porter had worked with the president to write a statement he would accept. Porter, Hope Hicks, and newly minted press secretary Sarah Sanders had all urged the president to give the speech as written—unequivocally condemning the white supremacists and telling the country that the federal government would aggressively prosecute the perpetrators of the violence. It was up to Kelly to make sure it happened.

On Monday, two days after the killing of Heather Heyer, the president interrupted his working vacation in Bedminster to come back to Washington for the day. The Oval Office and much of the West Wing were undergoing renovations, so his meetings that day were conducted in the White House residence.

The meeting was on the second floor, in a grand space overlooking the South Lawn known as the Treaty Room, where the FBI director and attorney general gathered with the homeland security advisor to brief the president on the federal investigation into the violence at Charlottesville. John Kelly was there, and so were a couple of other aides. My description of this meeting is based on conversations with three of the people present, all of whom spoke on the condition I not use their names. One of the participants has shared with me contemporaneous notes on what happened.

The president sat at an enormous desk known as the Treaty Table, which President Ulysses Grant used for his cabinet meetings and where the treaty ending the Spanish-American War was signed in 1898. Attorney General Sessions and FBI director Wray sat in two chairs directly across from the president. Homeland Security Advisor Bossert and Chief of Staff Kelly sat around a coffee table off to the side. Two other aides stood by the door to the room.

As the meeting began, Sessions told the president what the federal investigation would entail. There was some discussion about whether they could declare the attack that killed Heyer an act of domestic terrorism. But the president quickly took over the meeting. He wasn't interested in getting a briefing on the investigation. He had other things on his mind.

The protestors, the president said, were being unfairly treated. The majority of them, he insisted, were there for a good reason—they did not want to see the statue of Robert E. Lee taken down.

Turning to Sessions, the president asked whether he thought the statue of Lee should come down. Sessions said the decision should be up to the local community. In this case, by the way, it was the Charlottesville city council that had voted to take down the Lee statue.

But the president was just getting started.

According to notes from the meeting, the president, sitting there at Ulysses Grant's old conference table, declared that Robert E. Lee was "the greatest strategic military mind perhaps ever." He also praised Confederate general Stonewall Jackson. He made it clear the KKK and neo-Nazis were "bad" but he seemed to dismiss that as too obvious a point. The issue for Trump was that the protestors in Charlottesville were taking up a good cause by fighting to keep the statue of Robert E. Lee in a prominent place.

"Next will be Washington and Jefferson," he said, and, looking around to everyone in the room, he asked, "Does anyone think this is fair?"

Nobody jumped in to agree with the president or to challenge him.

Nobody in the room suggested to him that praising Confederate generals was an inappropriate thing for a president to do under any circumstances, let alone after all that had gone down in Charlottesville just two days before. In fact, Kelly chimed in to agree with him on the greatness of the Confederate generals and on his point about Washington and Jefferson. But the president wasn't really looking for feedback. This was a monologue, not a discussion. FBI director Wray tried several times to bring the conversation back to the briefing on the federal investigations and told the president it was imperative that he specifically name the KKK and neo-Nazis as groups behind the violence. But the president kept going, talking about the brilliance of the Confederate generals and the ridiculousness of the effort to remove their statues.

There was nobody in that room willing to confront the president and tell him the issue was not that the people marching alongside neo-Nazis were being unfairly criticized. The protests had been led by virulently racist groups that had provoked the violence that killed Heather Heyer; that's what had shocked the nation. John Kelly was new to the job. And so was Christopher Wray, who had just been named FBI director two weeks earlier, following Comey's dismissal. Bossert had been on the job longer, but he wasn't particularly close to Trump. And Sessions's standing with the president had been precarious for months, since his decision to recuse himself from the Russia investigation and his failed resignation attempt.

As the meeting ended, the president looked to the two staffers standing by the door.

"Do you want to see the Lincoln Bedroom?" he asked.

And with that, the group walked out of the room, stepped to the right, and went into the Lincoln Bedroom. Just moments after praising Confederate generals Robert E. Lee and Stonewall Jackson, the president was gushing about Abraham Lincoln. Pointing to the unusually large bed and full-length mirror, he talked about how tall

Lincoln was. He showed off the handwritten version of the Gettysburg Address, which he said was regarded as "the greatest speech ever," and, with glee, told them all how newspapers at the time panned it as a terrible speech. To those in the room, the implication was clear: The fake news hated Lincoln then just like they hated Trump now. As he would later say in an interview with George Stephanopoulos: "Abraham Lincoln was treated supposedly very badly. But nobody's been treated badly like me."

The president pointed to a desk in the room.

"That's where he wrote it," he said, referring to the Gettysburg Address.

"No," Kelly interjected. "He actually wrote it on the train ride from Washington to Gettysburg."

Kelly hadn't taken issue with the president's rant just minutes earlier about the brilliance of Confederate generals and how protestors marching with neo-Nazis were being treated unfairly, but here he was interrupting the president's story about the Gettysburg Address and bluntly correcting him. And, in this case, it was Kelly who was wrong. Historians debate many things about Abraham Lincoln, but they agree he did not write the speech on the train. He wrote most of it in Washington during the two weeks before he went to Gettysburg, and he wrote the final lines after he arrived there. None of it was penned during the bumpy train ride. Kelly was repeating a widely debunked myth. In this case, it was actually the president who was closer to the truth.

From the Lincoln Bedroom, the president went downstairs to deliver the speech his senior advisors wanted him to deliver. He had vented in private about how unfairly the Unite the Right protestors had been treated, but when he came before the cameras in the Diplomatic Reception Room on the ground floor of the White House residence, he did exactly what his advisors said he must. He read a

statement specifically and unequivocally condemning the white supremacists.

"Racism is evil," he said. "And those who cause violence in its
name are criminals and thugs, including the KKK, neo-Nazis, white
supremacists, and other hate groups that are repugnant to everything
we hold dear as Americans."

The president's remarks were carried live on all the cable news
channels and as a special report on the broadcast networks as well.

When he was done speaking, the president walked into the hallway with his aides, including Kelly, Bossert, Porter, Hicks, and Sanders. They ducked into the nearest room with a television—a small
room on the ground floor used as the office of the White House doctor, Ronny Jackson—to watch how the speech he had just delivered
was being received.

Jackson's office had more than one television, which made it
possible for the president to see how his speech was playing on
Trump-friendly Fox News and also on CNN and MSNBC.

He was outraged by what he saw. His first comments on Charlottesville had been criticized, especially on CNN and MSNBC, for
not specifically condemning the hate groups, and now that he had
done exactly that, he was being criticized again.

Commentators on both networks were calling his comments too
little, too late. He was also slammed for beginning his comments
with glowing words about the economy and his trade agenda before
turning to Charlottesville. On Fox News, the new comments were
called "a course correction," implying he had done something wrong
with his first comments.

The president listened for a few minutes and then turned to
his aides.

"This is fucking your fault," he said. "That's the last time I do that."

It was quite a start for John Kelly as chief of staff. Over the course of the next several hours, the president stewed about the way his remarks were received. He said over and over again that it had been a mistake to make the second statement because in doing so, he was effectively acknowledging there was something wrong with the first one. He was convinced it made him look bad. It emboldened his enemies.

It was the very next day that things got a whole lot worse—for John Kelly and for Donald Trump.

During an impromptu press conference the president held that next day in the lobby of Trump Tower, he said many things that offended even some of his most fervent supporters.

He wasn't supposed to be talking about Charlottesville. He had just finished a meeting upstairs in his residence—his first trip back to Trump Tower since becoming president. There at his dining room table he'd met with some of the top officials in the Trump administration, including Treasury Secretary Steve Mnuchin, Transportation Secretary Elaine Chao, Office of Management and Budget Director Mick Mulvaney, and Chief of Staff Kelly, as well as Porter, Sanders, and Hicks. They had met for some ninety minutes to talk about the administration's effort to come up with a plan to improve America's infrastructure. As they concluded the meeting and headed toward the elevator to come down to the lobby, the plan was clear: The president would make short remarks about infrastructure. There would be no questions.

But two minutes before they got in the elevator, the president asked for copies of his two statements on Charlottesville. Specifically, he wanted the sections in both statements that condemned bigotry and hate. Just in case he was asked, he said, he wanted to show that he had condemned bigotry in both statements. He was still infuriated at the suggestion that his second statement was an acknowledgment that there was something wrong with the first one.

Porter got printouts of the two statements and handed them to the president. But Hicks and Sanders both reminded the president: no questions.

Down in the lobby, the president made comments on infrastructure as planned. And then came the inevitable questions. Not about infrastructure, of course, but about Charlottesville. Within minutes he was telling the world exactly what he had said in his private meeting the day before in the White House residence.

"I noticed that Stonewall Jackson's coming down," he said. "I wonder, is it George Washington next week, and is it Thomas Jefferson the week after? You know you really have to ask yourself, where does it stop?"

A day after reading the carefully crafted statement condemning the white supremacist groups, the president was back once again saying there was blame on both sides—drawing a moral equivalency between the white nationalists and the people staging a counterprotest against them. And the president offered a defiant defense of those protesting alongside the neo-Nazis and Klansmen, saying there were "very fine people on both sides."

The phrase "very fine people" drew swift condemnation across the political spectrum. Business leaders resigned from White House advisory groups. Chief economic advisor Gary Cohn privately told people he was horrified by the president's words and was considering resigning.

To almost everyone listening, the remarks were shocking.

On Fox News, Republican pundit Gianno Caldwell put it starkly the next day: "Last night, I couldn't sleep at all because President Trump, our president, has literally betrayed the conscience of our country."

Republican lawmakers lined up to condemn the president's words and to correct him. Senate Majority Leader Mitch McConnell scolded the president in a statement, saying, "There are no good neo-Nazis." Mitt Romney blasted the president for suggesting there were good and bad people on both sides in Charlottesville, saying, "No, not the same. One side is racist, bigoted, Nazi. The other opposes racism and bigotry. Morally different universes." And the president's friend Senator Lindsey Graham said his comments were "dividing Americans, not healing them.

"Through his statements yesterday, President Trump took a step backward by again suggesting there is moral equivalency between the white supremacist neo-Nazis and KKK members who attended the Charlottesville rally and people like Ms. Heyer," Graham said.

The cameras caught John Kelly off to the side, grimacing with an unmistakable look of anguish on his face, as the president sang the praises of Confederate generals and praised those who had marched with the neo-Nazis. But Kelly had no reason to be surprised. He had heard it all less than twenty-four hours earlier. And while he had encouraged the president to say something else, neither he—nor the FBI director or the attorney general, who were also there—had challenged anything he said.

They'd decided instead to placate him—to allow him to vent in private so that he would read the carefully crafted statement they wanted him to read in public. Kelly learned a lesson about Donald Trump. You may be able to advise him and steer him away from bad ideas or toward good ones. You might even get him to read a script from time to time. But the Trump Show is an unscripted program. Ultimately, the star will say whatever is on his mind, the consequences be damned.

As he left Trump Tower, the president seemed totally unaware of the crisis he had just caused for himself. Kelly didn't tell him he had made a mistake by going on a rant about Confederate generals and the "very fine people" on both sides of the ugliness in Charlottesville.

Nobody did. What good would it do? Would they talk him into making another "course correction"? Not likely.

The president was irritated about all the hostile questions. As he headed back to Bedminster, he admonished his aides, telling them the questions he had just been peppered with were proof he had made a mistake by delivering the second statement that specifically condemned the white supremacists. Instead of accepting the second statement, reporters had demanded to know why he didn't make it sooner.

Charlottesville was a turning point for the president. He had long believed it is a mistake to back down or apologize or to acknowledge *a mistake*. But as he had done when the *Access Hollywood* video came out during the campaign, he'd listened to his advisors. They had talked him into making the second statement. It wasn't quite an apology, as his response to the *Access Hollywood* video had been, but he saw it that way. Watching the reaction, he was convinced of two things: 1) He hadn't gotten any credit for saying the words everybody had said he had to say, and 2) The weakness he'd displayed by giving in to demands for the second statement had only emboldened his enemies to attack him harder.

He would never again let anybody talk him into admitting a mistake or doing anything with even the faintest hint of an apology. There would be no more course corrections.

Two months after Charlottesville, I flew down to Puerto Rico ahead of President Trump's visit to survey the ravages brought by Hurricane Maria. The scene was horrific. The lush green of the island was gone, most of the vegetation blown away. The trees still standing were barren. I visited with a man named Hector Garcia, who was still living in a house ripped in half by the storm—most of the roof and front wall blown off, the kitchen and living area on the second floor entirely exposed to the elements. I walked with him around what was left of his home, stepping over exposed pipes, tangled electrical wires, scattered clothing, and a stray mattress. Like 90 percent of people on the island, he had no electricity. He showed me the bag of supplies he had received from FEMA—water, toothpaste, a toothbrush, and some canned food—the sum total of the government help he had received so far. The hurricane had hit almost two weeks earlier.

Garcia had no idea that President Trump was visiting the island, but when I told him, he and his wife said they were grateful he would be there. A hopeful sign, they believed, that help would be on the way.

"He is coming because he knows we are in crisis," Garcia told me.

His confidence in the president may have been misplaced. A few days before making the trip, the president had talked about the challenge FEMA faced with its recovery operation, because Puerto Rico "is an island surrounded by water—big water, ocean water."

Upon arrival, the president toured the devastation and visited a FEMA distribution center inside a church, declaring, "There's a lot of love in this room." He helped hand out supplies to hurricane victims, but things got strange when he started tossing rolls of paper towels as if he were shooting free throws on a basketball court. And when he met with Puerto Rico's governor, he congratulated him on the death toll, which, at that moment, stood at sixteen confirmed deaths. The president pointed out that many more had died during Hurricane Katrina in 2005.

"Sixteen versus literally thousands of people," he said. "You can be very proud."

By the end of the day, the death toll had been revised to over thirty. And once the carnage was fully accounted for a year later, the official government death toll was over three thousand.

And, in an unusual move for a presidential visit to a hurricane disaster area, he brought his budget director, Mick Mulvaney. Introducing him at the meeting with the Puerto Rican governor, he said: "I hate to tell you, Puerto Rico, but you've thrown our budget a little out of whack."

I reported all of this, without editorial comment, in the story I filed that evening for ABC's *World News Tonight*—the tossing of paper towels, the congratulatory comments on the death toll, the complaint about the budget. I also pointed out that the governor of Puerto Rico said he was grateful for the president's visit and that a US Navy hospital ship had just arrived to provide additional help.

Trump apparently watched my story after he left the island. He wasn't happy. In fact, he ordered Hope Hicks, who had been promoted to White House communications director a few weeks earlier, to "call fucking [John] Santucci and ask him why his network fucking hates me." She did. And John, who had moved from being one of the best-sourced embedded reporters on the Trump campaign to being one of the best-sourced reporters in the ABC Washington bureau, dutifully passed the message along. The complaint didn't bother me. The White House could not point to anything specific in my report that was wrong, and I knew it was neither inaccurate nor misleading.

The handling of Hurricane Maria was yet another indication that no matter how much discipline Kelly tried to impose on the West Wing, Trump would be the one calling the shots—and tossing the paper towel rolls.

CHAPTER SEVENTEEN

MEET THE NEW BOSS

As John Kelly settled in as chief of staff, the retired four-star marine general set out to impose some military-style order on a West Wing that hadn't had much order at all while Reince Priebus was chief of staff. But there was one key player on the president's team who Kelly seemed to think brought a little too much military discipline to his job: National Security Advisor H. R. McMaster.

McMaster's style often rubbed the president the wrong way. A burly, muscle-bound three-star general, McMaster came across as equal parts drill sergeant and intellectual—and neither part appealed to the president. His rat-a-tat briefings were carefully organized, thorough, and thoroughly boring to the commander in chief. As McMaster motored through his talking points, he gave the impression he was lecturing the president as if he were a young army captain under his command. As McMaster went through his briefings, the president would often look at the others in the room and roll his eyes, as if saying, "Will this guy ever get to the point?"

In the Trump White House, McMaster stood out as a senior

advisor willing to challenge the president when he believed he was mistaken. He also firmly believed that once the president gave an order, it was his duty to carry it out, even if he disagreed with it. Kelly saw things differently.

During one meeting in the fall of 2017, Trump had even less patience than usual with McMaster. Interrupting McMaster's presentation on the deteriorating situation in Venezuela, where anti-American dictator Nicolás Maduro was clinging to power, the president demanded a war plan. One of the options he had in mind was a naval blockade of Venezuela, which didn't make sense for a lot of reasons, including the fact that Venezuela is not an island. McMaster told the president a war plan wasn't necessary at this point, that there were several options to explore that did not involve military action. The president didn't like the answer and demanded to see a war plan put together—now.

"I will pass that order on to the Pentagon immediately, Mr. President," McMaster said.

As the meeting broke up, McMaster walked briskly down the hall to his office. Kelly hustled after him.

"What the hell are you doing?" Kelly asked.

"I am going to carry out an order from the commander in chief," McMaster answered.

Kelly told him to stand down and not to pass the president's order on to the Pentagon.

The incident, which was described to me by one senior White House official who was there and confirmed by another, was perfectly representative of Kelly's approach to serving as Donald Trump's chief of staff. As Kelly said privately shortly after taking the job when asked if he would be able to control the president, "If I was to write a book on what I've done in the last three weeks, I'd call it *Tweets Not Sent, Decisions Not Made.*"

I asked McMaster about the incident long after he left the White House.

"I didn't need John Kelly to tell me how to do my job," he told me.

McMaster said he didn't remember the specific meeting, but "there were all sorts of incidents like that" where Kelly would want to slow-walk or ignore a request from the president rather than directly confront him.

McMaster believed Kelly was constantly pacifying and undermining the president because he didn't want to directly challenge him. In McMaster's view, directly challenging the president when he disagreed with a decision was his duty, but once the president made a decision, it was also the duty of a senior advisor to carry out that order. If he undermined an order from the commander in chief, even one he disagreed with, McMaster believed he would be undermining the Constitution. The people had elected Donald Trump; they hadn't elected John Kelly or H. R. McMaster. And the unelected chief of staff is not among the checks and balances envisioned by James Madison.

But Kelly, along with fellow retired four-star marine general James Mattis at the Pentagon and Secretary of State Rex Tillerson, considered himself part of an axis of adults—reining in a president and presidential advisors they saw as dangerously undisciplined and inexperienced. Or as Senator Bob Corker, who was then the Republican chairman of the Senate Foreign Relations Committee, put it: "I think Secretary Tillerson, Secretary Mattis, and Chief of Staff Kelly are those people that help separate our country from chaos."*

Kelly himself cultivated this idea. On more than one occasion he gravely told me that when I wake up each morning, I should be

---

*Corker made this comment on October 4, 2017, to a group of reporters on Capitol Hill. Four days later on Twitter, Corker said, "It's a shame the White House has become an adult day care center."

thankful that James Mattis was there at the Pentagon serving as secretary of defense. His tone suggested Mattis was saving the world from Donald Trump's most dangerous impulses. He also privately called Rex Tillerson "Saint Rex of Texas," suggesting he was serving a martyr's cause being Donald Trump's secretary of state. And Kelly clearly thought he was doing the same.

At a crowded sports bar in Manila, the final stop on Trump's first trip to Asia as president, Kelly told me the most important thing he did was tell the president no.

"No. Don't tweet that. No. Don't change your policy on that. No, no, no."*

Kelly sought to bring chain-of-command discipline to the White House from his first days on the job. When he moved into his office, he brought along Kirstjen Nielsen as his top aide and instructed her to take over a connecting office that then belonged to Steve Bannon, the president's stridently ideological chief strategist. Kelly wasn't firing Bannon, but he was effectively banishing him from the West Wing. About a week later, Bannon submitted his letter of resignation, effective two weeks after that. He didn't have much choice. At one point before Bannon left, Kelly was asked if Bannon would be attending a meeting on Afghanistan policy.

"No," Kelly said. "There will be no children in the room."

Kelly took other steps to impose order. He banned personal cell phones from the White House. And he ended the open-door policy to the Oval Office, where it seemed just about anybody could pop in

---

*Kelly told me this during an off-the-record conversation, but while I was writing this book, he agreed to allow me to quote this and other previously off-the-record remarks he made while he was chief of staff.

on the president. You had to go through Kelly. His message to the staff: Every person who *needs* to talk to the president will; every person who *wants* to talk to the president will not.

At Kelly's early-morning senior staff meetings, he would call on each senior advisor to give a brief update on his or her area of responsibility. He almost always called on Ivanka Trump and Jared Kushner last. Kelly was sending an unmistakable message that he was the one now in charge. When it came to policy and White House operations, even family would have to go through Kelly.

From the start, Kelly would tell just about anybody who asked that he hated the job. He called it the toughest and most important job he had ever had. He also said it was the job he enjoyed the least, telling me once he hadn't experienced a moment of joy during his time as chief of staff. He was there to serve the country, he would say. The implication seemed to be that he was serving by protecting the country from its president.

Kelly had been on the job for just nine days when Trump made his famously apocalyptic threat against North Korea—threatening "fire and fury" in response to a story about North Korea's rapidly advancing nuclear program.

President Trump issued the threat without telling Kelly or anyone else it was coming. In fact, it came when the president had invited the press to come in for a quick photo op at a meeting he was having on the opioid epidemic at his golf resort in Bedminster, New Jersey. As the cameras were about to be escorted out of the room, a reporter asked the president about a story in *The Washington Post* saying that North Korea had successfully developed a nuclear warhead small enough to be put on a ballistic missile with a range long enough to hit the US military base in Guam. This was an especially worrisome development because North Korea had also been developing missiles believed to be capable of reaching the continental United States.

"North Korea best not make any more threats to the United States," he said, his body tense, arms tightly crossed in front of his body. "They will be met with fire and fury and frankly power, the likes of which this world has never seen before."

The taunt was not planned. The implications had not been discussed with his national security team. Nobody knew it was coming.

As he made the threat, the president looked down at a sheet of paper before him, but the paper said nothing about North Korea. It was a list of talking points about the administration's plans to deal with the opioid epidemic. The comments that put the world on edge were completely ad-libbed and exactly the kind of thing Kelly rightly wanted to avoid. He was quickly learning the lesson that all who served at the pleasure of the president had to: Donald Trump would not be controlled.

Two weeks later, Kelly privately explained one of his central challenges was getting the president to understand the implications of his decisions. "He needs to understand that eighteen- and nineteen-year-old people are going to die. This is big-boy and big-girl shit," Kelly said. "You have to understand people will die because of these decisions."

His approach, he explained, was to "overwhelm him with facts"—something that Kelly said was necessary because the president would often say things to him that just weren't true.

"The president will say, 'I heard from a friend,'" Kelly said, "and we will say, 'That's not true.'"

Kelly succeeded for a while in imposing a degree of order on the West Wing. He was able for a time to control the flow of information and people into the Oval Office. But his experience during that first month—with the impromptu "fire and fury" comments provoking an international crisis and the impromptu comments on Charlottesville a week later provoking a domestic crisis—showed Kelly had no more success in controlling Trump than Reince Priebus had.

For all his efforts to bring discipline to the White House, Kelly himself showed little restraint in expressing his own frustrations. He vented to almost anybody. At one point, a young lawyer, just out of law school, visited the White House and was introduced to Kelly, who showed him the Oval Office. Kelly, seeing the young lawyer was in awe of the surroundings, offered a different take.

"This place is my hell," Kelly told him.

Kelly could say "no, no, no" all he wanted, but on North Korea especially, the president would always be calling his own shots. During his first year in office, that meant, rhetorically at least, pushing the country to the brink of war. A month after his "fire and fury" threat, the president was at the United Nations branding Kim Jong Un "Rocket Man" and making the starkest warning an American president has ever made on the world stage.

"The United States has great strength and patience, but if it is forced to defend itself or its allies, we will have no choice but to totally destroy North Korea," he said. "Rocket man is on a suicide mission for himself and for his regime."

The warning that North Korea would be destroyed if it attacked the United States was not exactly unprecedented. Bill Clinton had essentially said the same thing nearly twenty-five years earlier when asked about the prospect of North Korea's developing and using a nuclear weapon.

"We would quickly and overwhelmingly retaliate," President Clinton said during a trip to the Korean Demilitarized Zone in 1993. "It would mean the end of their country as they know it."

But the name-calling and the threat to "totally destroy" North Korea was alarming, especially coming in a speech before the United Nations General Assembly.

In an effort to take a step back from the brink, Secretary of State Tillerson reached out to North Korea in the aftermath of the president's UN speech, hoping to establish some kind of dialogue beyond the public exchange of doomsday threats.

During a visit to Beijing two weeks after the UN speech, Tillerson told reporters the Trump administration had had direct communications with the North Koreans.

"We are probing, stay tuned," he said.

He added: "We ask, 'Would you like to talk?' We have lines of communications to Pyongyang—we're not in a dark situation, a blackout."

This was the first indication of diplomatic outreach to North Korea by the Trump administration. It was striking because it came in the immediate aftermath of the president's personal taunts aimed at Kim Jong Un and his dire threat to "totally destroy" North Korea.

But within hours, the president himself seemed to undermine all of Tillerson's suggestions of a diplomatic outreach to North Korea with a short tweet:

> **Donald J. Trump**
> @realDonaldTrump
>
> I told Rex Tillerson, our wonderful Secretary of State, that he is wasting his time trying to negotiate with Little Rocket Man . . .
>
> 10/1/17, 10:30 AM

Six months later, Tillerson would be gone and the president would be moving in a dramatically different direction—once again, calling the shots on his own, his national security team scrambling to keep up.

The first indication of Trump's coming turn on Kim Jong Un

came when the president made a five-nation trip to Asia in November 2017, only six weeks after he dressed down Tillerson on Twitter for attempting to talk to the North Koreans. Meeting with South Korean president Moon Jae-in in Seoul, he said for the first time he would be open to talks with North Korea. There was no more talk of fire, fury, or totally destroying North Korea.

But for me, the most striking moment of that trip came when the president visited Da Nang, Vietnam, to attend a summit of Asian-Pacific leaders. While Trump was attending the summit, I made arrangements to meet with one of the president's senior advisors at the Hyatt Regency resort where the White House staff was staying. The traveling White House corps was staying in another part of town, but together with my ABC News colleague Devin Dwyer, I was able to get through security and into the resort where the president was staying to have my off-the-record meeting with this official.

As Dwyer and I walked on the grounds of the luxury resort, we saw the president's top advisors in a way we had never seen them before. On a veranda surrounded by palm trees and overlooking the crystal-blue pool, we saw speechwriter and immigration hard-liner Stephen Miller wearing shorts, smoking a cigarette, and playing pool—by himself. A few steps from the pool table, Sarah Sanders was trying on a winter coat, which was funny because it was nearly ninety degrees. But she was with a local Vietnamese tailor who was taking her measurements for a custom-tailored coat that would be ready by the time Air Force One left Vietnam.

And as we sat down at a table with the senior official, I looked back to the entrance of the resort and saw two people walking toward the veranda wearing Asian conical hats—the kind you see workers wearing in rice paddies. As they got closer, I saw who was wearing the hats: Hope Hicks and White House staff secretary Rob Porter. They had just returned from a hike.

It was quite a scene. The president was at the summit, along with Chinese president Xi Jinping, Russian president Vladimir Putin, and the other Asian-Pacific leaders. It was a high-level meeting, and most senior staff were not permitted to attend. It didn't matter. Those left behind seemed to be having a good time, and the president would be making his own decisions anyway.

CHAPTER EIGHTEEN

MAD MEN

On March 3, 2018, President Trump attended the Gridiron Dinner and did something truly out of character. He made fun of himself.

"So many people have been leaving the White House, it's actually been really exciting and invigorating," he said. "I like turnover. I like chaos. It really is good. Now the question everyone keeps asking is, 'Who is going to be the next to leave: Steve Miller or Melania?'"

This was a rare Trump performance that was not before the cameras. For over a century, Gridiron Dinners have been attended by a who's-who of Washington power players—including every president since Grover Cleveland—but they are never televised. That was unfortunate for Trump, because his speech was filled with genuinely funny jokes, including this one on North Korea:

"I won't rule out talks with Kim Jong Un," he deadpanned. "I just won't."

Pause.

"As for the risk of dealing with a madman, that's his problem, not mine."

Everybody laughed, perhaps a little too loudly for the president. The joke was funny, but what nobody in the room knew, possibly including the president himself, was that it was more than a joke. He really was on the verge of agreeing to the first-ever meeting between a US president and a North Korean dictator.

Five days after the Gridiron Dinner, Donald Trump did something else he had never done before, at least not with any reporters present: He ducked his head into the White House briefing room. It was 5:27 P.M. and I was in the ABC White House booth up against a deadline, writing my script for that evening's six thirty P.M. newscast on a big economic story—the president had just signed a proclamation imposing tariffs on imported steel (25 percent) and imported aluminum (10 percent). The announcement pleased American steelworkers, but it had rattled markets, annoyed US allies, irritated Republican leaders in Congress, and led to the abrupt departure of the president's top economic advisor, Gary Cohn.

The president's tariff announcement was made amid all the usual Trump White House chaos. Several news outlets had reported early that morning that the tariffs were coming, but the White House press office had told reporters, emphatically, there would be no trade announcement that day. The official White House schedule put out by the press office included nothing about a trade announcement. But not long after the official White House schedule went out, the president tweeted he would be making a trade announcement that afternoon, proving once again that the only true spokesperson for Donald Trump is Donald Trump and that his Twitter feed is often a more reliable source of information about his plans than anything put out by his press office.

It all added up to a big story—new tariffs and major real-world ramifications for the economy and for our relations with our European and Asian allies. And there was White House drama to go along with it—warring factions in the West Wing and a presidential tweet taking the president's own staff by surprise. There was even some unintended comic relief. As the president announced the steel tariffs, he was surrounded by steelworkers. A steelworker and union leader named Scott Sauritch from West Mifflin, Pennsylvania, told a story about how imported steel had cost his father, Herman, his job. Trump came back to the podium and told him, "Your father, Herman, is looking down. He is very proud."

"Oh, he's still alive," the steelworker replied.

"He is?" Trump said. "Well, then he is even more proud of you."

But when the president ducked his head into the briefing room a couple of hours later, he wasn't there to talk about anything to do with steel and aluminum tariffs.

The president came into the briefing room with a scheduling announcement. Not a White House scheduling announcement, but one involving a foreign government.

"At seven o'clock, South Korea will make a major statement on a big subject," he said.

It was early evening, and there weren't many people in the briefing room—only a few camera crews and a handful of reporters. Those who were there were quite startled. As the videographers grabbed their cameras and went toward the president, a South Korean cameraman with a thick accent started screaming at the president something about the Nobel Peace Prize. The president slid the door shut and retreated to the West Wing.

It all happened so quickly that by the time I ran the fifteen or so yards from the ABC News booth to the White House briefing room, the president was gone. At this point, a bunch of reporters who had also missed the president's appearance hustled through the blue door and up toward Press Secretary Sarah Sanders's office to see what that was all about.

I stayed behind. After all, I had a deadline fast approaching and needed to finish my story. From the confines of the ABC booth, however, I could keep an eye on the blue briefing-room door—we have a robotic camera in the briefing room that is always on and the live video feed comes to a monitor above my desk. While a bunch of my colleagues were trying to get answers out of Sarah Sanders about what was going on, I got an email from fellow ABC News correspondent Martha Raddatz. A national security source had told Martha that the South Korean announcement would be regarding "the parameters" of negotiations with North Korea over its nuclear weapons, adding that US officials were "pretty skeptical." Martha also noted that the South Korean national security advisor was in DC. Would he make the announcement? If so, where? We called the South Korean embassy. No answer.

As the reporters streamed back into the briefing room, I went out to see what they had learned from Sarah Sanders. Short answer: not much. As it turned out, the president's quick visit to the White House briefing room had caught her by surprise too. He had walked right past her office on the way to the briefing room but hadn't stopped to tell her what he was doing. Sanders told the reporters there would be a written advisory going out soon. I went back to the ABC White House booth to record the voice-over for my story on the steel and aluminum tariffs and to make a few calls to try to figure out what South Korean announcement the president was talking about.

Unable to learn anything more, I decided to go up to the press secretary's office to see if Sanders had any more information to share. At this point, I had less than twenty minutes before I needed to be in front of the ABC News camera on the North Lawn for a live report that would be seen by the roughly nine million viewers of ABC's *World News Tonight with David Muir.*

As I walked through the blue door by the podium and made my way up toward the press secretary's office, I was startled to see the president himself. He was standing there just outside the door to the colonnade with Vice President Pence, Sarah Sanders, and the VP's chief of staff, Nick Ayers.

When the president saw me, he motioned for me to come over.

"Are you going to cover the South Korean announcement?" he asked.

"Of course, sir," I answered, still not sure what he was talking about. "What is it? Where is it?"

"You'll see."

"Is this about negotiations?" I asked.

"It's almost beyond that," he said, and then added: "I hope you give me credit."

"Give you credit for what?" I asked. "Can you at least tell me where this announcement is happening?"

"He never gives you credit," said Sanders.

The situation was bizarre. I was now about fifteen minutes away from my live report on the North Lawn about the big trade announcement, but the president was making it sound like something even bigger was coming. And there I was in the Rose Garden colonnade, trying to get answers but finding myself in a debate with the president and his press secretary about giving the president "credit" for whatever was about to happen as the vice president stood there silently nodding his head. Then things got even stranger.

Turning to his vice president, the president launched into the story about how I had interviewed him at the Old Post Office building in 2014—the story he has told over and over again in my presence.

"He interviewed me as if I was a presidential candidate," he told Pence. "He took a lot of heat for it, but he got great ratings."

I was standing with the president, vice president, and press secretary right around the corner from where a bunch of White House reporters were scrambling to figure out what the momentous announcement the president had said was coming actually was. In fact, the White House briefing room was on the other side of the wall from where we were standing. But nobody in there had any idea I was right there, just a few feet away, talking to the president.

Instead of getting any useful information—I still didn't know if the mysterious South Korean announcement would be in Seoul or in Washington—I was listening to the president reminisce about an interview I had done four years earlier. And I was nervously watching the time. If I didn't get out to the ABC camera position on the North Lawn soon, I would miss my time slot on *World News Tonight*.

What the president would not tell me was that he had just met the South Korean national security advisor, who relayed an offer from Kim Jong Un to have a one-on-one meeting. To the surprise of the South Koreans and the president's own national security team, President Trump had accepted the offer on the spot and told them they should make the announcement right there at the White House.

With time running out, I made one last attempt to find out what was happening, said goodbye to the president, and hustled out to the North Lawn. Just as I got my microphone and earpiece in place and *World News* was coming on the air, Sarah Sanders put out a notice that the South Korean national security advisor would be making an announcement from the White House driveway in thirty minutes.

She confirmed the announcement would be about talks, but I assumed it would be lower-level talks. Nobody contemplated the idea that President Trump, who had threatened Kim Jong Un with fire and fury and taunted him as Little Rocket Man, would have agreed to unconditional talks with the world's most despised and dangerous despot.

The announcement itself was stunning. The South Korean national security advisor, standing in front of the main entrance to the

West Wing, told reporters about the invitation he had brought from Kim Jong Un and that President Trump had accepted. He said the summit would be in June, just three months away.

The president had agreed to meet directly with Kim Jong Un, and as far as we could tell, the only conditions were that North Korea would suspend its nuclear and missile testing while the details of the meeting were worked out.

Two months later, everything seemed in place for a summit. The White House announced a date and location: June 12 in Singapore. Mike Pompeo had helped lay the groundwork with a secret trip to Pyongyang to meet with Kim Jong Un in April, just a week before he was confirmed as secretary of state.

Kim Jong Un wasn't the only adversary the president reached out to during this time period. He had also scheduled a series of off-the-record meetings with senior executives of the very news organizations he had branded enemies of the people. Among those invited to lunch with the president at the White House during the late spring and summer of 2018 were A. G. Sulzberger of *The New York Times,* Robert Albritton of Politico, and several other news organizations. The lunch meetings were held in a small dining area adjacent to the Oval Office with a bank of televisions on one wall invariably turned on and tuned in to the cable news channels. Press Secretary Sarah Sanders usually joined the president during these lunch meetings.

One day in late May 2018, a New York–based news executive was preparing to go to the White House for lunch when a major news story broke: President Trump had abruptly called off the summit with Kim Jong Un, citing North Korea's "open hostility" and ominously warning that the US military stood ready to defend America's interests. The statement, dictated by the president, reminded Kim that the United

States possessed nuclear weapons "so massive and powerful that [the president] pray[ed] to God they [would] never have to be used."

The president's statement caught the world by surprise, especially South Korea, which had pushed hard to make the summit happen, and Singapore, which was preparing for the immense security challenges of hosting the summit.

The president, however, seemed to shrug off the upheaval caused by his decision to cancel the summit. It was business as usual; his lunch meeting with the news executive was still on. In fact, Press Secretary Sanders called as the news was breaking on North Korea to ask the executive if he was allergic to shellfish.

"The president is thinking of having shrimp salad," the White House press secretary explained.

It's hard to know what was more surprising about this: that the president and the press secretary were taking time to work out the lunch menu minutes after the world appeared to have taken a step closer to nuclear war, or the fact that a president known for his love of junk food was planning to have shrimp salad for lunch. Whatever the case, lunch was still on.

The president had a good reason for canceling the summit. The day before, North Korea had reacted angrily to comments from National Security Advisor John Bolton and Vice President Mike Pence about following the "Libya model" for disarmament—a model that had ultimately ended with the brutal killing of Libyan leader Muammar Gaddafi. The North Korean statement called Pence "a political dummy" and warned that the United States had a stark choice: "Meet us at a meeting room or encounter us at nuclear-to-nuclear showdown." And it wasn't just the threats and insults. The North Koreans had also failed to show up to a key meeting to plan logistics for the summit and were not responding to phone calls.

The president's abrupt move to cancel the summit seemed to

throw the North Koreans off balance and caused an equally abrupt change in tone from Kim Jong Un, who responded with a conciliatory statement saying he still wanted to have the summit.

The next day, May 25, the White House made a senior National Security Council official available to answer questions from reporters about all things related to North Korea. This was a so-called background briefing, which means reporters could quote what the official said but we could not use his name. It took place in the White House briefing room. Deputy Press Secretary Raj Shah explained the ground rules:

"This briefing's going to be on background. It's off camera, not for broadcast," Shah said, adding that the briefer could "be referred to as a senior White House official."

This is a common practice that I have witnessed in every White House I have covered—the press office making top officials available but demanding they not be quoted by name. The practice often annoys reporters, who would prefer to name the officials we talk to, but Barack Obama's press office did this all the time. So did George W. Bush's. And Donald Trump's office was only continuing the practice.

I asked the official, who had been directly involved in the effort to set up the summit meeting, if it could still happen as scheduled. He chuckled and said, "We've lost quite a bit of time that we would need," adding, "June twelve is in ten minutes." The tone of his response was unmistakable: It would be virtually impossible to pull the summit off as planned.

But in another case of Trump whiplash, the president announced a few hours later that his administration was back in touch with the North Koreans and the summit could possibly happen as planned after all. In reporting the president's sudden reversal of his reversal, *The New York Times* quoted the senior administration official who had just suggested it would be virtually impossible to get the meeting back on track.

That prompted this remarkable tweet from the president.

Donald J. Trump
(@realDonaldTrump)

The Failing @nytimes quotes "a senior White House official," who doesn't exist, as saying "even if the meeting were reinstated, holding it on June 12 would be impossible, given the lack of time and the amount of planning needed." WRONG AGAIN! Use real people, not phony sources.

5/26/18, 11:21 PM

Use real people? This "senior administration official"* was a true flesh-and-blood Trump administration official. The only reason he was not named by *The New York Times* or any other news organization that attended the briefing is because Trump's own press office insisted he not be named. It was a bizarre episode and a perfect illustration of one central fact about the president's attacks on the news media: Much of the news he derides as fake news comes right out of his own White House. And when it comes to North Korea, the episode revealed another immutable fact: The president himself was driving the policy. If the president had been following the advice of his own top advisors, the summit meeting simply would not have happened.

---

*The anonymous official's name is Matthew Pottinger, the senior director for Asian affairs on the National Security Council. If the president is going to accuse reporters of using "phony sources" when they abide by White House ground rules, then I believe those ground rules no longer apply.

It would still be several days until the summit was officially back on. North Korea, so eager to salvage the meeting, dispatched a delegation led by one of the most intimidating figures in Kim Jong Un's government, Vice Chairman Kim Yong Chol, to the United States. He was the former head of North Korea's intelligence services and believed to be responsible for masterminding an attack on a South Korean naval ship that killed forty-six sailors in 2010. The Trump administration had to waive sanctions placed on Vice Chairman Kim to allow him to enter the United States. After his arrival at Kennedy airport, he was escorted by the US Diplomatic Security Service everywhere he went, driven in a black SUV first to Manhattan for dinner with Secretary of State Mike Pompeo and then all the way to the White House.

The arrival at the White House was awkward. No North Korean official had set foot in the White House in eighteen years. Chief of Staff John Kelly greeted the SUV at the South Portico. There were four people in the North Korean delegation, but only two of them were allowed into the White House—Vice Chairman Kim and his translator. The other two had to wait outside in the SUV, just a few yards from the reporters in the White House press pool.

The North Koreans had brought a letter from Kim Jong Un in an enormous envelope, but before it was given to the president, it was tested for poisons. After all, the North Koreans know how to conduct assassinations with poison; Kim's own half brother had been killed in Malaysia just fifteen months earlier by North Korean agents using VX nerve gas.

The meeting with the president was supposed to be brief—twenty minutes on the schedule—and take place just inside the door leading to the South Lawn, the diplomatic room. But at the last minute, President Trump changed the plan, inviting Vice Chairman Kim and his translator into the Oval Office. The meeting wasn't brief, lasting some eighty minutes. National Security Advisor John Bolton, who had so offended the North Koreans with his "Libya model" comments, was nowhere to be seen. A beaming Donald Trump posed for photos with the giant letter from Kim Jong Un.

When the meeting was finally over, the president escorted Vice Chairman Kim and his translator back out to the SUV and greeted the two members of the delegation who had been forced to wait outside. They posed for more photos and the president talked to the press pool, announcing that the summit was indeed back on. We would be going to Singapore after all.

The sensitivity surrounding the planning of this summit was unlike that for any other. No North Korean dictator—not Kim's father or grandfather—had ever embarked on a trip like this. In fact, Kim had to arrange to borrow an airplane from China—an American-made Boeing 737, no less—because North Korea had no aircraft capable of safely making the trip. Kim also arranged to bring all his own food and chefs to prepare meals out of fear of being poisoned. And the South Korean newspaper the *Chosun Ilbo* reported Kim brought his own toilet to "deny determined sewer divers insights into the supreme leader's stools." This was shaping up to be one of the strangest diplomatic meetings in American history.

Shortly before the summit began, a senior US official told me another one of Kim's concerns was whether there would be a coup attempt back home while the summit was under way. What would they do with Kim if that happened?

"Maybe we can send him to Gitmo," the official joked.

The summit in Singapore was one of the most unlikely meetings of world leaders ever witnessed. On one side, there was Kim Jong Un, a thirty-four-year-old tyrant who had ordered the killing of his half brother, his uncle, and countless others and who had left North Korea only once since taking over as the supreme leader seven years earlier. On the other side was Donald Trump.

As I waited for the two of them to come before the cameras for their first handshake, I couldn't quite believe the backdrop— American and North Korean flags, side by side.

The three previous US presidents had alternated between periods of punishing North Korea and negotiating, but none of them would ever agree to allow a North Korean dictator to share a stage with an American president without major concessions. The Bush administration had gone to great lengths to avoid even low-level talks directly with North Korea, insisting on working through the so-called six-party talks, which also included China, Japan, South Korea, and Russia.

President Trump's decision to allow Kim Jong Un to share a stage like this without any commitment to dismantle his nuclear program was widely criticized by foreign policy experts, including some who had helped guide the policies of Trump's predecessors. The critics raised legitimate concerns, but there was a fundamental truth here: Some of the brightest foreign policy minds of our time had helped Bill Clinton, George W. Bush, and Barack Obama confront the North Korean threat, and they had all failed spectacularly. Over the course of those three administrations, North Korea methodically developed a nuclear program and a missile program that steadily increased in sophistication and lethality. By the time Donald Trump was sworn in, North Korea possessed an arsenal of twenty to thirty nuclear weapons or perhaps more. And it has developed intercontinental ballistic missiles believed to have the range to hit the United States. The freewheeling, by-the-gut approach Trump tried in Singapore may ultimately fail too, but it's also true that the carefully considered approach of the highly experienced foreign policy experts guiding the policy before Trump certainly did fail.

At a summit with many strange moments, for me the strangest came at the very end, when President Trump opened a press conference up to the entire global press corps in Singapore covering the summit. The presser was held in a cavernous room about the size of a basketball arena, with about two hundred fifty or so reporters and cameras present, including a large contingent from China's state-controlled media.

I had a seat in the second row. Shortly before the press conference started, the president's advisors came into the room and occupied the seats in the front row, Secretary of State Mike Pompeo directly in front of me. As the assembled press waited quietly, expecting the president to come out at any minute, there was a loud sound—an electronic percussion of some kind, the bass shaking the room—and suddenly two jumbotrons above the stage started showing a video—rapid-fire images of mass movements of peoples, the Colosseum in Rome, the Lincoln Memorial, the Taj Mahal, the pyramids, North Korean performers, children playing with virtual reality technology, skyscrapers—and a narrator speaking a foreign language. Was it Korean? Was it Chinese? My first thought was hackers had somehow broken into the system controlling the large monitors on the stage. Had the North Koreans hijacked Donald Trump's press conference to play a propaganda video? As the video played on, it included images of Kim Jong Un waving to adoring crowds and then Donald Trump doing the same thing. The video lasted about four minutes, ending with a logo for something called "Destiny Pictures" and then starting again, this time in English.

"Seven billion people inhabit the planet Earth. Of those alive today only a small number will leave a lasting impact," the narrator began. "And only the very few will make decisions that renew their homeland and change the course of history."

And with that line, images on the screen of Donald Trump and

Kim Jong Un. Nobody had hacked into the system. This was a US-made video created to mimic the propaganda videos produced by the North Koreans. And it was bizarre.

As the English version of the video played out, ABC broke into regular programming for a special report on the president's upcoming press conference. I could hear anchor David Muir in my earpiece setting the scene, and then I heard him calling on me to ask what was going on with the video.

I stood up and looked in the direction of our camera, one in a sea of cameras in the back of the room. It was a strange moment. The video was playing loudly behind me. I was standing in front of Secretary of State Pompeo, and aside from the camera operators and Secret Service agents, I was the only person in the vast room who was not sitting down, and I was trying to speak loudly enough to be heard over the video.

All I could do was describe the scene to Muir and to confess I had absolutely no idea why the video was playing or what exactly it was.

As soon as the English version ended, President Trump walked onto the stage. In his opening remarks, he said nothing about the video, instead launching into a summary of what had taken place at the summit.

I later learned the decision to play the video was another last-minute call by the president shortly before the press conference, sending his staff scrambling to see if they could make it happen on such short notice. As for the video, it was created at the direction of the National Security Council by a private contractor. The president played it for Kim Jong Un on an iPad during their one-on-one meeting.

He played the video for Kim the way a real estate developer might present a video to a potential investor. Using the propaganda images like those regularly featured on North Korean state TV, the video spelled out the virtues of a nuclear deal for Kim Jong Un. By making a deal with Trump to get rid of his nuclear weapons, he would change the course of history. He would make his nation wealthy beyond his wildest dreams. On the other hand, if he failed to take that chance, it could mean Armageddon—and the video showed rocket launches and images of the apocalypse.

Trump told his aides that Kim loved the video, which is why he decided to play it at the start of his press conference.

The summit ended with an agreement from the North Koreans to "work toward complete denuclearization of the Korean peninsula," but there was no timetable set and no specific agreement to disman-tle any of its nuclear program. The North Koreans did not even agree to give a full accounting of their nuclear program, which would be a necessary first step before crafting an agreement to dismantle it. Nevertheless, the president offered one final concession before leaving Singapore, announcing that the United States would cease its annual large-scale joint military exercises with South Korea. Those military exercises had long infuriated the North Koreans and now Trump was putting them on hiatus—without getting anything in return.

When he landed back in Washington, the president declared vic-tory with a tweet.

Donald J. Trump
(@realDonaldTrump)

Just landed—a long trip, but everybody can now feel much safer than the day I took office. There is no longer a Nuclear Threat from North Korea. Meeting with Kim Jong Un was an interesting and very positive experience. North Korea has great potential for the future!

6/13/18, 5:56 AM

Not exactly. North Korea had paused its nuclear testing and its threats to the United States, but the threat remained. The North Korean nuclear arsenal was exactly as it had been before the summit started. In fact, US intelligence assessed that the program continued to grow in the months after the summit.

CHAPTER NINETEEN

TRUTHINESS

On April 13, 2018, the White House press corps was on high alert for possible United States–led military airstrikes against Syria. Syrian dictator Bashar al-Assad had been accused, once again, of using chemical weapons to attack civilians in an area controlled by the Syrian opposition. We had good reason to believe the United States–led attack would come that night. Pentagon reporters had quietly been told by senior Defense Department officials that they probably should not go home—a clear signal airstrikes would be coming soon. The British government, which would participate in the attacks, had provided the same guidance to news organizations in London.

At about seven P.M., a group of reporters from NBC, ABC, the Associated Press, and Reuters gathered in Press Secretary Sarah Sanders's office seeking off-the-record guidance on what might be coming that night. Should we stick around? Will the president address the nation if airstrikes are launched tonight? Should we be prepared for that to happen?

Sanders looked at the reporters in her office and said flatly—off the record*—there would be *no airstrikes* that night. To emphasize the certainty of what she was saying, she put on her coat, grabbed her bag, and declared she was going home. And with that, Sanders said goodbye to the reporters and walked out.

It was a lie.

Sanders wasn't going home. She walked out of her office and into a hallway leading to another part of the West Wing. She went a few yards and then, out of sight of the reporters, turned into another room, took her coat off, and set up to work in a part of the White House where she would not be seen by any reporters. Two hours later, the president addressed the nation.

"My fellow Americans," the president said, "a short time ago, I ordered the United States armed forces to launch precision strikes on targets associated with the chemical weapons capabilities of Syrian dictator Bashar al-Assad."

Fortunately, nobody had believed the lie Sanders had told. At ABC, we'd discussed what she had said but decided to disregard it. In fact, every major television network disregarded her guidance and had a correspondent on the North Lawn of the White House as they carried the president's remarks live.

I later confronted Sanders about what she had said. I told her that lying—especially lying like that on an issue of national security— destroys a press secretary's most important asset: credibility. If reporters can't trust the off-the-record guidance given by the White House press secretary, how can we trust what she says on the record? And the lie was dumb as a communications strategy. What if we had believed her? What if the White House press corps had followed her

---

*Once again, I firmly believe that if a source says something off the record that is a lie, it is no longer off the record. The implicit trust behind the arrangement has been broken.

fake lead and gone home? There would have been nobody present to report on the president's speech.

She told me she had been instructed (she didn't say by whom) to lie in order to protect the security of the mission and the safety of the troops involved. In that case, I told her she should have said no comment. She insisted that if she had said no comment, it would have been seen as a signal that military action was about to happen and somebody would have reported airstrikes were coming. That simply is not correct.

The Pentagon had essentially confirmed the airstrikes were coming by telling reporters not to go home. The British, who were taking part in the military operation, had done the same thing. And nobody reported anything until it happened. The only knowledgeable party to lie about it was the White House press secretary, and she passed the lie on to her staff, who repeated it to other reporters.

I explained to her that I had covered many military deployments over the years—as both a White House reporter and a Pentagon reporter—and had never seen a government spokesman lie as blatantly as she had. Reporters understand the importance of not putting US troops in jeopardy. Many of us have been embedded with US troops on dangerous operations where our survival could have depended on the security of the mission.

"I might do it differently next time," Sanders told me. "Hopefully there won't be a next time."

Sanders had not lied out of malice or to score political points but out of the misguided belief that she needed to lie to protect a military operation.

Her deputy, Hogan Gidley, on the other hand, told an equally brazen off-the-record lie to reporters later in the year with no such benign intentions.

As I waited for a train to leave Union Station early in the morning on September 24, 2018, I got an urgent call from my ABC colleague Devin Dwyer: "Get off the train. Axios is reporting Rosenstein has resigned."

The Axios report, by Jonathan Swan, said that Deputy Attorney General Rod Rosenstein had "verbally resigned" to Chief of Staff John Kelly in anticipation of being fired by the president. The report caused an immediate frenzy. After all, Rosenstein was the person overseeing Robert Mueller's special counsel investigation. I had just boarded an Amtrak train bound for New York to attend President Trump's appearance before the United Nations General Assembly.

Adding to the frenzy surrounding Swan's report, Justice Department spokesperson Sarah Isgur Flores had confirmed to me and other White House reporters that Rosenstein had indeed gone to the White House that morning to meet with Kelly. He had gone into the meeting, she told me, expecting to be fired. In fact, I was told Rosenstein was still there. Other reporters had heard the same thing and went to ask Deputy Press Secretary Hogan Gidley whether Rosenstein had indeed come over to the White House to resign.

"Off the record, let me offer you this: He is not here," Gidley said.

But he was there! And a short while later, TV cameras spotted Rosenstein on the White House grounds.

And Gidley knew Rosenstein was there. He later explained that he had just seen Rosenstein leaving John Kelly's office and assumed he was leaving the White House. In other words, Gidley only intended to be wildly misleading. In fact, Rosenstein had not left and was sticking around for another meeting.

It turned out that Swan's report wasn't exactly right. Rosenstein did offer to resign and had gone into that meeting with Kelly expecting he was about to be fired. But in the end, his resignation was not accepted. Swan later amended his story with this note: "By saying Rosenstein had 'verbally resigned' to Kelly rather than 'offered his resignation,' I conveyed a certainty that this fluid situation didn't deserve. It's an important nuance, and I regret the wording."

Gidley offered no such regret for telling reporters something he knew was, at best, intentionally misleading.

Despite this and other high-profile exceptions, Sarah Sanders was a much more reliable source of information than her predecessor— and far more reliable than her boss.

Anthony Scaramucci, Trump's short-lived communications director, described the president's relationship with the truth this way: "He has a reality distortion field around himself, where he curves facts towards himself."

Former defense secretary James Mattis had another way to describe Donald Trump's relationship to the truth. Mattis privately described Trump as "impervious to facts."

The president's incessant telling of untruths has been well documented and started long before he went into politics. He lies even when telling the truth would actually make him look better.

"I think what he has done at times, which has been unfortunate, is, in my view, lie about things that he hasn't needed to lie about," Chris Christie, a friend and supporter of Trump's, told CNN in February 2019. "That's worse in many respects."

In October 2018, Congress passed a bill to deal with the opioid epidemic. For Trump it was a rare bipartisan accomplishment, an opportunity to show he could work with Democrats.

But at a rally in Ohio, instead of taking credit for bringing Democrats and Republicans together to deal with a major public health crisis, he said the bill passed with "very little Democratic support."

The facts: The bill passed 393–8 in the House and 98–1 in the

Senate. Democrats overwhelmingly supported it. The only vote against the bill in the Senate was cast by Republican Mike Lee of Utah.

Some of Trump's untruths grow with time. Back in March 2018, he accurately described a pay raise he had signed off on for members of the military, saying the new Defense Department appropriations bill "include[d] the largest pay raise [the military had] received in more than eight years."

That was entirely correct. The Defense Department appropriations bill he signed gave servicemembers their biggest salary increase (2.4 percent) since President Obama signed off on a 3.4 percent increase for 2010.

A few weeks later, he made a slight exaggeration, telling servicemembers the raise was their "largest pay raise in over a decade."

But by May 2018, the slight exaggeration had bloomed into an outright falsehood as he told a group of military spouses that servicemembers had received a raise for the "first time in ten years."

In fact, military servicemembers have received pay raises every year for the past thirty years. The president had told the troops something that was just not true. The headline in the *Military Times* read: "Trump Seems Confused about Military Pay, Claims Troops Received No Raises for a Decade."

But even as fact-checkers called out the president's falsehood, it kept growing.

Visiting Iraq in December 2018, he told the troops, "You haven't gotten one in more than ten years—more than ten years. And we got you a big one. I got you a big one. I got you a big one." And he said this: "You just got one of the biggest pay raises you've ever received." He suggested the pay raise for 2018 was 10 percent; in fact it was 2.4 percent.

And it wasn't one of the largest pay raises ever. During two of

Obama's eight years in office, the military received higher pay increases, as they did in six of George W. Bush's years in office. In 2002, for example, the military received a pay increase of 6.9 percent, nearly three times the increase in 2018.

During the 2016 campaign, Trump had made a long-forgotten promise to always tell the truth.

"In this journey, I will never lie to you," he had pledged during an August 2016 rally in Charlotte, North Carolina. "I will never tell you something I do not believe."

I asked him about that promise one week before the midterm elections in 2018 during a short interview backstage before a rally in Tampa, Florida.

"You made a promise," I reminded him. "You said, 'I will never lie to you.' Can you tell me now, honestly, have you kept that promise?"

I was taken aback by his answer.

"Well, I try. I do try. I think you try too. You say things about me that aren't necessarily correct. I do try, and I always want to tell the truth. When I can, I tell the truth."

When I can, I tell the truth.

George Washington may have never said, "I cannot tell a lie," but Donald Trump did say, "When I can, I tell the truth."

It reminded me of what a college friend once said to me: "I would only lie to you if I had to."

I then asked the president about one of his most recent untruths— that the United States is the only country in the world with birthright citizenship (where you are automatically a citizen if you are born here). In fact, there are at least thirty-three countries with birthright citizenship, including Canada and Mexico, per the Library of Congress.

"Well, I was told that," he said.

Fact-checking this president is a full-time job. *The Washington Post* has a team of fact-checkers, led by veteran journalist Glenn

Kessler, that diligently checks virtually every public assertion made by the president. Kessler is a tireless and fair journalist who does not shy from calling out untruths uttered by either Democrats or Republicans. By mid-2019, Kessler's team had documented more than ten thousand false or misleading statements by the president—an ignominious record unlikely to be matched by any other public figure.

So it shouldn't be surprising to hear a casual disregard for the truth from those charged with speaking for a president who seems to have an aggressive disregard for the truth. Behind the scenes, Sarah Sanders did not display the outright hostility toward reporters that Sean Spicer did. In fact, most White House reporters will tell you that Sanders generally made a good-faith effort to provide reliable information to White House reporters. But in her on-camera briefings, Sanders all too often told reporters, and by extension, the public, things that were not true.

In his report on Russian election interference, Special Counsel Robert Mueller took the unusual step for a prosecutor of calling out the press secretary for something she said at a White House briefing, but Mueller's account actually understates the extent of what Sanders said.

In his report, Mueller noted that in the aftermath of the firing of FBI director James Comey, Sanders had suggested "countless members of the FBI" had told the White House they had lost confidence in Comey. When Mueller asked Sanders about that under oath, she said it had been "a slip of the tongue." And that a similar statement she made in an interview about rank-and-file FBI agents' losing confidence in Comey was made "in the heat of the moment" and "not founded on anything."

But what Mueller does not mention is that Sanders was asked about this in a White House briefing the very next day. And not only did she repeat the untruth, she elaborated on it. In light of what she told the special counsel, this is an especially damning exchange with *New York Times* reporter Michael Shear. Here is the White House transcript:

> SHEAR: And one last question, just to follow up on the FBI thing. And I'm not trying to be overly combative here, but you said now today, and I think you said again yesterday, that you personally have talked to countless FBI officials, employees, since this happened.
>
> SANDERS: Correct.
>
> SHEAR: I mean, really? So are we talking—
>
> SANDERS: Between like email, text messages—absolutely.
>
> SHEAR: Like fifty?
>
> SANDERS: Yes.
>
> SHEAR: Sixty, seventy?
>
> SANDERS: Look, we're not going to get into a numbers game. I mean, I have heard from a large number of individuals that work at the FBI that said that they're very happy with the president's decision.

She was just making it up. As she told the special counsel, her comments on the FBI rank and file were based on nothing. A spokesperson for the president of the United States should not be making things up, even if the president himself has a tendency to do just that.

CHAPTER TWENTY

OPPOSITION PARTY

O n Halloween in 2018, I traveled to Florida to interview President Trump backstage before a rally at the Hertz Arena just outside Fort Myers. It was six days before the midterm elections. The president was campaigning for the Republican candidates for Senate and governor of Florida. As the interview wrapped up, the president wanted to know if I would be sticking around for his speech.

"Are you going to watch?" he asked. "It's going to be a good one."

Yes, I would be watching the speech—that's my job. In fact, I was going right from the interview to the arena to join the rest of my colleagues in the press corps. Before I left, he brought me to another room backstage to say hello to the two Florida Republican candidates who would be joining him at the rally: Governor Rick Scott, who was running for the Senate, and Representative Ron DeSantis, who was running for governor.

"Meet the great Jonathan Karl of ABC News!" he said as we walked into the room.

I shook hands with DeSantis and Scott and their wives. As I turned to leave, the president asked again if I would be watching his speech. I assured him again: Yes, I would be out there with the rest of the press corps.

I then walked into the arena and made my way through the crowd to the press area in the middle of the floor. As with any Trump rally, there were more than a dozen television cameras and about three or four dozen reporters crowded into the area known as the press pen— surrounded on all sides by enthusiastic Trump supporters.

President Trump took the stage a few minutes later to the booming sounds of Lee Greenwood's "God Bless the USA." When the song ended, the crowd broke out into loud cheers of "USA! USA!" This was an older, almost entirely white, and highly energized crowd. Trump began with a couple of lines about "the great state of Florida," but he quickly turned to a much more serious, somber subject.

Reading from teleprompters, he said he first wanted to talk about the horrific shooting at the Tree of Life synagogue in Pittsburgh that had happened just four days earlier. A middle-aged man shouting anti-Semitic slurs and armed with an AR-15–style assault rifle and three handguns had opened fire on Jewish worshippers, killing eleven of them. The president had visited the synagogue the day before the rally, a visit welcomed by the rabbi at Tree of Life but protested by others, some of whom chanted, "Words matter," as Trump arrived. Pittsburgh's Democratic mayor had asked the president not to come, citing his divisive rhetoric.

The crowd in Fort Myers grew quiet as the president condemned the shooting, calling it "an evil anti-Semitic attack" and affirming "our unbreakable solidarity with the Jewish people." He then told them about the visit he had just made to Pittsburgh. Apparently, he was outraged that news coverage included reference to the protestors as well as his meeting with the rabbi and the police officers who were wounded when they took down the shooter.

"After this day of unity and togetherness," he said, "I came home and sadly turned on the news and watched as the far-left media once again used tragedy to sow anger and division."

And with that the crowd started booing and jeering, breaking out into loud chants of "CNN sucks! CNN sucks!" He paused, nodding his head as he listened to the chants. At Trump rallies, "CNN sucks!" can serve as a specific attack on CNN reporters or, just as frequently, a shorthand way to attack all mainstream news organizations.

"And when we talk about division," he said, gesturing to the press area, "this is a big part of the division right there."

Presidential attacks on the press are a fixture of every single Trump rally, but this one felt different to me. And strange. In practically the same breath, he condemned both a horrific anti-Semitic massacre that killed eleven people and the press. And we were still only about three minutes into his speech!

I also felt like I had whiplash. I had just been backstage with the president. He had just been showing me off to his guests—"the great Jonathan Karl!"—and urging me not to miss his speech. And now—just ten minutes later—he was getting thousands of his supporters to taunt and jeer in my direction.

It was a stark example of the Dr. Jekyll–and–Mr. Hyde routine Donald Trump has performed with the news media since the early days of his presidential campaign. One minute he courts reporters and news organizations, craving approval and attention. The next minute, he lashes out. This is partly because he wants the attention but hates the criticism. But there is also some strategy here: He wants to define the media as the opposition party.

Just six days into the Trump presidency, Steven Bannon, who at the time had the lofty title of "chief strategist" at the White House, dubbed the media the "opposition party" in an interview with . . . *The New York Times*. Reporter Michael Grynbaum accurately and dispassionately reported Bannon's words without editorial comment, which essentially proved Bannon wrong. Would a true opposition party really do that? The president himself seemed to like what Bannon told *The New York Times*, and by the next day, he too was calling the news media the opposition party, a label he has regularly used ever since.

Less than a week later I ran into Bannon in the East Room of the White House at the event where President Trump announced Neil Gorsuch as his first Supreme Court nominee.

"That was quite an interview with the *Times*," I said. "Opposition party? Really?"

Bannon told me he actually believed the press was being reasonably fair and was doing a pretty good job of covering President Trump's first days in office. But, he explained, the media is a much more convenient opponent than the Democrats—a better opposition party for Trump than the real opposition party. Why? Because, he said, Trump needs to appeal to key constituencies of the Democratic Party, especially union workers upset with trade deals long supported by both parties—the white working-class voters who delivered the margin of victory in Michigan, Wisconsin, and Pennsylvania. Why alienate them by attacking their party? As for "you guys" in the press, he said, you are unpopular with everyone.

Trump himself has offered a different reason for going after the news media. He explained the reason with remarkable candor to Lesley Stahl of CBS before she interviewed him for *60 Minutes* after the 2016 presidential election. She asked him why he keeps attacking the press.

"I said, you know that is getting tired, why are you doing this— you're doing it over and over and it's boring," Stahl said, recounting the moment at a journalism forum in May 2018. "He said you know why I do it? I do it to discredit you all and demean you all, so when you write negative stories about me no one will believe you."

If people believe the news is fake, they won't believe the negative stories. If people believe the press is the opposition party, news stories are seen as no more trustworthy than political attack ads. Maybe that's why Trump said his supporters would continue to support him even if he shot somebody on Fifth Avenue*—they wouldn't believe news coverage of the shooting.

At the White House, the president sometimes seems to be lashing out at reporters with such ferocity it's as if he wants to provoke a counterattack. He is trying to make the reporters who cover him behave like the opposition he says we are.

The attacks can be unnerving. I have had the president glare at me in the Oval Office and say, "That was a stupid question." From behind the Resolute Desk, surrounded by government officials and before the TV cameras, he has called me biased and unfair. It's tempting to respond or hit back. If you do, it becomes a story about the conflict between a reporter and the president—in other words, exactly what he wants.

Some of the president's harshest attacks have been against women who report on his administration. During a Rose Garden press conference, he called on my fellow ABC News White House correspondent Cecilia Vega, and as she waited for the microphone to be handed to her, the president said, "She's shocked that I picked her. She's like in a state of shock."

"I'm not," she answered. "Thank you, Mr. President."

"That's okay, I know you're not thinking. You never do," he said, having apparently misheard what she said.

One of the president's more bizarre attacks on a reporter came

---

*President Trump made this comment during a campaign speech in Sioux City, Iowa, on January 23, 2016: "You know what else they say about my people? The polls, they say I have the most loyal people. Did you ever see that? Where I could stand in the middle of Fifth Avenue and shoot somebody and I wouldn't lose any voters, okay? It's like incredible."

against another of my ABC colleagues on November 2, 2018. ABC News reporter Karen Travers asked the president about a new poll that found 49 percent of Americans believed he was encouraging politically motivated violence.

"No," the president replied. "You're creating violence by your question."

Karen, who is as evenhanded and unbiased a reporter as I have ever met, was a little stunned to hear the president of the United States accuse her of "creating violence." She replied with a single word.

"Me?"

"You are creating—you—and a lot of the reporters are creating violence by not writing the truth."

During one forty-eight-hour period in November 2018, the president harshly criticized three African American women who report on the White House. He called April Ryan of American Urban Radio Networks a loser, denounced a question from Yamiche Alcindor of *PBS NewsHour* as a "racist question," and insulted CNN's Abby Phillip. The president's attack on Phillip came as he was taking questions on the South Lawn of the White House before departing on Marine One. She was actually following up on a question I had just asked the president about how he wanted newly appointed Acting Attorney General Matt Whitaker to handle Special Counsel Robert Mueller.

"Do you want Matt Whitaker to rein in Robert Mueller?" she asked. It was a good question. After all, the president had just fired Attorney General Jeff Sessions in large part because he had refused to rein in the Mueller investigation.

"What a stupid question that is," he snapped. "What a stupid question."

And then, wagging his finger in Abby's face, the president tried to humiliate her in front of the cameras.

"I watch you a lot," he said. "You ask a lot of stupid questions."

Abby Phillip's response revealed a lot about her integrity as a journalist. She could have been intimidated. She could have taken offense and gone on the counteroffensive. She could have accused the president of attacking her because she was an African American woman (and, to be clear, this was part of a pattern of insulting African American women).

Instead, she ignored Trump's taunt and tried again to get an answer to her question. Without answering, he turned away and walked off to board Marine One.

Later I asked Abby about the incident. She said she took the president's response as a sign her question had struck a nerve and therefore, she believed, she was on to something. And she figured the larger attack—"You ask a lot of stupid questions"—was just another one of his insults aimed at CNN generally.

"I didn't take it personally. I figured it had more to do with CNN," she told me.

She stayed focused on the real story—the potential for the new acting attorney general to interfere with the special counsel investigation—and refused to allow the president to make her the story instead. In the months that followed, Abby would ask many more questions of the president, none of them stupid.

In the midst of a government shutdown in 2019, President Trump put me on the spot, in a particularly jarring way. He had called the press pool into the Oval Office to witness his signing a bill to combat human trafficking. At the end of the bill signing, I asked about the hundreds of thousands of federal workers who were being forced to work without pay because of the government shutdown.

"Mr. President," I asked, "what do you say to those federal

workers—security guards, Secret Service agents, TSA agents—who are now going without pay?"

He looked at me and said the federal workers had been "terrific" and he insisted most of them supported him on the fight that was causing the shutdown. The president was refusing to sign the appropriations bills to fund the government because the bill for the Department of Homeland Security did not include money for construction of a wall on the southern border. But the Homeland Security bill was just one of six different funding bills that were in limbo—unsigned by the president.

A bipartisan group of senators had called on him to sign all of the other spending bills while the dispute over homeland security played out. That way, the rest the of the government could reopen while he fought with Democrats over funding to build the wall.

"Why not sign the other bills, though? So some of these workers can get paid, and the government—"

"You think I should do that?" he asked.

"You can—"

"No, no, do you think I should do that, Jon?"

The president, sitting at the Resolute Desk and flanked by the vice president, two cabinet secretaries, and a dozen other senior government officials who were standing around him, was trying to get me into a debate, to offer my personal opinion on his fight with Congress.

"Well, it's not for me to say that," I answered.

"I mean, I watch your one-sided reporting. Do you think I should do that? Hey, Jon—no, seriously, Jon, do you think I should just sign?"

I started to explain the reasons the bipartisan group of senators was giving for him to do just that. He kept interrupting, demanding my opinion.

"Well, the argument—"

"No, no, tell me. Tell me."

"If you sign these bills that have nothing to do with border security—"

"Jon, do you think I should just sign?"

"I'm saying that, if you sign that, these workers can start getting paid, the government can start—"

"So you would do that? If you were in my position, you'd do that?"

"I'm not in your position," I said, amazed the president was asking what I would do if I were the president. "I'm asking if that's something you would do."

"I'm asking you, would you do that if you were in my position? Because if you would do that, you should never be in this position. Because you'd never get anything done."

That line got a laugh out of those around him, including Homeland Security Secretary Kirstjen Nielsen and Vice President Pence. It was truly bizarre: The president of the United States was telling me I should never be president of the United States.

I laughed out loud when I saw how Fox News reporter Brian Flood—accurately—reported the story:

> President Trump dressed down ABC News chief White House correspondent Jonathan Karl on Wednesday, telling the reporter he wouldn't make a good commander in chief.

But this was also a test. He was goading me into being a partisan player in his battle with Congress. He was also accusing me of "one-sided reporting." If I had taken the bait and given my opinion, I would have proven him right; I would have been acting like the opposition party, not like a reporter.

At a forum sponsored by Axios in 2018, longtime White House reporter Mike Allen asked Ivanka Trump if she thought the news media was the enemy of the people. She laughed at the question but
answered firmly in the negative: "No, I do not believe the media is the
enemy of the people."

At the White House briefing later that day, Sarah McCammon of
National Public Radio asked Press Secretary Sarah Sanders about Ivanka's apparent disagreement with her father's oft-repeated attack that
the media is the enemy of the people. Sanders didn't directly criticize
the president's daughter, but she rattled off a list of Trump administration actions she thought got insufficient media coverage and said, "It's
completely understandable for the president to be frustrated."

Was the press secretary really justifying the label "enemy of the
people" by saying that the president wasn't getting enough positive
news coverage? To virtually every reporter in the room, the answer was infuriating. But then CNN's Jim Acosta asked Sanders a
follow-up question that made many of the reporters in the room,
including me, uncomfortable too.

"I think it would be a good thing," Acosta said, "if you were to say,
right here, at this briefing, that the press, the people who are gathered
in this room right now, doing their jobs every day, asking questions
of officials like the ones you brought forward earlier, are not the enemy of the people. *I think we deserve that.*"

Acosta was entirely correct that the White House press secretary
should be able to say that the people she works with every day are not
traitors or enemies, as the president has so often said. But by person-
alizing the issue the way he did, Acosta was missing the larger point.
The "enemy of the people" slur is more than an attack on the

reporters in the briefing room. This isn't about Jim Acosta or any of the individuals who cover the White House. A free and independent press is an essential component of American democracy. Frankly, who cares if the president insults us as individuals?

As Acosta went on, Sanders became more agitated. It sounded more like a therapy session than a White House briefing—Acosta and Sanders taking turns portraying themselves as victims. As she refused to absolve Acosta and the rest of us of being enemies of the people, Sanders offered another litany of complaints, including the personal attacks and threats she had received.

"As far as I know, I'm the first press secretary in the history of the United States that's required Secret Service protection," she said. "The media continues to ratchet up the verbal assault against the president and everyone in this administration."

There was no way Sarah Sanders was going to disagree with her boss from the White House podium, no matter what his daughter had just said. "I'm here to speak on behalf of the president," she said, "and he's made his comments clear."

A few minutes later, Acosta quietly left the room. Not many people noticed; CNN's seat is right by the door and the briefing was almost over. It's not unusual for a reporter to leave a briefing early, but Jim later said he left in protest.

As soon as Sanders left, Acosta was back in the briefing room to do a live report on CNN. And now he was calling for a real protest. A protest led by reporters.

"There's no government official here but I'll say that the press is not the enemy of the people," he said. "And, you know, I think maybe we should make some bumper stickers. Make some buttons, you know, maybe we should go out on Pennsylvania Avenue like these folks who chant 'CNN sucks' and 'fake news,' maybe we should go out, all journalists should go out on Pennsylvania Avenue and chant 'We're not the enemy of the people,' because I'm tired of this."

It was a moment that could have been scripted by the president. Here was the chief White House correspondent for a major news network playing right into the explicit Trump strategy of portraying the press as the opposition party. Reporters should protest outside the White House? Really? I appreciate Jim's passion in taking offense to the label "enemy of the people"—I share it—but the surest way to undermine the credibility of the White House press corps is to behave like the political opposition. Report the facts. Investigate. Ask the hard questions. Don't give speeches from the White House briefing room and, for heaven's sake, don't talk about holding protests against the president in Lafayette Park.

There are times when I have wanted to get on my soapbox just like Acosta did. There are times when it is entirely appropriate to be indignant and aggressive, to call out hypocrisy and dishonesty. And there's been no shortage of either in this White House. I didn't become a reporter to dutifully record the words of people in power. I became a reporter, in part, to hold those in power accountable.

There are opinion journalists who make no secret of taking sides and who are also excellent journalists. On the left, Rachel Maddow regularly does genuinely news-making enterprise reporting on her MSNBC show. On the right, Byron York of the *Washington Examiner* regularly does solid political reporting. They are part of a breed of opinion journalists whom you want to pay attention to because, regardless of whether you agree or disagree with their views, you will learn something by listening to them.

But as a reporter for a major news organization assigned to cover the White House, I don't believe I should act like an opinion journalist. There is a central role for journalism that strives to be objective, fair, and unbiased. As a White House correspondent, if I come across like a political opponent to the president, I have failed. As the president himself told Lesley Stahl, the reason he goes after the press is that he wants to be able to cast doubt on genuine reporting. Negative story? What do you expect from the opposition party? As reporters, we make that strategy destructively effective if we act like the opposition.

The president seems to genuinely enjoy sparring with Jim Acosta. He taunts him, insults him, provokes him, but he keeps calling on him. He doesn't mind raising his profile because Acosta has a role in the Trump Show. For those Trump supporters chanting "CNN sucks," Acosta is a perfect villain.

But in November 2018, Acosta managed to really get under the president's skin, and the White House responded with more than insults. With the president's approval, Press Secretary Sarah Sanders revoked Acosta's press pass and banned him from the White House.

I don't always agree with Acosta's approach to covering the beat, but this was a direct assault on the First Amendment, and just about everybody in the White House press corps rallied to his defense. Even Fox News put out a strongly worded statement condemning the White House decision to take away his press pass.

At issue was Acosta's behavior during a press conference in the East Room of the White House the day after the midterm elections. It had been a tough night for the president and his party; Republicans had decisively lost control of the House of Representatives. I was at the press conference, sitting a few seats from Acosta. As soon as the president called on him, I knew we were in for a confrontation. Acosta didn't exactly begin with a question.

ACOSTA: I wanted to challenge you on one of the statements that
     you made in the tail end of the campaign in the midterms,
     that this—
TRUMP: Here we go.
ACOSTA: Well, if you don't mind, Mr. President—
TRUMP: Let's go. Let's go. Come on.

Acosta was standing just a few feet from the president, directly in
front of the presidential podium. From my vantage point, it looked as
if the two of them were about to engage in something between a debate and a bar fight. They went back and forth over the anti-immigrant
rhetoric the president had used while campaigning for Republicans
during the midterms, particularly his warnings about a caravan of
migrants traveling toward the United States from Central America.

ACOSTA: [You said] this caravan was an invasion. As you know,
     Mr. President—
TRUMP: I consider it to be an invasion.
ACOSTA: As you know, Mr. President, the caravan was not an
     invasion. It's a group of migrants moving up from Central
     America towards the border with the US.
TRUMP: Thank you for telling me that. I appreciate it.

They went back and forth several more times. Then the president
went after Acosta.

TRUMP: I think you should—honestly, I think you should let me
     run the country, you run CNN, and if you did it well, your
     ratings would be much better.
ACOSTA: But let me ask, if I—if I may ask one other question—
TRUMP: Okay, that's enough.

And with that the president called on Peter Alexander of NBC News. But Acosta wasn't ready to stop. He started to ask a question about another subject—the Russia investigation. A White House intern tried to grab the microphone from him. Acosta resisted. And then the president really let loose.

"I'll tell you what," he said, glaring at Acosta. "CNN should be ashamed of itself having you working for them. You are a rude, terrible person. You shouldn't be working for CNN."

By the end of the day, the White House had revoked Acosta's credentials and announced he would no longer be allowed on White House grounds. Press Secretary Sarah Sanders claimed the action was taken because Acosta had put his hands on the intern who tried to take away the microphone. That wasn't true. In fact, two days later, the president himself undermined that explanation by saying he wasn't particularly concerned about Acosta's treatment of the intern.

"He was not nice to that young woman," he told reporters on November 9. But, he added, he didn't hold it against Acosta "because it wasn't overly, you know, horrible."

Shortly after the White House took away Acosta's credentials, the White House Correspondents' Association (WHCA) asked for an emergency meeting with Press Secretary Sarah Sanders and Deputy Chief of Staff for Communications Bill Shine. At the time, I was the vice president of the WHCA. Because our then-president, Olivier Knox, was traveling, I took the lead in the meeting, calling for Acosta's credentials to be immediately reinstated.

It was a contentious meeting. I made it clear that we were not there to either criticize or defend Acosta's behavior. We were there to fight for his right to have access to the White House. Revoking his press pass crossed a red line. Acosta's behavior was no longer the issue. The issue was the White House's banning a reporter it didn't like. By the end of the meeting, it was obvious they would not back down.

Acosta's ban from the White House would be permanent. Furthermore, they said he would not be allowed to attend events at the president's upcoming trip to Paris.

Shine told me the only way Acosta would be allowed back on White House grounds was if he had an ironclad guarantee that Acosta would never again act the way he had in the press conference. A guarantee?

"Can I be rather blunt about something?" Shine asked me. "I am not going to put myself—I'm not going to let Sarah put herself—in a position where a month from now he does it again, we get called to the Oval, and the president looks at us and says, 'You told me you fixed it.' That's never happening to me. Jim Acosta does not have any control over my reputation with the president of the United States."

Our appeal to the White House to reverse course was going nowhere. CNN went to court to sue to get Acosta's press pass reinstated. The White House response to the lawsuit was even more disturbing than the revocation of Acosta's press pass. The legal response, written by Department of Justice lawyers, made no mention of Acosta's treatment of the intern, which Sanders had said was the reason for Acosta's ban. Instead Justice Department lawyers argued that the president has absolute power to decide which reporters are allowed on White House grounds.

"The President and his staff have absolute discretion over which journalists they grant interviews to, as well as over which journalists they acknowledge at press events," the Justice Department wrote in its response to CNN's lawsuit. "That broad discretion necessarily includes discretion over which journalists receive on-demand access to the White House grounds and special access during White House travel for the purpose of asking questions of the President or his staff."

In fact, the Justice Department argued, the president could ban the entire press corps from the White House:

"No journalist has a First Amendment right to enter the White House."

As a reporter who has covered the White House on and off for two decades, I thought this was a terrifying argument, and it was especially disturbing that it was being made by the US Department of Justice on behalf of the president.

The White House Correspondents' Association filed an amicus brief with the court to support the CNN lawsuit. The brief, written by George Lehner, who has long served as the pro bono lawyer for the WHCA, is a powerful statement in defense of the freedom of the press. It also makes it clear the Acosta case was about much more than Jim Acosta. It is worth quoting at length.

First, the WHCA amicus brief outlines the clear implications of the president's argument as put forth in the Justice Department response to the CNN lawsuit:

> The President of the United States maintains that he has absolute, unbridled discretion to decide who can report from inside the White House. Under the President's view of the law, if he does not like the content of an article that a journalist writes about him, he can deny that journalist access to the White House. If he does not like the viewpoint that a journalist expresses about him, he can deny that journalist access to the White House. If he decides that a journalist's story is "fake news," he can deny that journalist access to the White House. In fact, according to the President, if he alone considers a journalist a "bad" or a "rude" person, he can deny that journalist access to the White House.

The WHCA amicus brief addressed the far-reaching implications of the president's argument—implications not just for reporters or news organizations but for American democracy.

> Simply stated, if the President were to have absolute discretion to strip a correspondent of his [press] pass, the chilling effect would be severe and the First Amendment protections afforded journalists to gather and report news on the activities of the President would be largely eviscerated. White House correspondents would have to choose between avoiding reporting or questioning that could upset the President, on the one hand, and risk the loss of a [press] pass—a requirement of the job—on the other hand. Forcing those who cover the President to make such an untenable choice is not something the First Amendment can tolerate. Nor can the First Amendment—or our democracy as a whole, for that matter, tolerate yielding to the President the power to effectively choose who does and who does not cover him.

Those were the far-reaching implications of the Trump administration's argument. During oral arguments before the judge, CNN lawyer Ted Boutrous addressed the more immediate issue of the White House's complaint about Acosta's behavior. Boutrous suggested that if the president had a problem with the way Acosta acted at press conferences, he should look in the mirror.

Donald Trump, Boutrous argued, "is the most aggressive, dare I say rudest, person in the room. . . . He encourages that kind of rough-and-tumble discussion."

And then Boutrous made a prediction: "Knowing Trump, he'll probably call on Mr. Acosta the day he gets his press pass back."

CNN won the first round of the legal fight, as the judge ordered the White House to give Acosta back his press pass while the lawsuit went forward. Soon after that, the White House gave in entirely. Instead of fighting the CNN lawsuit, the White House announced new rules of decorum that would essentially ban reporters from asking follow-up questions without the express permission of the president or whatever White House official was taking questions. The rules were quickly ignored. The important thing was that the case was over. Acosta was no longer banned from the White House.

The very next day, the president took questions from reporters on the South Lawn. And, yes, he called on Jim Acosta.

CHAPTER TWENTY-ONE

THE McCAIN OF IT ALL

As a reporter covering the Trump White House, I have had many bewildering days. One of the most confounding to me was the Monday after John McCain died.

I showed up for work and noticed that the flag over the White House was not at half-staff.

Why would the flag not be at half-staff following the death of someone widely seen as an American hero?

The president had a busy day scheduled, and I was the network pool correspondent, which meant I would be in close proximity to him for all of it. For the first event, the president invited pool reporters in for a call with the president of Mexico. At the end of the call, I asked the president an easy question.

"Mr. President, any thoughts on John McCain?"

He did not look at me. I asked again. He crossed his arms tightly around his chest, scowled, and looked forward, refusing to answer my question or make eye contact with me. As the president's aides escorted us out of the room, I tried again.

"Any thoughts on the legacy of John McCain, Mr. President?"

I didn't know what to expect, but I didn't think he would completely ignore such an easy and obvious question. And yet, I received no answer. A little later, he welcomed President Uhuru Kenyatta of Kenya to the White House. As the two leaders posed for the cameras in the Rose Garden, I tried again. Still no answer. A few minutes later, I was in the Oval Office as the president began his meeting with President Kenyatta. This time I was standing right behind the couch to the president's left, immediately over the First Lady's shoulder. Again, I asked about John McCain. After he ignored me again, I tried a slightly different question.

"Do you think John McCain was a hero, sir?"

Silence.

"Nothing at all about John McCain?"

I was standing a mere five or six feet away from the president, but once again, he stared ahead, scowling and refusing to look in my direction.

The president's failure to either lower the White House flags or say anything about McCain's passing was becoming a bigger story with his refusal to answer my questions. Vice President Pence, Chief of Staff John Kelly, and several other top White House advisors privately urged him to offer a few words on McCain's service to the country. By midday, Denise Rohan, national commander of the American Legion, which represents nearly two million veterans, had put out an open letter to the president urging him to honor McCain by lowering the flags to half-staff:

> Senator John McCain was an American hero and cherished member of The American Legion. As I'm certain you are aware, he served five and a half years as a prisoner of war in North Vietnam and retired from the U.S. Navy

at the rank of Captain. He then served in the U.S. Congress for more than three decades.

On the behalf of The American Legion's two million wartime veterans, I strongly urge you to make an appropriate presidential proclamation noting Senator McCain's death and legacy of service to our nation, and that our nation's flag be half-staffed through his internment.

I would have one more chance that day to get a response myself. There was one last event on the president's public schedule: a meeting with President Kenyatta and his staff in the Cabinet Room. I tried again.

"The American Legion has asked you to lower the flags to half-staff. Any reaction to the American Legion? Any reaction to the American Legion asking you to put out a proclamation about John McCain?"

Again no response, no eye contact. So, I asked a final question:

"Why won't you say anything about John McCain?"

Still nothing.

I had asked the president ten times about John McCain, and ten times he had ignored me. By the end of the day and after my last attempted question, he did respond to the American Legion and lowered the flags, but he never spoke about McCain's legacy.

The bravery and sacrifice of McCain were beyond question. During the Vietnam War, his A-4 Skyhawk subsonic jet was shot down. He ejected, landed in the middle of a lake in the North Vietnamese capital with a broken arm and leg, and was beaten badly after he was pulled out of the water. He spent five and a half years in the notorious Hanoi Hilton prison camp, where he endured more torture. When his tormentors tried to release him before his fellow POWs, he refused because he knew they were trying to score propaganda points by giving preferential treatment to the son of a famous admiral (McCain's father was the commander of US forces in the Pacific during the Vietnam War). Despite all of that, at a campaign forum in Iowa in 2015, Trump declared McCain was not a war hero.

"He's not a war hero," he said. "He was a war hero because he was captured. I like people who weren't captured."

Trump's attacks continued even after McCain was diagnosed with terminal brain cancer. In light of all that, I shouldn't have been surprised by the president's behavior after his death. But this was a clarifying moment for me. I had a closer relationship with McCain than with any other major national political figure I had ever covered.

I never had more fun, or less sleep, covering a presidential campaign than I had covering John McCain's run for president in 2000. I spent countless hours traveling around New Hampshire riding in the back of his Straight Talk Express bus, sitting with McCain in a seemingly never-ending, rollicking press conference. McCain talked so much, I sometimes found myself running out of paper, taking notes on napkins from Dunkin' Donuts. There was a joke back then that McCain's base was the press. And there was something to that. While he sometimes griped about my reporting, there was no question that I genuinely admired him, and so did most of the reporters who covered him.

It wasn't his politics or policies. It wasn't even his openness to reporters like me—although that was certainly a factor. What I came to admire most about McCain was that he stood for something more important than politics. To me, the central message of McCain's life was his oft-repeated challenge to each and every one of us to dedicate our lives to a cause greater than ourselves. From somebody else, that might have sounded trite or canned, but I found it genuinely inspiring coming from a guy who spent five and a half years as a prisoner of war and who needed help each day to put on his shirt because the torture he'd endured left him unable to lift his hands over his head.

Superficially, McCain had several things in common with Donald Trump. Like Trump in 2016, McCain ran a presidential primary campaign in 2000 fueled in large part by free media coverage. Like Trump, he was often unpredictable and impetuous. Like Trump, he could say viciously harsh things about his opponents. And like Trump, he took great joy in driving Republican Party leaders crazy.

But in reality, the two men were as different as fire and ice. John McCain's call to serve a cause greater than oneself was a direct affront to the politics of narcissism practiced by Donald Trump.

On the Saturday night John McCain died, I was on a farm in central Virginia at a music festival waiting for the band Dead & Company to take the stage. As soon as the news broke, I got a call from ABC News special events producer Marc Burstein, telling me ABC would be going on the air with a special report about John McCain and he wanted me to call in. I started walking as fast as I could away from the stage and the crowd and out onto a dark field.

The special report began with a pretaped McCain obituary I had already written and produced months earlier. One of the unusual things about my job is that I have written the obituaries of many people who are still very much alive and whom I continue to cover. Writing McCain's obituary had been particularly difficult because I knew it would air all too soon. My obituary ended with an excerpt from McCain's last major speech. His body weak and voice struggling, he talked about his career of public service with the emotion of somebody who knew he was likely giving his last speech.

"I've tried to deserve the privilege the best I can," he said. "And I've been repaid one thousand times over with adventures and good company, with the satisfaction of serving something more important than myself, of being a bit player in the extraordinary story of America. And I am so grateful."

After my obituary ended, Tom Llamas, who was anchoring the special report, called on me to make some additional comments over the phone. At first, I was holding back tears, but after a minute or so, I was smiling, firm in the knowledge that McCain, who was also one of the funniest people I ever covered, would have found my situation hilarious. There I was, standing in the middle of a field in the dark, as far from a music festival stage as I could get, reminiscing on national television about his life in politics. And, to top it off, the band playing off in the distance was called Dead & Company.

While President Trump disrespected McCain's memory in the days after his death, McCain, ever the fighter, hit back much harder from the grave. McCain had ignored Trump's personal attacks in his final years, but he detested almost all that Trump stood for—the scapegoating of immigrants, the coziness with Russia, the insulting of America's allies. He made his views clear while he was alive, and he planned a memorial service to send one final message to the world on the danger of Trumpism.

First, he wrote a statement he instructed to be read after his death. With these last words, the man who spent so long in a Vietnamese prison camp said he loved his life—all of it—and would not trade the worst day of it for the best of anybody else's.

"I owe that satisfaction to the love of my family," he said. "And I owe it to America. To be connected to America's causes—liberty, equal justice, respect for the dignity of all people—brings happiness more sublime than life's fleeting pleasures. Our identities and sense of worth are not circumscribed but enlarged by serving good causes bigger than ourselves."

And then, a message unmistakably about the man in the White House.

"We weaken our greatness when we confuse our patriotism with tribal rivalries that have sown resentment and hatred and violence in all the corners of the globe. We weaken it when we hide behind walls, rather than tear them down, when we doubt the power of our ideals, rather than trust them to be the great force for change they have always been."

McCain had made it clear before he died that he did not want Donald Trump at his memorial. The feeling was undoubtedly mutual. But McCain did ask Trump's chief of staff John Kelly and his defense secretary Jim Mattis—both retired marines and two of the most prominent people in Trump's cabinet—to take part. The two men escorted McCain's widow, Cindy, to pay her final respects at the Vietnam Memorial and accompanied her to the National Cathedral for the memorial service. The visual message was powerful. McCain seemed to be telling the world not to worry too much, that in Trump's own cabinet, there were people dedicated to causes far greater than Donald Trump.

Inside the National Cathedral, the service was McCain's final political masterpiece. He had fought bitterly and lost to both George W. Bush and Barack Obama. He had continued to fight, challenge, and more than occasionally annoy them after they got to the White House. But he'd invited both men to deliver eulogies. Barack Obama noted the irony: "What better way to get a last laugh than to make George and I say nice things about him to a national audience?"

But these were political differences, not the kind of fundamental disagreement McCain had with Trump about the meaning of America.

Neither President Bush nor President Obama mentioned Trump by name. They didn't have to. McCain, his body lying in the flag-draped coffin on the altar in the National Cathedral, had sent his final message to America.

"If we are ever tempted to forget who we are, to grow weary of our cause," President Bush, looking toward McCain's coffin, said, "John's voice will always come as a whisper over our shoulder—we are better than this, America is better than this."

President Obama spoke of the intense political disagreements he'd had over the years with McCain, but he also said, "We never doubted the other man's sincerity or the other man's patriotism, or that when all was said and done, we were on the same team. We never doubted we were on the same team."

Could any of them say the same about Trump? McCain seemed to offer the answer with Trump's conspicuous absence from the service—the one major American political figure who was not welcome.

CHAPTER TWENTY-TWO

CALLING THE SHOTS

The president added a big name to his communications team during the summer of 2018. Former Fox News executive Bill Shine became the deputy chief of staff for communications. Shine had worked at Fox News since its inception in 1996, rising to become the executive responsible for the network's entire prime-time lineup before being forced out in the wake of the sexual misconduct scandal that brought down his mentor Roger Ailes.

Shine was a controversial figure who had worked for and managed some of the biggest egos in the media business. Even after the Ailes scandal, he was responsible for the top-rated prime-time news lineup on cable television. With his hiring, it appeared the Trump Show had a new executive producer, but it didn't take long for Shine to learn who was calling the shots on communications issues big and small in the White House.

In late November, President Trump met with his advisors before heading out to Marine One for the first leg of a trip to Argentina for a G20 summit meeting. News had just broken that former Trump lawyer Michael Cohen had told the special counsel that he had been working with the Russians during the 2016 presidential campaign on a deal to build a Trump Tower in Moscow. The story looked bad for the president, who had firmly denied having any financial dealings in Russia.

As usual, there was a group of White House reporters waiting on the South Lawn, hoping to ask the president questions before he boarded Marine One. Shine suggested to the president that he should walk straight to the helicopter and avoid the questions.

"You're right," the president told Shine. "I won't answer questions."

And then the president walked out of the Oval Office and toward Marine One. He looked over to the waiting reporters, paused briefly, and then walked over to them and answered questions—lots of them. Totally ignoring his deputy chief of staff for communications, he spoke at length about Cohen, calling him a liar and ensuring the story would dominate news coverage even more than it already did.

Shine may not have been steering White House communications strategy, but several news profiles early in his tenure described his efforts to improve the way presidential events at the White House appeared on television. A *Washington Post* profile referred to Shine as "the lighting guy." But even in this area, the president was the one calling the shots.

When a network camera crew came into the Oval Office in January 2019 to set up for a prime-time address the president was giving on immigration, they were surprised to see the president come by—twice—to help with the setup hours before his speech. While the network crew tested out the camera angles and lighting, the president sat in the chair behind the Resolute Desk.

As President Trump sat behind the desk, he asked that the monitors be turned toward him so that he could see how he appeared on the screen. The commander in chief asked for adjustments to the camera angles and lighting to minimize the reflection from the windows behind him. And he dictated how he wanted the camera to zoom in when he started speaking. During an Oval Office address, the camera usually starts out on a wide angle and then zooms in as the speech gets started. President Trump said he wanted two zooms— start wide, zoom in halfway and stop, and then zoom in the rest of the way.

While Bill Shine watched silently from the back of the room, President Trump was playing producer and director of his own prime-time address.

After the address was over, the president called the video camera crew over to take a photo with him behind the Resolute Desk. He motioned to Vice President Pence, who had been watching from behind the cameras, to join the photo. Pence walked over and stood by the president's left side and began to pose for the picture, but the president didn't like the shot. Without looking at his vice president, he tapped firmly on the desk with his right hand. Pence obeyed the signal and moved over to the president's right side.

On October 11, 2018, the president woke up and made a phone call to his favorite television show—*Fox and Friends*. Even by the standard of Donald Trump interviews on Fox News, this was a long one. To be sure, there was a lot to talk to the president about. For one thing, a Category 4 hurricane—Hurricane Michael—was barreling across the Gulf of Mexico and about to make landfall on the Florida panhandle. It was also less than a month to the midterm elections and things were looking bad for the president's party. And there was a big international story: *Washington Post* columnist Jamal Khashoggi had gone missing in Turkey, and there was mounting evidence he had been murdered in the Saudi Arabian consulate in Istanbul.

The interview wasn't exactly hard-hitting. At one point cohost Ainsley Earhardt asked the president to wish her father a happy birthday.

"If you wish him a happy birthday," she told the president, "it would be the best birthday present I could ever give him."

As the hosts tossed softball questions at him, the president marveled about how much ink he got in *The New York Times*.

"You know, over the years," he told the *Fox and Friends* hosts, "I probably appeared on the front page of *The New York Times* probably four or five, six times in my entire life. Now if I have less than three or four stories on the front page, I'm saying, gee, I guess they didn't have much to write about."

Finally, after the president talked live over the phone on Fox News for forty-three minutes, cohost Steve Doocy told him it was time to go.

"Go run the country," Doocy told the president.

The president's official schedule on this day was an unusual one. In the morning, he was signing an environmental bill where he would be joined by Republicans and Democrats, including staunch Trump critic Senator Sheldon Whitehouse (D-RI). After that, the president would be joined by Kid Rock, Skunk Baxter of the Doobie Brothers, Mike Love of the Beach Boys, and several other musicians for the signing of the Music Modernization Act. And it was also reported— but not on the president's public schedule—that he would be having lunch with rapper Kanye West.

As it turned out, ABC News was representing the TV networks in the White House pool, which meant I would be there for any event where the president decided to allow television cameras. Early in the morning, the White House press office confirmed Kanye would indeed be having lunch with President Trump—and he would be joined by NFL Hall of Famer Jim Brown.

Kanye would be having lunch with the president, but I was told it would be a "closed press" event—there was no way the television cameras would be allowed into the lunch, not even for a short photo op.

At the first event in the Oval Office, the president took several questions. I asked him about the reports Saudi Arabia was responsible for Khashoggi's disappearance.

"Do you think they should pay a price if it turns out that the Saudis are responsible?" I asked.

"There'll be something that has to take place," he said. "First, I want to find out what happened. And we're looking. Again, this took place in Turkey. And to the best of our knowledge, Khashoggi is not a United States citizen. Is that right? Or is that—"

"He's a permanent resident," I said.

Even before all the evidence was in, the president was laying the groundwork for giving Saudi Arabia a pass on the brutal murder of a *Washington Post* columnist. As he answered my question, it became clear he was already ruling out sanctions against Saudi Arabia.

"We don't like it, Jon. We don't like it. And we don't like it even a little bit," he said. "But as to whether or not we should stop a hundred and ten billion dollars from being spent in this country, knowing they have four or five alternatives, two very good alternatives—that would not be acceptable to me."

As the press pool was being escorted out, I asked one more question.

"Will we see you with Kanye later?" I asked. "Will you bring us back in?"

I had already been given an answer to that question by Sarah Sanders and the press office. But now, as usual, it was Donald Trump who was acting as the White House communications director.

Responding to me as the press pool was walking out of the Oval Office, the president overruled the press office.

"Yes," he told me. "We're going to have you come in for Kanye for just a couple of seconds, okay?"

And, sure enough, about two hours later, we were brought back into the Oval Office for the president's meeting with Kanye West—a "photo op" that would last more than twenty minutes and turn into the strangest happening I had ever witnessed in the White House.

I sent an email to the television networks describing what was happening. My note started like this:

Warning—there is some cursing: motherf#*&, bulls—, balls.

Also: Kanye gave me a hug as I left the Oval.

Let's just say it was a most unusual pool spray

Kanye West—a legendary rap artist and one of the top-selling musicians of all time—sat across from the president wearing a red Make America Great Again hat. Next to him was NFL Hall of Famer Jim Brown, one of the greatest running backs of all time.

The meeting started out low-key. Brown, speaking softly, told the president he liked what he was doing with North Korea.

Kanye chimed in: "You stopped the war," he said. "You, day one, solved one of the biggest problems."

And with that, Kanye West took over the conversation. As he spoke for ten minutes straight, I furiously took notes on my phone, trying to accurately relay what was happening to the rest of the network producers and correspondents, but it was no use. This was pure stream of consciousness, a Kanye West tour de force. He spoke of a nonviolent drug offender serving six consecutive life sentences. He mused about repealing the Thirteenth Amendment ("We don't have thirteen floors, do we?"). He spoke about his sky-high IQ and getting incorrectly diagnosed with bipolar disorder. At one point, he leaned across the desk to show the president a picture of a plane he said should replace Air Force One.

"This right here is the iPlane One. It's a hydrogen-powered airplane. And this is what our president should be flying in," he said.

The president turned to where I was standing on the right side of his desk and said, "Can we get rid of Air Force One?"

I shook my head.

"No? You don't like that idea?"

Kanye kept going. He was speaking with passion, but it wasn't exactly easy to follow what he was saying.

"Well, we're going to have Apple, an American company, work on this plane with . . . But you know what I don't like about—it's not that I don't like—what I need *Saturday Night Live* to improve on, or what I need the liberals to improve on is, if he don't look good, we don't look good. This is our president."

"It's true," the president said.

"He has to be the freshest, the flyest, the flyest planes."

As he went on, I simply couldn't keep up. But there was one part that stood out: when Kanye West described the significance of the Make America Great Again hat he was wearing.

"It was something about putting this hat on, it made me feel like Superman," he said. "You made a Superman. That's my favorite superhero. And you made a Superman cape for me."

And he really shocked everyone in the room—including the Secret Service—when he got up, walked around to the other side of the desk, and gave the president a hug.

The whole scene was surreal. But especially that. Kanye West was the guy who jumped onstage at the 2009 MTV Video Music Awards to protest Taylor Swift's getting the award for best female video instead of Beyoncé. He was the guy who declared on national television,

"George Bush doesn't care about black people," during a live broadcast on NBC to raise money for victims of Hurricane Katrina. And now he was praising Donald Trump—calling his signature campaign hat a "Superman cape"?

"Can I just ask a quick question of Kanye?" I asked as the marathon photo op was wrapping up.

"Yes," the president said. "Please."

"So, you had said, of President Bush, that he doesn't care about black people," I said, looking at Kanye sitting across from President Trump. "And you've heard some people say that about this president. What do you—how do you respond to that?"

His answer was long.

"I think we need to care about all people. And I believe that when I went onto NBC, I was very emotional, and I was programmed to think from a victimized mentality, a welfare mentality. I think that with blacks and African Americans, we really get caught up in the idea of racism over the idea of industry."

He brought up police brutality.

"You know, we talk about police murders, which we definitely have to discuss, and we have to bring nobility to the police officers and make—the police officers are just like us. But there's this whole hate-building, right? And that's a major thing about racial tension. And we also, as black people, we have to take a responsibility for what we're doing. We kill each other more than police officers. And that's not saying that the police officer is not an issue, because they are in a place—a position of power. But sometimes they're in a place of law enforcement. They need to be law-power. It's force versus power. And when you—you shouldn't have to force people to do that."

And he talked about liberals.

"One of the moves that I love that liberals try to do—the liberal would try to control a black person through the concept of racism, because they know that we are very proud, emotional people. So when I said 'I like Trump' to, like, someone that's liberal, they'll say, 'Oh, but he's racist.' You think racism could control me? Oh, that don't stop me. That's an invisible wall."

But he hadn't really answered my question, so I tried another.

"You reject those who say he's racist?"

"You had one question," he said. "I answered your question. I don't answer questions in simple sound bites. You are tasting a fine wine. It has multiple notes to it. You better play four-D chess with me like it's *Minority Report*. Because it ain't that simple. It's complex."

And with that I was left speechless. Kanye West had compared himself to a fine wine and challenged me to play "four-D chess" in the Oval Office.

As the press was being escorted out, I went over to ask Kanye one more question. But before I could speak, he said, "Come over here, man, give me hug!"

And with that hug ended the strangest event I had witnessed at the White House—or perhaps anywhere else.

As the surreal meeting with Kanye West went on in the Oval Office, I looked around to see how Chief of Staff John Kelly was reacting. What did the no-nonsense, retired four-star marine general think of the Kanye Show? But as I looked around, Kelly was nowhere to be found. Rumors of Kelly's imminent departure from the White House had been circulating for months and were now an almost daily oc-currence, but in truth, he had already started to check out.

During his final weeks as chief of staff, Kelly's contempt for the president was on open display. In the first week of December, Defense Secretary Jim Mattis came in for a meeting in the Oval Of-fice on the Pentagon's budget. As they discussed the modernization of the US nuclear arsenal, the president professed a mastery of nuclear science.

"I know more about nuclear weapons than anybody," he said. "I know more about them than all you people."

Muttering under his breath, Kelly said to himself, "Jesus, this fucking bastard."

Kelly was standing behind Mattis, who was sitting in front of the president's desk. The president didn't hear him, but another official in the room did and that official told me about it.

As the president considered his options for replacing Kelly, there was speculation among people close to him that he might decide to go without a chief of staff. After all, the president had already basically been doing the job himself. In early December 2018, Kelly himself gave the president some advice about choosing his next chief of staff.

"Do not hire an ass-kisser," Kelly told the president. "If you do, you will get impeached."

The job was eventually offered to Office of Management and Budget director Mick Mulvaney—sort of. Mulvaney was made "acting chief of staff." As Mulvaney explained it, this meant that if it worked out, he would stay on in a permanent capacity; if it didn't work out, he would move on to something else or go back to his old job.

From the start, Mulvaney made it clear he would have a very different approach to the job than John Kelly or Reince Priebus. As he put it, his job was not to manage the president but to manage the staff. The idea of controlling the president—which both Kelly and Priebus had tried to do with limited success—was out. Mulvaney wouldn't try to limit the people coming into the Oval Office, and he wouldn't try to push the president in any particular direction.

As soon as he took the job, Mulvaney called the senior White

House staff to Camp David for a weekend retreat. As he discussed the plans and challenges for the coming year, Mulvaney quoted from a book that he suggested everybody should read.

The book Mulvaney recommended: *A First-Rate Madness: Uncovering the Links Between Leadership and Mental Illness*.

The author is Nassir Ghaemi, the director of the Mood Disorders Program at Tufts Medical Center. He puts forth a counterintuitive thesis: Some of history's greatest leaders have been mentally ill, while some of the worst have been perfectly sane.

It's a fascinating thesis considering that the book was recommended by Donald Trump's acting chief of staff.

"This book argues that in at least one vitally important circumstance *insanity* produces good results and *sanity* is a problem," Ghaemi writes in the book's introduction. "In times of crisis, we are better off being led by mentally ill leaders than by mentally normal ones."

Ghaemi goes through a series of case studies and argues that some of the most effective leaders—ranging from Abraham Lincoln and General William T. Sherman to Winston Churchill and Franklin Delano Roosevelt—suffered from varying degrees of mental illness, while some eminently sane individuals—General George McClellan and Neville Chamberlain, for example—proved to be abysmal failures in challenging times.

So, why did Mulvaney find this book so relevant that he recommended it to Donald Trump's top advisors? Take a look at how Ghaemi describes the behavior of individuals with the mental disorder mania:

> Decisions seem easy; no guilt, no doubt, just do it. The trouble is not in starting things, but in finishing them; with so much to do and little time, it's easy to get distracted. . . .

Sex becomes even more appealing . . . affairs are common; divorce is the norm. . . .

A key aspect of mania is the liberation of one's thought processes. . . . This emancipation of the intellect makes normal thinking seem pedestrian. . . .

Mania is like a galloping horse: you win the race if you hang on, or you fall off and never even finish. In Freudian terms, one might say that mania enhances the id, for better or worse.

Such are the characteristics of mentally ill individuals with mania, Ghaemi argues, and often of great leaders too.

"Much of what passes for normal is not found in the highly successful political and military leader, especially in times of crisis. If normal, mentally healthy people run for president," Ghaemi argues, "they tend not to become great ones."

The new acting chief of staff seemed to be saying President Trump was mentally ill—and that this was a good thing. The corollary to that theory: Don't try to control the man in the Oval Office. What you think is madness is actually genius.

Donald Trump is not mentioned in *A First-Rate Madness*—the book was published five years before he launched his presidential campaign. But after I learned of Mulvaney's interest in the book, I reached out to the author and asked him how Trump would fit into his thesis.

"I think Donald Trump fits into my thesis perfectly," Ghaemi told me. "I believe that he clearly has mild manic symptoms all the time, as part of his personality ('hyperthymic temperament'). These symptoms consist of decreased need for sleep (a core feature) with high physical energy (including high sexual drive), talkativeness, distractibility, high sociability, and high self-esteem (often focused on by critics as 'narcissism'), along with being prone to impulsive decisions or behavior (typically sexual indiscretions and impulsive spending). His lifelong personality fits this profile exactly."

So, Mulvaney, in recommending the book, got this much right: Donald Trump fits the author's definition of mental illness. His behaviors are consistent with a condition called hyperthymia. That's the same condition Ghaemi believes many great leaders—including Churchill and FDR—also had. But those were great leaders during times of crisis.

"But the flip side is that in times of noncrisis, those leaders are less effective than normal leaders, especially because of the negative risks of manic traits (being too impulsive, hubristic, and unrealistic)," Ghaemi told me. "Such persons are at their weakest in noncrisis situations, when norms need to be followed. They are not effective administrators, and not well organized. If manic traits occur alone, without any evidence of depressive episodes or symptoms (as apparently with Donald Trump), manic leaders can be very unempathic toward those they oppose, and unrealistic (decisions might be creative but just wrong)."

In reading *A First-Rate Madness*, Mulvaney may have thought he had found the hidden greatness behind Donald Trump's most unsettling behaviors—the early-morning tweets, the lack of discipline, the sexual indiscretions, the erratic decision-making—but if he had read a little closer, he would have seen Ghaemi also argues there are dire exceptions to the rule. Those hyperthymic traits can help create a great leader in times of crisis or, in some cases, a really bad one.

"Some people with manic-depressive illness are unrealistic (even psychotic), unempathic, and unresilient," he writes. "We shouldn't romanticize this condition; in its most extreme forms, it is highly disabling and dangerous."

CHAPTER TWENTY-THREE

NO GUARDRAILS

In September 2018, *The New York Times* published an anonymous article in its opinion section with a provocative headline: "I Am Part of the Resistance Inside the Trump Administration."

The *Times* described the author as "a senior official in the Trump administration whose identity is known to us and whose job would be jeopardized by its disclosure."

In the article, the anonymous official, who appeared to be a high-level Republican political appointee, described a president who was erratic and unstable but who was prevented from doing serious harm to the country by his own top advisors.

"[M]any of the senior officials in his own administration are working diligently from within to frustrate parts of his agenda and his worst inclinations," the anonymous official wrote.

"I would know. I am one of them."

The article set off a mad and unsuccessful frenzy to find the source of the betrayal. Two days later, the president declared he wanted Attorney General Jeff Sessions to hunt down the anonymous author of the op-ed article.

"Jeff really should be investigating who the author of that piece was because I really believe it's national security," the president told reporters traveling with him on Air Force One.

"Is there an action that should be taken against *The New York Times* for publishing it?" a reporter asked him.

"Well, we're going to see," he answered. "I'm looking at that now."

Putting aside the president's suggestion that a newspaper could be punished for publishing an editorial, one of the most striking things about it was the timing: The op-ed appeared just as whatever "resistance" there was in the Trump inner circle appeared to be gone or fading away.

The words of the op-ed sounded familiar. During that first year of the Trump presidency, I heard several of the president's senior advisors say essentially the same thing. Looking back, I count a half dozen senior White House officials saying to me some variation of this: *If you think what's happening is out of control, you should see the things we stop from happening.*

But by the fall of 2018, it was clear that Chief of Staff John Kelly's attempt to impose order on the West Wing had failed. The president had come to resent his efforts to limit who could get into the Oval Office. And others who had been willing to challenge him were gone, including economic advisor Gary Cohn and Secretary of State Rex Tillerson. White House Counsel Don McGahn, who had refused the president's demand to have Special Counsel Robert Mueller fired, was on the way out too and would be officially gone within a month. Defense Secretary Jim Mattis was still at the Pentagon, but his ability to influence the president suffered a severe blow after the publication of Bob Woodward's book *Fear,* which came out in early September. Woodward reported that Mattis had told associates the president acted like "a fifth or sixth grader" and that "secretaries of defense don't always get to choose the president they work for."

After Woodward's book came out, the president's first instinct was to go after the author, tweeting, "Isn't it a shame that someone can write an article or book, totally make up stories and form a picture of a person that is literally the exact opposite of the fact, and get away with it without retribution or cost." But while he was musing about getting retribution against Bob Woodward, he never again trusted Mattis.

If there had been a "resistance" inside the Trump administration as described in the *New York Times* op-ed, you might think it would have thwarted the "zero tolerance" policy on illegal immigration that led to one of the biggest stains on the Trump presidency: the forced separation of young children from their parents at the border.

Homeland Security Secretary Kirstjen Nielsen is often portrayed as the architect of the child separation policy, but she was not. The policy was put into effect with little fanfare on April 6, 2018, with a memo from Attorney General Jeff Sessions. The Sessions memo declared, "Illegally entering this country will not be rewarded, but will instead be met with the full prosecutorial powers of the Department of Justice."

In the past, most of those who crossed the border illegally and had no criminal record would be given a summons to appear in court and released until the court date. Now the attorney general had decreed that every single person crossing the border illegally should be arrested and detained. Because of a 1997 court ruling, however, children could not be detained for more than twenty days. That meant the children had to be taken away from the adults and sent elsewhere while their adult family members were held in detention facilities as the lengthy legal process played out.

Sessions had long been a hard-liner on immigration, but this policy was driven from the very top. From his first days in office,

President Trump regularly asked to see numbers on illegal border crossings. For the first year of his presidency, those numbers went down. But by the spring of 2018, border crossings were on the rise.

Two weeks after the Sessions memo, a front-page article in *The New York Times* detailed gut-wrenching stories of young children being taken away from their parents at the border. The article described the ordeal faced by a young woman from Honduras and her eighteen-month-old son.

> On Feb. 20, a young woman named Mirian arrived at the Texas border carrying her 18-month-old son. They had fled their home in Honduras through a cloud of tear gas, she told border agents, and needed protection from the political violence there.
>
> She had hoped she and her son would find refuge together. Instead, the agents ordered her to place her son in the back seat of a government vehicle, she said later in a sworn declaration to a federal court. They both cried as the boy was driven away.

Back at the White House, however, the president was focused on the numbers. And the number of migrants crossing the border illegally was still going up.

On May 9, the president convened a cabinet meeting to talk about the situation at the border. The meeting went off the rails quickly when the president called on Attorney General Sessions to speak.

"The problem at the border, Mr. President, is that we are not being tough enough," Sessions said.

Nielsen and others had called for hiring more immigration judges to deal with the backlog of asylum cases. Sessions said that was not the problem.

"I think it is ridiculous to have more judges," Sessions said. "We have to be stronger at the border and just not let them in."

The president turned and glared at Nielsen.

"Why are we letting them in?" he demanded.

Nielsen started to explain that anybody who sets foot on US soil has a right to ask for asylum and to have that request heard in a court of law. And, obviously, border patrol agents can't go into Mexican territory to intercept migrants before they enter the United States.

"Why can't you just be tougher like Jeff is saying?" the president said, his voice rising. "He just said we can send them right back."

Nielsen continued to explain the limits of what she could do under current law.

Nobody can be sent back until a judge determines whether they have a legitimate reason to seek asylum in the United States. If a judge rules they are not eligible for asylum, they can be deported. But because there are so many cases and not enough judges, it takes months for those cases to be processed.

"I'm sure the attorney general would acknowledge that anybody who touches US soil has a right to due process," she said.

As Nielsen tried to explain the basics of immigration law, the president got more and more angry. He was now screaming at his secretary of homeland security. And she kept trying to explain.

"The problem is you are too weak!" the president thundered.

Nielsen calmly continued to explain. One solution, she said, was to get an agreement with Mexico to hold migrants from Central America while they wait for their asylum requests to be processed in the United States.

Every time Nielsen spoke, the president got angrier. Jared Kushner, who was in Nielsen's line of sight, started shaking his head, signaling to her to stop talking. Others in the meeting did too, but she kept talking and the president kept getting angrier.

The outburst made everybody uncomfortable. The president was humiliating a cabinet official, and nobody spoke up to defend her or push back in any way.

Nielsen had seen the president angry before, but this was different. Another official at the meeting told me the president was so agitated there was legitimate concern about his health—as if he might literally have a stroke right there in the Cabinet Room.

After the cabinet meeting ended, Nielsen went to see Vice President Pence to ask him what she should do. She didn't see how she could continue doing her job under those circumstances. If she did what the president demanded, she would be breaking the law. Pence downplayed the president's outburst. He didn't see any problem at all. The president is just frustrated and blowing off steam, he told her. He'll calm down. It will be fine, he said. Just do your job.

One month later, as the horrific stories of family separations mounted, Nielsen got a call while she was flying back to Washington from an event in New Orleans. It was Press Secretary Sarah Sanders. She told her the White House wanted her to publicly address the outcry over what was happening with the children at the border.

As soon as she landed in Washington, Nielsen went to the White House. When she got there, Sanders told her they wanted her to have a press conference right away, right there in the White House briefing room. Nielsen didn't think it was a good idea. Chief of Staff John Kelly said she shouldn't do it because Sessions was the one behind the policy, not her. She went in to briefly see the president in the Oval Office.

"Just go out there and be tough," he said.

The decision had already been made. And with that, Nielsen went into the White House briefing room for an utterly disastrous press conference that solidified her image as the public face, and villain, of the policy behind the separation of children from their parents at the border.

Her staff didn't prepare her for it. Nobody in the White House press office prepared her for it. Shortly before she walked into the briefing room, ProPublica had posted a shocking video of a detention facility in McAllen, Texas, filled with children. Their faces were blurred, but on the video you could clearly hear the anguished cries of the children separated from their parents. But Nielsen had not seen the video and did not even know about it. Nobody had told her.

As the press conference got under way, my ABC News colleague Cecilia Vega asked her about the video of the children.

"Have you seen the photos of children in cages?" Vega asked. "Have you heard the audio clip of these children wailing, that just came out today?"

Nielsen's response was clinical—and ice cold.

"I have not," she said. "But I have been to detention centers. And again, I would reference you to our standards. I would reference you to the care provided not just by the Department of Homeland Security but by the Department of Health and Human Services."

"But is that the image of this country that you want out there," Vega asked, "children in cages?"

"The image that I want of this country is an immigration system that secures our borders and upholds our humanitarian ideals. Congress needs to fix it."

The answer sent a chill through the White House briefing room; she expressed no concern for the children. The child separation policy would finally be revoked two days later—but only after the public outcry became so intense that First Lady Melania Trump weighed in against a policy that the president's own top advisors had done nothing to rein in.

Over the course of the next several months, the president would tell Nielsen two dozen times that the zero-tolerance policy—and with it family separation—needed to be reinstated. On two occasions Melania Trump was present.

"Darling, we cannot do that," the First Lady said.

Nielsen remained secretary of homeland security for a total of sixteen months. As secretary, Nielsen had oversight of a vast agency of more than 240,000 federal employees responsible for everything from aviation security to natural disasters to cybersecurity. Only about 20 percent of the Department of Homeland Security is focused on immigration and border security, but those issues represented nearly 100 percent of Nielsen's conversations with the president.

On one crucial issue—protecting US elections from another hostile attack from a foreign power—Nielsen had only one substantive conversation with the president. It did not go well.

The conversation came on July 27, 2018. With mounting evidence that Russians were poised to interfere in another American election, the national security team convened a meeting about it in the situation room. As Nielsen began to speak about what her department was doing to combat a cyberattack on election systems in the United States, she reassured the president that everybody agreed that there was no evidence that the Russians or any foreign power had hacked into voter systems and changed votes.

The president interjected and told her to make sure everybody knew that nothing the Russians did in 2016 affected the results of the election. He had beaten Hillary Clinton fair and square.

As Nielsen continued to speak about the threat in the upcoming elections, the president changed the subject. Enough about election security. He wanted to talk about his border wall. The meeting ended after about twenty minutes. Only five minutes were spent talking about securing American elections against another hostile attack by a foreign power. Five minutes. Although there would be other lower-level meetings on the issue, the subject of election security never again came up in a meeting of the president and his secretary of homeland security.

There are few issues more important than protecting America's elections from foreign interference. But Donald Trump saw any mention of the issue—even a discussion of protecting the next election—as an attempt to question the legitimacy of his victory in 2016.

If there was any doubt that President Trump did not see foreign interference as a legitimate concern, it was erased when he was interviewed by George Stephanopoulos in June 2019. Asked what he would do if a foreigner offered him information on a political opponent, he said, "I think I'd take it." Not only would he take it, a month later he would seek it out, asking the president of Ukraine to investigate Joe Biden and setting in motion the events that could lead to his impeachment.

CHAPTER TWENTY-FOUR

MAD MEN REDUX

In February 2019, I traveled to Vietnam for the second summit meeting between Donald Trump and North Korean dictator Kim Jong Un. When I checked into the Meliá hotel in Hanoi, I found a note in my room from the hotel management:

> We would like to inform you that the security scanner will be installed at our hotel lobby by the diplomatic protocol of Vietnam due to the visit of a Head of State staying at our hotel. Please also note that the security will be reinforced in all areas at the hotel.

This was strange. The entire city was essentially shut down in advance of the summit. I knew President Trump wasn't staying in my hotel. He would be arriving the next day and staying at the JW Marriott. Could Kim Jong Un—North Korea's famously reclusive dictator—also be staying at the Meliá hotel? There was no way that could happen.

After all, it wasn't just me staying at this hotel. The hotel's main ballroom had been transformed into a so-called White House filing center—equipped with workspaces for about one hundred reporters along with monitors and fiber-optic cables to send video from the summit back to the American television networks. And on the hotel rooftop, there were platforms equipped with lights and video cameras for television correspondents like me to do our live reports. Only about a dozen reporters were staying at the Meliá, but the entire US press corps would be working there during the summit.

If Kim Jong Un was also going to be staying at the Meliá hotel, surely somebody would have told us.

I assumed the note from hotel management was either a mistake or a prank and went to sleep. I had just spent almost exactly twenty-four hours traveling from Washington to Vietnam and was dead tired.

While I was falling asleep, wondering what head of state could be staying at my hotel, Kim Jong Un was on a sixty-hour train ride from Pyongyang to Vietnam. North Korea may have nuclear weapons and advanced missiles, but it doesn't have quality airplanes. As with the first Trump/Kim summit in Singapore, there was no North Korean aircraft capable of making the trip. So, rather than rely again on the Chinese to lend him one, as he had done the first time he met with President Trump, Kim opted to take the train.

It was a long journey, to be sure, but the train was outfitted to accommodate a supreme leader, equipped with plush private cabins, North Korean chefs, and satellite TV.

The TV turned out to be a problem.

Somewhere during the marathon train ride, the supreme ruler was watching cable news coverage of his upcoming summit meeting. He noticed a correspondent reporting from the rooftop of a hotel in Hanoi. He was then informed that the correspondent he was watching was standing on the roof of the very hotel where he would be staying in Hanoi. In fact, he was told, the entire US press corps would be working out of the hotel for the duration of the summit. The arrangement had actually been approved by a member of the North Korean delegation, but nobody had told Kim.

The reclusive North Korean dictator was apparently apoplectic about the idea of sharing a hotel with a horde of American journalists. The Vietnamese government got a panicked phone call from a North Korean official traveling on the train with Kim. He had an ultimatum: Get the American reporters off the roof of Chairman Kim's hotel, or the train would turn around and Kim would return to Pyongyang.

This set off a diplomatic red alert that went from Kim Jong Un's train to the office of the Vietnamese president to the Trump national security team and back to my hotel room in Hanoi.

By the time I awoke at dawn the next morning, Rebecca Wasserstein, the director of the White House Travel Office, had sent out an urgent alert to the entire traveling US press corps:

> Due to technical issues, the White House Press Filing
> Center will be relocated. . . .

Well, yes. The "technical issues" were really one issue. An outraged madman armed with nuclear weapons was heading in our direction and there was no way in hell he was going to allow a hundred or so American reporters to be working right there in his hotel.

With great expense and even greater hassle, the entire US press operation was moved out of Kim's hotel. We would have to work and broadcast from elsewhere. After some intense negotiating, the few of us who were staying in the hotel were able to keep our rooms. For me and a small group of my fellow White House correspondents, this made for a strange couple of days in Hanoi, sharing the Meliá hotel with Kim Jong Un.

Kim had rented out the two top floors of the hotel and brought his own food, chefs, and kitchen equipment to prepare his meals. That meant nobody saw him except when he was entering or exiting the hotel. But his goons were everywhere. The tables surrounding the piano bar in the shiny marble lobby were filled with stern and unsmiling North Korean security guards.

Everybody was told to avert their eyes whenever Kim came in or out of the hotel. Hotel employees were under strict orders to never look at him. At one point, I was alone in the elevator when it stopped and six North Koreans, including a woman who was clearly the person in charge, came in. I can't say with 100 percent certainty who she was. But from the corner of the now-crowded elevator, it appeared I was sharing a ride with Kim Jong Un's sister. The men with her seemed distressed by my presence. She, however, didn't seem concerned in the least.

From the start, the summit seemed unlikely to produce an agreement. In fact, in the aftermath of Trump's first meeting with Kim in Singapore eight months earlier, the relationship had become more strained. Secretary of State Mike Pompeo had planned to travel to Pyongyang in August to meet with Kim, but President Trump had postponed the trip at the last minute, blaming China for a lack of progress on denuclearization talks. The meeting was rescheduled for November, but then Kim Jong Un abruptly disinvited the secretary of state.

The only real diplomatic activity going on was an occasional exchange of letters between Trump and Kim. The president spoke about them often, even at political rallies.

"He wrote me beautiful letters, and they're great letters," Trump said at a rally in West Virginia in September 2018.

But while the president often talked about the "beautiful letters" from Kim, neither he nor the White House revealed what they said.

I was intrigued. "Beautiful letters" from the world's most notorious dictator? What could they say? For months, I tried to find out.

Eventually I had a chance to see Kim's letters to the president. I was not permitted to take notes, but I was given the chance to read through English-language translations of the six letters Kim had sent the president before their second summit meeting.

Reading them, I could see instantly why the Donald Trump called them "beautiful letters." The letters are each addressed to the president as "Your Esteemed Excellency." They vary in length, but all of them praise the president's political skills and talk of a new era of relations between the United States and North Korea. Kim doesn't include much substance, but he never fails to offer best wishes for the president's family and his health. The longest letter was sent in December 2018. In that letter, Kim explains why he abruptly disinvited Secretary Pompeo to Pyongyang in November. The primary reason, Kim writes, is that the only person who can truly represent the president's mind is Trump himself. And with this, Kim Jong Un hit upon an essential truth about the Trump presidency.

The two-day Trump/Kim summit began with dinner at the historic Metropole hotel in downtown Hanoi. The Metropole is an elegant place to talk about nuclear weapons. Walking into the lobby, you feel like you are walking back in time to when Vietnam was a French colony. The architecture is French colonial, the restaurants have Michelin-starred chefs, and the legendary Bamboo Bar has fifteen-dollar beers. Scores of famous guests have stayed there over the years. Charlie Chaplin celebrated his honeymoon there in 1936. Jane Fonda stayed there in 1972, when she was protesting the Vietnam War with the Vietcong (there's a bomb shelter beneath the Bamboo Bar). John McCain stayed there when he returned to Hanoi years after the war.

The Trump/Kim dinner was an intimate one. President Trump was joined by Secretary of State Mike Pompeo and Acting Chief of

Staff Mick Mulvaney. Kim Jong Un was joined by Vice Chairman Kim Yong Chol and North Korean Foreign Minister Ri Yong-ho. They sat in a private room at a round table, female translators at their sides. Food security was carefully monitored by both parties: The North Koreans took responsibility for the appetizer (shrimp cocktail), the two sides jointly handled the main course (steak), and the Americans handled dessert (chocolate cake).

Except for a brief photo op at the start, the dinner was private, but here is what I have learned about how the conversation went.

The dinner began with some small talk about the American and North Korean flags, which were flying together over the city. After an explanation that each star on the American flag stands for a state, Kim's vice chairman asked if the Americans were going to be adding any additional states and, by extension, more stars to the flag. One of the Americans joked that Greenland was for sale. When the joke was not understood as a joke, there was a clarification from the American side: No, the United States is not going to be adding any more states.*

In that case, the vice chairman said, the Americans should announce publicly that the United States was not trying to add more territory.

Toward the end of the dinner, Kim Jong Un outlined the offer he was bringing to the summit. North Korea would agree to dismantling its Yongbyon nuclear facilities, which were believed to be just one component of the North Korean nuclear program, in exchange for the immediate lifting of all sanctions put in place since 2016.

---

*Apparently, the North Koreans were not alone in thinking the idea of buying Greenland was not a joke. On August 16, 2019—almost six months after the Trump/Kim dinner in Hanoi—the *Wall Street Journal* broke a remarkable story: President Trump had been repeatedly asking advisors to look into buying Greenland, which is a territory of Denmark. At first, the White House insisted the president was never serious about it, but the president himself soon proved he was entirely serious by canceling a planned trip to Denmark after the Danish prime minister declared Greenland was not for sale.

When President Trump told him he couldn't accept that offer, Kim appeared taken aback, surprised to hear the offer so quickly rejected. The dinner ended soon after that.

Over the course of the following day, the North Korean proposal did not change at all. Kim wouldn't budge and showed absolutely no interest in the other issues the United States was prepared to discuss. He didn't want to talk about a peace declaration, something that had long been a North Korean demand. He didn't want to talk about opening liaison offices—a North Korean office in Washington and a US office in Pyongyang. He wanted one thing and one thing only: an end to economic sanctions.

At the last photo op, reporters asked Kim several questions, making the North Korean side uncomfortable. After the pool reporters were escorted out with some commotion while continuing to shout questions, Trump turned and asked a question of Kim: "Do you have that problem in your country?"

"I think you know the answer to that question," replied Kim, the absolute dictator of a country where there was no free press and shouting a question at the leaders would almost certainly result in a trip to a prison camp, or worse, for whoever did the shouting.

The closed-door discussion that followed proved as fruitless as the meetings that preceded it. The president told Kim he would like to cancel the closing lunch they had planned to attend next. They shook hands, and the North Koreans quickly left the room without retrieving Kim's water glass, as they had usually done. A member of the White House team took the glass and asked one of the intelligence analysts on the delegation if they needed it, presumably thinking it would have traces of Kim's DNA that the CIA might find useful.

"That's okay. We're good," the analyst said. Apparently they already had that base covered.

One key Trump advisor was neither surprised nor disappointed with the breakdown of the Hanoi summit: National Security Advisor John Bolton. He thought the talks were a terrible idea to begin with and had predicted the Hanoi summit would be a failure. For Bolton, the only downside was that it didn't end more acrimoniously. President Trump showed no anger and left Hanoi saying he wanted to continue his dialogue with Kim Jong Un.

Three weeks after Hanoi, Bolton saw an opportunity to drive a stake through the idea of negotiating with Kim Jong Un. Two Chinese-based shipping companies had been caught trading with North Korea in violation of US and UN sanctions. Violations of this kind were common and usually handled without fanfare. But Bolton convened two National Security Council meetings to lay out a plan to publicly announce the violations and to add the offending companies to a list of sanctioned organizations.

According to a source who attended both meetings, Bolton was asked at each meeting if President Trump had signed off on the strategy. After all, the president had told his national security team that he did not want to do anything to surprise or provoke North Korea while he was pursuing his diplomatic opening with Kim Jong Un. The source tells me Bolton, clearly irritated, responded that he was the national security advisor and was, of course, acting consistently with the president's desires.

The enforcement actions against the two Chinese-based companies were announced with fanfare by the Treasury Department as a senior official on the National Security Council briefed the White House press corps on the action, portraying it as part of the president's maximum-pressure campaign on North Korea. Bolton himself touted the move on Twitter.

Bolton knew the sanctions announcement would provoke the North Koreans, and if the age-old pattern of North Korean behavior held, they would do something provocative in return.

But hours after the sanctions were announced, the president stepped in and reversed the whole thing. On Twitter, of course.

Donald J. Trump
@realDonaldTrump

It was announced today by the U.S. Treasury that additional large scale Sanctions would be added to those already existing Sanctions on North Korea. I have today ordered the withdrawal of those additional Sanctions!

3/22/19, 1:22 PM

As the national security advisor, Bolton may have felt it was important to ratchet up the pressure after the failed Hanoi summit. He may have wanted to put an end to the idea that further talks would yield anything more. But regardless of his title, the real national security advisor when it came to North Korea was Donald Trump, not John Bolton.

Four months after the Hanoi summit, Donald Trump was heading back to Asia to attend a G20 meeting in Japan and a meeting with South Korea's president in Seoul. The day before I flew to Japan, I asked two different senior officials about rumors President Trump could meet with Kim Jong Un. I was told it was not impossible, but the officials said it was highly unlikely. President Trump did plan to make a visit to the Demilitarized Zone on the border between the Koreas, but Trump and Kim had exchanged another round of letters and there was no mention of a meeting at the DMZ.

Once the president arrived in Japan, there was still no talk about a Kim Jong Un meeting, but he did have an odd meeting with Vladimir Putin. As reporters were coming in for the photo op at the beginning of the meeting, Trump leaned over to Putin and motioned in the direction of the press.

"Fake news," he said. "You don't have this problem with Russia that we have. You don't have it."

"Yes, yes," Putin, smiling, responded in English. "We have, too. The same."

It was like a little comedy routine, except Trump was joking with a leader who has been accused of ordering the killing of journalists who have dared criticize his government.

After their opening remarks, the comedy routine continued on another serious subject when an American reporter asked President Trump if he would tell Putin not to meddle in the 2020 election.

"Of course I will," Trump responded. And then, with a smile, he turned to Putin and said, "Don't meddle in the election, President. Don't meddle in the election."

After the cameras left, the joking continued. A source familiar with the conversation tells me Putin began his conversation with President Trump and the US delegation by telling a joke about a short man raping a tall woman. That's right, the Russian president began the conversation with a joke about rape. Not only was the joke wildly inappropriate, it left the Trump team puzzled. After the joke was translated into English, the US delegation looked perplexed, unable to understand the meaning of the punch line.

Before leaving Japan for South Korea, President Trump tweeted his extraordinary invitation to Kim Jong Un to rendezvous with him at the DMZ. The Twitter invite caught both Acting Chief of Staff Mick Mulvaney and National Security Advisor John Bolton by surprise.

> **Donald J. Trump**
> @realDonaldTrump
>
> After some very important meetings, including my meeting
> with President Xi of China, I will be leaving Japan for
> South Korea (with President Moon). While there, if
> Chairman Kim of North Korea sees this, I would meet him
> at the Border/DMZ just to shake his hand and say Hello(?)!
>
> 6/28/19, 6:51 PM

North Korean state-controlled media responded to the tweet by calling the invitation "interesting," but there was no indication at first of whether Kim would accept. Before flying out to South Korea, President Trump held a press conference in Japan. I asked about the prospect of Kim's RSVPing with regrets.

"Will it be a bad sign if he doesn't show up?" I asked.

"No. Of course, I thought of it because I know if he didn't, everyone would say, 'Oh, he was stood up by Chairman Kim.' No, I understood that," he answered, adding, "He follows me on Twitter."

"He follows you on Twitter?" I asked.

"I guess so, because we got a call very quickly."

The North Koreans did in fact call after the president's tweet.

A source involved in the communication later told me the North Koreans reached out through a lower-level channel to say Kim Jong Un would not be able to respond to the invitation unless it was in writing. A Twitter invite did not count.

So, while the president was in meetings at the G20, the president's team crafted a formal, written invitation, which the president signed between meetings.

Now the challenge was getting the invitation delivered. A US official called the North Koreans to arrange delivery, but the North Koreans did not pick up the phone. Several more calls went unanswered. The letter traveled aboard Air Force One when the president flew to Seoul and was promptly transported to the DMZ. But still, the North Koreans were not picking up the phone. Finally, somebody on the South Korean side of the DMZ pulled out a bullhorn and called over to the North Koreans to tell them to pick up the phone. They did, and the letter was handed over.

After some back-and-forth, the North Koreans agreed to the meeting. And just eighteen hours later, the president shook hands with Kim Jong Un at the line separating North and South Korea. The scene was chaotic because there had been virtually no advance preparations. President Trump walked with Kim over to the North Korean side, making history as the first sitting US president to set foot in North Korea. As they walked back to the South Korea side, they appeared uncertain where they were going.

This wasn't a full-blown summit meeting. Trump had pitched it as a quick hello. But in reality it was a performance. Trump knew the meeting would dominate global news coverage, and it did. The nature of his invitation contributed to the drama by making it a diplomatic cliffhanger: Would he or would he not show up?

To Trump this was never about the substance; it was about the show. Trump and Kim spoke for about forty minutes, but there was no agreement beyond a commitment to keep talking. After all the fanfare, the North Korean nuclear program stood exactly where it had before. Trump was criticized for once again giving Kim Jong Un a great moment on the world stage without getting any concessions. And one person close to the president was also unhappy. John Bolton skipped the trip to the Demilitarized Zone, opting instead to fly to the capital of Mongolia for meetings that had nothing to do with Kim Jong Un.

EPILOGUE

It's a reporter's job to be skeptical of those in power, but for all the spinning and stonewalling I have encountered in a career covering politics, the disregard for the truth that I have witnessed at the Trump White House is qualitatively different. I have seen senior officials in the Trump White House—taking a cue directly from the president—willing to just make things up. And at the same time, the president himself has waged a sustained campaign to make people think the truth is a lie whenever he doesn't like the truth or it makes him look bad. This isn't the dodging and weaving you expect to see from politicians, including presidents. This is an assault on truth itself.

Against this backdrop, acts of truth-telling and candor stand out. When Acting White House Chief of Staff Mick Mulvaney went into the briefing room on October 17, 2019, and sealed the president's fate on impeachment, he bluntly and boldly told the truth. The press conference was called to announce the decision to hold the 2020 G-7 summit at the Trump National Doral in Miami, a move that would bring world leaders to one of the president's prized properties. Mulvaney was there to explain that the administration had gone through a thorough search to choose the best location to hold the summit, but he acknowledged an inconvenient truth: It was Trump himself who said the summit should be held at his own resort. There would be no congressional investigation necessary to determine that the president drove a decision to use the power of the presidency for personal profit, bringing lots of foreign money into the Trump Organization and probably violating the Constitution's prohibition on foreign gifts in the process. It was a brazen, unapologetic—and amazingly honest— acknowledgment of something that could be yet another impeachable offense.*

But Mulvaney made an even more candid, and truthful, acknowledgment when I asked a question that went to the heart of the impeachment inquiry already under way in the House of Representatives.

"You were directly involved in the decision to withhold funding from Ukraine. Can you explain to us now definitively why?" I asked. "Why was funding withheld?"

At the very moment I asked these questions, congressional investigators were interrogating Gordon Sondland, the U.S. ambassador to the European Union, in an effort to determine whether the aid had been held up to pressure Ukraine to investigate the president's political opponents. Ambassador Sondland had just said the president told him there was no quid pro quo, but he could not say whether the president was telling him the truth about that.

Enter Mulvaney. He gave a lengthy answer, telling me the president "is not a big fan of foreign aid" and listing three reasons he wanted the Ukraine funds cut off: 1) He was upset the Europeans were not contributing enough; 2) He was worried the money would be misspent because of corruption; and 3) "Corruption related to the

---

*The criticism of the decision was so intense that it caused the president to do something he almost never does: He backed down and announced two days later, in a tweet, that he would not be holding the G-7 summit at his resort after all.

DNC server."* That third item was what he had asked the Ukrainian president to investigate. And here was Mulvaney saying that was one of the reasons aid was held up. And he was emphatic on this point: "Absolutely. No question about that. But that's it. And that's why we held up the money."

This sounded like a stunning admission of something the president himself had denied, so I asked him to clarify—twice. The second time I spelled out the implications of what he said, giving him an opportunity to take it back.

"But to be clear," I said, "what you just described is a quid pro quo. It is: Funding will not flow unless the investigation into the Democratic server happens as well."

"We do that all the time with foreign policy," Mulvaney said. "And I have news for everybody. Get over it. There is going to be political influence in foreign policy."

Get over it.

His fateful answer outraged White House lawyers. They were watching it live in the West Wing and believed he had just undermined a crucial pillar of the president's defense. Mulvaney's response was a disaster politically and legally, but it was also stunningly

---

*This refers to one of the wackiest conspiracy theories I have ever heard. It goes something like this: During the height of the 2016 convention, the Democrats faked the hack of the DNC computer system, releasing thousands of politically embarrassing emails just as Hillary Clinton was preparing to accept the presidential nomination. They then hired a company called CrowdStrike to investigate and pin the blame on the Russians. When the FBI came in to investigate, CrowdStrike hid the DNC server in Ukraine because that's where one of the company's co-founders is from (actually, co-founder Dmitri Alperovitch is a Russian-born American citizen, but nothing about the theory is backed up by facts). So the whole thing was a setup to make it look as if Russians were helping Trump. Tom Bossert, who served as President Trump's homeland security advisor until April 2018, says he repeatedly explained to the president that the conspiracy theory had been thoroughly debunked. As Bossert told George Stephanopoulos in September 2019, "I am deeply frustrated with what [Rudy Giuliani] and the legal team is doing and repeating that debunked theory to the president. It sticks in his mind when he hears it over and over again, and for clarity here, George, let me just again repeat that it has no validity."

truthful. Remember: Mick Mulvaney is the one person who would definitely know why the president held up aid to Ukraine because he is the official whom the president ordered to do it.

The reaction to Mulvaney's candor was immediate. Speaker of the House Nancy Pelosi called it a confession. Mulvaney's words were relayed to the congressional investigators who were interrogating Ambassador Sondland in a security briefing room on Capitol Hill. Sondland told investigators that what Mulvaney described would be inappropriate. And my colleague Mary Bruce broke the news to Senator Lindsey Graham while he was in front of the cameras answering questions from reporters, leaving him practically speechless.

"Mick Mulvaney just said what you said?" Graham, shaking his head, asked Mary. "I don't know. I don't know."

Mulvaney seemed a little slow to realize the firestorm he had ignited. Shortly after the briefing was over, I sent him a text message.

"It was good to have you in the briefing room," I said. After all, there hadn't been a White House briefing for months.

"It's never boring, that's for sure," he replied.

Former Trump Communications Director Anthony Scaramucci, who had become one of the president's fiercest critics, had a starkly different take on my exchange with Mulvaney, predicting it would doom the Trump presidency.

"The question that saved America," Scaramucci texted me.

But five hours after his remarkably candid press conference, Mulvaney, under pressure from the president's lawyers, put out a written statement that attempted to deny what he had said on live TV. It was a ridiculously deceitful statement. And it was entirely consistent with the president's war on truth, denying truthful reporting because it made the president look bad.

"Once again," Mulvaney's written statement said, "the media has decided to misconstrue my comments to advance a biased and political witch hunt against President Trump. Let me be clear, there was absolutely no quid pro quo between Ukrainian military aid and any investigation into the 2016 election. The president never told me to withhold any money until the Ukrainians did anything related to the server."

But that was precisely what he told me and the rest of the world on live television.

A side-by-side comparison of Mulvaney's words in the briefing room and in his written statement five hours later makes clear Mulvaney was literally denying words that had come right out of his own mouth. Take a look:

Mulvaney's written statement: "The only reasons we were holding the money was because of concern about lack of support from other nations and concerns over corruption."

Mulvaney in the briefing room: "Three factors. I was involved with the process by which the money was held up temporarily. Three issues for that. The corruption in the country, whether or not other countries were participating in support of Ukraine, and whether or not they were cooperating in an ongoing investigation with our Department of Justice. That's completely legitimate."

It was disappointing to see Mulvaney, who was known as a straight shooter and had never lied to me, put his name to a statement that was absurdly false. But he was under enormous pressure to reverse himself. His candid answer to me in the briefing room destroyed the president's defense to a central allegation driving his impeachment. And the effort to undo the damage was directly out of the president's playbook: Label real news as "fake" if it makes Donald Trump look bad.

A couple of weeks before Mulvaney's fateful press conference, I was summoned to the Oval Office, with no advance notice, along with two other reporters—Zeke Miller of the Associated Press and Steven Portnoy of CBS News, both members of the White House Correspondents' Association executive committee.

We were brought into an empty Oval Office by White House Press Secretary Stephanie Grisham and Mulvaney, who asked us to sit in three chairs facing the president's desk—the famous Resolute Desk used by FDR, JFK, Ronald Reagan, and many other presidents. Grisham and Mulvaney then left to get the president, closing the door behind them.

It was already a strange moment: the three of us sitting alone in the Oval Office. No president. No staff. No Secret Service. Just three reporters. I leaned over to Zeke Miller and whispered, "There must be microphones in here, right?"

About a minute later—although it seemed much longer, as if we were frozen in time, silent and alone in the Oval Office—the door opened and President Trump entered, followed by Mulvaney and Grisham.

As President Trump shook my hand and took his seat behind the Resolute Desk, my mind raced back to the day I had first met him, almost exactly twenty-five years earlier, in his Trump Tower office. Back then I was a young and inexperienced reporter for a New York tabloid and he was just a flamboyant real estate developer showing off his most highly prized possession. Now I was the president of the White House Correspondents' Association and he was the president of the United States, facing the burdens of the presidency during a perilous time—for the country and for himself. As he sat down with us, markets were spooked by the escalating trade war with China, North Korea had just launched more missiles into the Sea of Japan, a category-five hurricane was heading toward Florida, and the president was just a couple of weeks out from an impeachment inquiry.

During our first meeting in 1994, he was seizing on the opportunity to make himself the center of attention—the screaming headline of the day's biggest story. Twenty-five years later, his priorities had not seemed to change at all, but the stakes were colossally higher.

He started off by asking about my plans for the White House Correspondents' Dinner. Before I could finish my answer, he went into a lengthy monologue about the 2011 dinner, which he attended. At that dinner, President Obama ridiculed him in joke after joke, poking fun at his campaign to make people believe Obama was not born in the United States and therefore not an American citizen. As he listened to Obama at that dinner, Trump scowled, visibly irritated as he was mocked and the crowd laughed loudly. Now, sitting in the Oval Office as president, Trump told me he actually was not offended in the least by Obama's jokes. He said he didn't like comedian Seth Meyers, who also spoke, but he wanted me to know that he really didn't mind Obama. If he had looked irritated, he explained, it was only because he knew the cameras were on him and he didn't want to be seen laughing. And, he told me, it was pure nonsense to say, as some have suggested, that he decided to run for president because he was so angry about what Obama had said about him.

As President Trump went on and on about the 2011 White House Correspondents' Dinner, it struck me that while we had been summoned to the Oval Office, nobody had told us why. Surely the president didn't carve out a piece of his day to talk about what had happened at a dinner nearly a decade earlier.

After talking about the correspondents' dinner for several minutes, he turned to the real purpose of the meeting.

The president had called us into the Oval Office because he was outraged about the media coverage he was getting, specifically a story of mine that had aired the evening before on *World News Tonight*. I already knew the story irritated him because minutes after it aired, he had tweeted about it:

> **Donald J. Trump**
> @realDonaldTrump
>
> Such a phony hurricane report by lightweight reporter
> @jonkarl of @ABCWorldNews. I suggested yesterday at
> FEMA that, along with Florida, Georgia, South Carolina and
> North Carolina, even Alabama could possibly come into
> play, which WAS true. They made a big deal about this . . .
>
> 9/2/19, 7:16 PM

The president called me a lightweight on Twitter, and about fifteen hours later had brought me and two of my White House Correspondents' Association colleagues into the Oval Office to reinforce the point.

Some context is important here. My story appeared on ABC during the Labor Day broadcast of *World News Tonight*. It didn't air until 10 minutes into the show. My report was short—1 minute, 33 seconds. The story began with comments he made about gun violence (expressing skepticism about the effectiveness of requiring tougher background checks for gun purchases). And I quoted from his comments that day during a FEMA briefing on Hurricane Dorian, which was heading toward the east coast of Florida.

His tweet took issue with roughly 14 seconds of that report. In my story, I said the president had misstated the storm's possible trajectory when he called on the people of Alabama to be careful, saying, "Alabama could even be in for at least some very strong winds and something more."

I wasn't giving my opinion; I was quoting the National Weather Service, which tweeted an apparent correction minutes after the president issued his warning to the people of Alabama:

> **NWS Birmingham**
> @NWSBirmingham
>
> Alabama will NOT see any impacts from #Dorian. We
> repeat, no impacts from Hurricane #Dorian will be felt
> across Alabama. The system will remain too far east.
> #alwx
>
> 9/1/19, 11:11 AM

Frankly, I didn't think the president's misstatement was a big deal. He had made a minor mistake. Then again, it isn't every day that a federal agency corrects the president, so I mentioned it at the end of my report. I had no idea that this short mention would provoke the wrath of the president.

In the Oval Office, the president told me my report was "pure bullshit." He didn't like that my story had also mentioned he played golf while the hurricane approached Florida, although he made a point to say that he had hit a great shot in the video we aired of him on the golf course. As he spoke, it was difficult to get a word in, but I did interject to tell him that it wasn't me who said he was wrong, it was the National Weather Service office in Alabama. The fact didn't register. The problem was my report.

Then he turned to another story that had enraged him: an article in *The Washington Post* over the weekend with the headline "Trump's Lost Summer: Aides Claim Victory, but Others See Incompetence and Intolerance."

He looked at us and said he had accomplished more than any other president. How could *The Washington Post* be writing this? he demanded. He said reporters don't even bother to call to check their facts anymore. I interjected, saying White House reporters routinely

call Stephanie Grisham for information and comment on their stories. I pointed out that I had done that with my story the previous
night on *World News.*

For a full twenty minutes, President Trump went on talking about
my story and the article in *The Washington Post,* insisting that he
wasn't getting any credit for his many accomplishments: confirming
so many judges, cutting regulations, getting Mexico to help reduce the
flow of undocumented immigrants across the border, and—above
all—the booming economy.

He told us that he had been perhaps the greatest president ever and
all he had to show for it was lousy press coverage. He wanted us—the
leadership of the White House Correspondents' Association—to do
something about it. But he was talking fast, leaving little room for
anybody else to get a word in. Finally, I interjected again.

I told him that it doesn't help when he calls the press the enemy of
the people. In fact, it is dangerous. "Some sick person might take your
words to heart," I told him.

"I hope people take my words to heart," he said, missing the point
that I was warning of possible violence against journalists less than a
month after mass shootings in El Paso, Texas, and Dayton, Ohio, had
killed more than thirty people. "I really believe the corrupt news is
the enemy of the people."

We were now nearly thirty minutes into this surprise meeting with
the president. Mick Mulvaney had already excused himself to attend
to something else, reminding the president that his trade negotiating
team was waiting outside to talk to him. Several minutes later, Mulvaney returned, accompanied by former Congressman Trey Gowdy.
As the two walked into the Oval Office, the president called out: "Paul!
Come on in and join us!"

"Mr. President, I have TREY Gowdy here to see you," Mulvaney
said, correcting the president as they walked into the Oval Office.

But the president wasn't going to admit to getting Trey Gowdy's name wrong any more than he was going to admit misstating the trajectory of a hurricane.

"Great!" the president said. "And please tell the other Paul I'll be with him soon."

And with that, the president restarted the conversation at the beginning, going back to his complaint about my "hurricane report" on the network news the night before.

The meeting finally broke up after about fifty minutes. At the beginning of the meeting, Stephanie Grisham had said it would be off the record. I am writing about it here because as the president said goodbye, he gave me permission to put it on the record, saying we could go out and tell people about what he said, adding, "Although I doubt it will do any good."

As we stood up to leave, the president shook our hands and thanked us for coming to see him, as polite now as he had been angry before. On the other side of the door, I saw the group that had been waiting to see him—son-in-law Jared Kushner, trade negotiator Robert Lighthizer, and economic advisor Larry Kudlow. It seemed as if they had been waiting for a while.

The rest of the week would be dominated by the increasingly ridiculous efforts by the president to insist he had never been wrong about the projection of Hurricane Dorian. When FEMA came in to brief him again in the Oval Office the next day, he took out a Sharpie pen and drew directly on the map, expanding the path of the hurricane's possible progression to include Alabama.

History will little note the president's deceptions to cover up a simple mistake he made about a hurricane's path, but it will long remember that he used the power of the presidency to blur the lines between truth and lies.

Donald Trump was a serial exaggerator long before he ran for president. It's how he built the brand. As a thirty-seven-year-old Donald Trump told *New York Times* sportswriter Ira Berkow in 1984, "Creating illusions, to an extent, is what has to be done." That's how he made the top floor of Trump Tower the 68th floor even though the building only has 58 floors. The floor directly above the 5th floor is the 14th floor, skipping 10 numbers, and—voilà—making a 58-story building appear to have 68 floors. Donald Trump hasn't changed since he pulled off that sleight of hand decades ago. But when he was lying about the number of stories in his buildings, it didn't really matter. When he uses the power of the presidency to convince his supporters they shouldn't believe what they see with their own eyes, it does matter.

Our democracy is built on trust. We distrust politicians, but we trust our ability to vote them out of office. We doubt the ethics of our leaders, but we trust our system of checks and balances—and the press—to hold them accountable. We trust the popular will of the people—and our ability to change course when the popular will is proven wrong or dangerously misguided. We trust the value of a dollar, even though it is a mere piece of paper backed only by our faith in the government that printed it. That's why I fear President Trump's war on truth may do lasting damage to American democracy.

Without some collective understanding and agreement about what is true—what is real news and what is fake—the trust that holds us together is imperiled. As former Senator Daniel Patrick Moynihan famously said, "Everyone is entitled to his own opinion but not to his own facts." Compare Moynihan's words with Donald Trump's during his speech to the Veterans of Foreign Wars convention in the summer of 2018: "What you're seeing and what you're reading is not what's happening." Or what his former campaign manager Cory

Lewandowski told Congress in 2019: "I have no obligation to be honest with the media because they're just as dishonest as anyone else."

Donald Trump didn't start the war on truth any more than he created the deep divisions in our country. The media landscape is a factor here. The proliferation of news outlets and the democratization of information through the internet give Americans the power to be more informed than ever, but also make it easier for us to feast on a diet of information that echoes and never challenges our biases and our beliefs. This deepens our divisions and makes them more difficult to overcome.

Donald Trump has poured rocket fuel on this deeply destructive trend. He may still be motivated only by an insatiable desire to promote himself, but his assault on truth is toxic and contagious. It infects those who support him and those who oppose him. And the contagion is global. Where previous presidents, Democrat and Republican, talked about exporting democracy and human rights around the world, the American president's words are now repeated by the voices of oppression. Instead of being a beacon of freedom—Reagan's "city on a hill"—and an inspiration to those fighting against repression, the repressors now echo Trump's taunts of "fake news" as they jail reporters and attempt to silence voices of dissent in their countries.*

What is at stake is the survival of our nation as a place where differing views are tolerated and debated, where election results are trusted and accepted, where people in power are held accountable, and where the truth is accepted, even when it challenges our beliefs and our biases. The Trump Show will eventually become a distant memory. The question is whether America will ever be the same again, whether we have become a nation of people who define truth in relative terms, accepting as true only what we want to believe,

---

*The Committee to Protect Journalists has documented this happening in several countries, including Kazakhstan, Egypt, and Russia.

yelling "fake news" at everything else, a nation so thoroughly divided we cannot agree on what is real. If we can't agree on reality and have no interest in seeking truth no matter where it leads, we have no hope of overcoming our divisions. Donald Trump the president is remarkably like Donald Trump the real estate developer I met more than a quarter century ago. But as a politician, he has made an alarming number of people act just like he does—not just his supporters, but also many of those who oppose him. Survey the political landscape, and you might just think the lesson of the Trump era is that you can deny inconvenient facts, slander those who disagree with you, renounce civility, and get away with it—and win.

That's a grim observation, but as I was finishing this book, I got an email that triggered a series of events that gave me renewed faith that a war on truth is doomed to fail, regardless of who is waging it.

The email was from a junior staffer in the White House press office named Janet Montesi. It was sent the day after I became president of the White House Correspondents' Association. Here it is:

> We've had the original WHCA charter in Upper Press for a
> few months and are not sure what to do with it. I believe it
> belongs to the Correspondents' Association—do you all
> have any insight as to where it should go?
>
> Thank you!
> Janet

I sprinted up to the White House press office, and there I saw a ratty old box, the corners frayed, the corrugated paper exposed along the edges. Inside was the long-lost founding charter of the White House Correspondents' Association, signed in 1914 by the eleven reporters who created the WHCA. Those reporters are long gone. Eight of the eleven news organizations they worked for are now defunct. The charter itself had been hung prominently at the White House since Woodrow Wilson was president, but it went missing in 2005 during a renovation of the White House briefing room. After a fruitless search that went on for more than two years, it was given up as lost.

How the charter was found and where it had been for nearly fifteen years remains a mystery. Janet told me "somebody" had dropped it off for Press Secretary Sarah Sanders and suggested it might be something she would want to hang on the wall outside her office. That didn't happen. Instead, it was left in the box and jammed behind the copy machine. Now that Sanders had stepped down as press secretary and Janet, who had worked at one of the desks by the copier, was moving on, she figured this document might be something significant to the WHCA.

After taking the charter to a secure location, my next stop was the National Archives to meet with David Ferriero, the archivist of the United States, to ask his advice on preserving this piece of our history and finding a safe home for it. I walked with him through the rotunda of the National Archives, where the original signed Declaration of Independence, the Constitution, and the Bill of Rights are on display. America's founding documents are well protected in titanium cases filled with argon gas and a high-tech system to ensure the humidity level inside the cases remains constant at 40 percent. Written by imperfect men with profound flaws, the documents look fragile and faded. The words "all men are created equal" are difficult to read, but they are there in the Declaration of Independence, written by a man who owned slaves a century and a half before women had the right to vote. The Bill of Rights enshrined freedom of the press but did so at a time when newspapers were partisan and, for the most part, didn't give a damn about fairness or objectivity. As those founding documents have faded with age, America has moved closer and closer to achieving the promise of their words. Walking through the rotunda of the National Archives, I lingered at the Bill of Rights. It struck me that there is a reason James Madison put freedom of speech and freedom of the press in the very first amendment. If we can't speak out, if we cannot challenge those in power, there is no guaranteeing the rights that follow.

The founding charter of the White House Correspondents' Association is part of that lineage—a small part but an important one. It too was written by flawed individuals, woefully lacking in the diversity that truly makes America great. But the charter represents something greater than the eleven reporters who signed it or the individual news organizations that employed them or the people who read their dispatches from Washington. That charter is a reminder that a free press has been right there in the White House for well over a century—in fact, for decades before the founding of the WHCA— asking questions of the most powerful people in our government, reporting on their actions, attempting to hold them accountable. The charter will fade, presidents will come and go, and so will the individual journalists and news organizations who report on them. But the desire to be informed and to seek out truth is as fundamentally American as anything written in those founding documents; it has and will continue to survive challenging times and flawed reporters just as surely as it will survive flawed presidents.

AFTERWORD TO THE PAPERBACK EDITION

"Why did you lie to the American people and why should we trust what you have to say now?"

T hat was my question to President Donald Trump on September 10, 2020. I intentionally kept the question general (lie about what?) because I believed it wasn't really about one lie. This was the central question of the Trump presidency—a presidency that began with a trivial lie (about the size of his inaugural crowd) and ended with a profoundly destructive one (about the integrity of our democracy).

In the pages of the hardcover edition of this book, I documented some of the serial untruths of Donald Trump and marveled at his tendency to lie even when he had no real reason to lie.

> *"Donald Trump lies for comic effect, he lies to make himself feel good, he lies to make you feel good, he lies because he likes to, he lies because he can."*

For the first three years of the Trump presidency, I was

determined not to be unnecessarily confrontational. When the president said something that was not true, I would correct the record. I never shied away from asking him questions he did not like, including more than a few that enraged him. I also believed it was my duty to treat him and his administration fairly. As a reporter covering any president, even one as controversial as this one, my personal opinions about his actions and his policies should be irrelevant. I am not the opposition party. I am not the resistance.

By the time I asked that question—*Why did you lie to the American people?*—the Trump presidency had taken its most sinister turn. Whatever the president's motives, the untruths he was telling were deadly. At the time I asked that question, Bob Woodward had just released audio tape of an interview he had done with President Trump in February 2020 that showed he wasn't just saying things that were untrue about the COVID-19 pandemic. He was saying things *he knew* were untrue. He was lying.

"This is deadly stuff," Trump told Woodward on February 7. "You just breathe the air and that's how it's passed." He added, "It's also more deadly than even your strenuous flu." And he even explained why he was lying to the public: "I always like to play it down. . . . I still like playing it down because I don't want to create a panic."

And yet, in public, the president was saying—and would continue to say for months—that COVID-19 was like the flu. That lie, repeated so often, would seep into the consciousness of millions of people, many of whom would go on to refuse to wear masks and refuse to take the threat seriously even after it killed hundreds of thousands of Americans.

Trump hated my question, and he got as angry at me as he had ever been in public.

"Such a terrible question and the phraseology," he said. "I didn't lie. What I said is: We have to be calm; we can't be panicked."

The next several minutes were intense, pitting me against the president. I went back and forth with him, armed with the clear evidence that he had knowingly lied to the public about a matter of grave importance. Here's a short segment of that exchange, with the words coming directly from the White House transcript:

THE PRESIDENT: And your question—the way you phrased that is such a disgrace. It's a disgrace to ABC Television Network. It's a disgrace to your employer. And that's the answer. Are you ready? Because I—

KARL: Are you saying you didn't lie?

THE PRESIDENT: I love—

KARL: I mean, you—you told him that you knew that—

THE PRESIDENT: Of course I didn't. Of course I didn't.

KARL: —it was "deadlier than the flu."

THE PRESIDENT: No, no. No, no.

KARL: And then you went out and told the American public that this was "just like the flu."

THE PRESIDENT: Let me tell you something: We've had flu years—

KARL: I mean, you told Woodward one thing and you told everybody else something else.

The president went on to both deny he was lying and, as he had with Woodward, to explain exactly why he lied.

About a month after Trump privately told Woodward how deadly COVID-19 is, he asked me and my White House Correspondents' Association (WHCA) colleagues Zeke Miller and Steve Portnoy to come into the Oval Office to discuss the upcoming White House Correspondents' Dinner. I thought it was a strange request, because, although I was president of the WHCA, I had not actually invited the president to the dinner. He had made a point of skipping our previous three dinners; I had not yet decided whether to invite him to this one.

The date was March 4, 2020. The coronavirus had reached the United States and was beginning to spread rapidly. There were only about 100 documented cases nationwide, but cases were popping up throughout the United States, including infections in Washington State, Oregon, New York, Rhode Island, North Carolina. And the level of concern was so high in California that while we were meeting with the president, Governor Gavin Newsom declared a state of emergency.

As I waited in the Oval Office for the president, I thought to myself, *Don't shake his hand.* I wasn't really thinking about my safety but about his. I had just been in New York. Fear of the virus had turned hand sanitizer into a prized and hard-to-get commodity. At this point, the health experts believed that shaking hands was one of the most likely ways to pass on the virus. So, no, I would not reach out my hand when the president walked into the room.

We sat alone in the Oval Office for a few minutes, waiting for him. As the president walked into the room, the three of us stood up and kept our hands at our sides. And he said, "Should we shake hands? What do you think?"

"It's up to you, Mr. President," I said.

"Ah, why not?" he answered, reaching out his hand. "What could I catch from you guys?"

That was the last hand I shook in 2020.

About twenty-five minutes into the meeting, Vice President Pence walked in with a message for the president about a meeting he had just attended on Capitol Hill about a coronavirus relief bill.

This was a deadly serious moment for the United States, but the president offered another joke about shaking hands.

"Mike has just been meeting with [coronavirus] victims at the hospital," he said. "Would you like to shake his hand?"

Of course, Pence had not been meeting with victims at the hospital and the president was just joking—about the pandemic. Just a week earlier, Pence had been appointed the head of the White House coronavirus task force. The health experts had not yet recommended wearing masks, but they had already been urging people to avoid unnecessary contact, like shaking hands.

My discussion with the president about the White House Correspondents' Dinner was off the record, but the question of whether or not he would attend quickly became moot. As the pandemic took hold, events of all sizes had to be canceled, including our dinner.

For the next few months, Trump had to stop holding political rallies, forcing him to find a new venue for the Trump Show: the White House briefing room. Before 2020, he had only set foot in the briefing room a couple of times and had never conducted a full press conference there. Beginning in March, he was in there virtually every day, holding press conferences that often lasted two hours.

For the first several weeks, President Trump conducted the briefings flanked by the medical experts on the coronavirus task force, including Doctors Anthony Fauci and Deborah Birx. This was a crisis that was affecting just about everybody. The death rate was rising, schools and businesses were shutting down, and grocery stores were running out of everything from canned food to toilet paper. So, naturally, much of the nation tuned in to hear what the White House was saying and doing about it all.

The Trump Show had become must-see TV and the president loved it. In late March, he tweeted out a quote from *New York Times* media reporter Michael Grynbaum marveling about the television ratings.

Donald J. Trump
@realDonaldTrump

"President Trump is a ratings hit. Since reviving the daily
White House briefing Mr. Trump and his coronavirus
updates have attracted an average audience of 8.5 million
on cable news, roughly the viewership of the season finale
of 'The Bachelor.' Numbers are continuing to rise. . . .

3/29/20, 1:48 PM

But while Trump delighted in his high ratings, he was also growing increasingly frustrated. The virus didn't respond to his bluster.
He predicted it would all go away, yet the numbers kept rising. He
declared that everybody who wanted a test could get a test, yet coronavirus tests were nearly impossible to get. In mid-March, a White
House reporter got very sick with all the telltale symptoms of
COVID-19. But even with help from the White House physician's office, it took two weeks for her to get test results.

As the news got grimmer, Trump started lashing out at reporters.
In the middle of one particularly harsh exchange he called me a "third-
rate reporter" and from the presidential podium declared, "You will
never make it." The outbursts were especially forceful not just because
they were seen by a massive television audience but also because these
were the most sparsely attended and intimate presidential press conferences in history. To accommodate social distancing, the normally
packed briefing room was limited to just fourteen reporters per press
conference, the assigned seats shared on a rotating basis among the
news outlets that usually attend White House briefings.

During one coronavirus task force press conference in late March,
the president walked out after answering a few questions and left

Vice President Pence to finish the briefing. Trump seemed irritated by some of the questions, but he wasn't just irritated. He was seething.

He left the briefing room and walked up to press secretary Stephanie Grisham's office. What happened next has never before been reported but was described to me by someone with direct knowledge of this remarkable display of presidential rage aimed at one of the top-ranked women in the West Wing. He was outraged that there were no friendly faces in the briefing room—nobody from Fox News and nobody from other conservative outlets like Newsmax and One America News (OAN) were in the rotation that day. Instead, sitting right there in the front row, was one of the reporters who irritated him most: Kaitlan Collins of CNN (who also happened to be one of the best reporters on the beat).

The president looked at his press secretary and made an extraordinary request.

"Go down there and get her out of there," Trump said.

He was ordering his press secretary to remove the CNN reporter *in the middle of a nationally televised news conference.* Grisham was never one to be shy about chewing out reporters. Although she never gave an on-camera briefing during her time as press secretary, she was as tough on reporters as anybody who ever held the job. But even for Grisham, this was too much to ask.

"Mr. President, I really cannot do that," she said.

And with that, the president erupted.

"That's because you are weak!" he said, glaring at her. "You are worthless!"

The next morning, Grisham summoned me, in my role as president of the White House Correspondents' Association, to her office to meet with Mark Meadows, who had just become Trump's fourth chief of staff. The WHCA assigns the seats in the briefing room, and

Grisham and Meadows, in the light of the president's explosion the night before, wanted me to give a seat to the reporter from OAN for the day's upcoming press conference. I politely declined. The president doesn't get to decide who does and does not attend press conferences at the White House, and it wasn't OAN's turn to have a seat in the briefing room.*

During this time, Trump was also venting about governors who had dared to criticize his response to the pandemic. One of the governors who infuriated him most in the early days of the pandemic was Jay Inslee of Washington State. Inslee had briefly run for the 2020 Democratic presidential nomination and Trump had been watching an early debate during which each candidate was asked to name the greatest national security threat facing the United States. Inslee's response really got to him: "Donald Trump."

On March 19, the website of the United States Naval Institute reported that the Navy was planning to deploy the Navy's massive hospital ship *Mercy* to Seattle to assist a medical system overburdened by the rapidly expanding outbreak of COVID-19 in the United States:

> *March 19—SAN DIEGO, Calif.—Hospital ship USNS Mercy (T-AH-19) was a hub of activity Thursday, as it took on a crew of civilian mariners and supplies ahead of deploying to assist West Coast civilian medical facilities hammered by COVID-19 cases.*
>
> *A Navy official told USNI News that, as of Thursday, Mercy is expected to sail to Seattle, Wash., though it could be redirected as needed. The governors of California*

---

*A couple days later, OAN's reporter started attending briefings even when OAN did not have a seat, standing in the aisle and flouting rules on social distancing. After that, OAN was permanently removed from the rotation and never again had a seat in the briefing room.

[Newsom] and Washington [Inslee] have both requested President Donald Trump to send the hospital ship to their respective states.

Shortly after that report, the president was meeting in the Oval Office with an outside political advisor when Vice President Pence came in to give an update on the *Mercy*. What happened in this meeting was described to me by someone who witnessed it and has never before been reported. Pence explained that the ship had been scheduled to go in for maintenance but that the Navy had quickly worked to equip it for a mission to help some of the overburdened hospitals on the West Coast. It would soon be ready to deploy. Pence added that he was working with the Navy and local officials to determine whether it should be sent to Washington State or to Los Angeles, which was now seeing an alarming rise in COVID-19 hospitalizations.

"Come on, Mike," the president said. "Don't you think we should send it to California? Gavin has been saying such nice things about me." In contrast to California governor Gavin Newsom, he said, Governor Inslee was a "showboater" and "a real jerk."

Pence clearly sensed the conversation was getting into dangerously inappropriate territory; you don't deploy a hospital ship based on political payback. He assured the president he was working to deploy the ship to wherever it could do the most good.

But Trump would have none of it.

"Molly!" he yelled, calling out to Molly Michael, his secretary, who sits at a desk in the area outside the Oval Office known as the outer oval.

"Molly! Get Gavin on the phone!"

A few minutes later Gavin Newsom was on the line. Newsom is a Democrat and had clashed with the president on other issues, but since coronavirus hit the West Coast, he had been praising the Trump White House for helping California deal with the pandemic. The president put him on speakerphone:

"Gavin!" the president said. "I'm here with Mike. We are trying to decide where to send the big hospital ship. Don't you think I should send it to you instead of that jerk in Washington? You've been saying the nicest things about me."

Newsom played it straight, telling the president to send the ship wherever it would do the most good.

On Sunday, March 22, the president opened his daily coronavirus press briefing by announcing that the USNS *Mercy*—"it's an incredible ship," he said—would be deployed to Los Angeles.

In the introduction of this book, which I wrote before the disastrous events of 2020, I posed this question:

> There are Trump supporters all over the country who look at the outrage of the day—the offensive tweet, the rapid-fire untruths—and ask this: Has Donald Trump made a mistake as profoundly damaging as the decision to invade Iraq to rid Saddam Hussein of weapons of mass destruction that he didn't have?

At the time, it seemed like a question about which reasonable people could disagree. I concluded, at the time, that Trump's war on truth could ultimately do more damage to our nation than any of the mistakes made by his predecessors:

> What is at stake is the survival of our nation as a place where differing views are tolerated and debated, where

election results are trusted and accepted, where people in power are held accountable, and where the truth is accepted, even when it challenges our beliefs and our biases.

The events of 2020 vividly showed the profound costs of Donald Trump's relentless assault on truth. He could not lie his way out of a pandemic, but his attempts to do so cost untold American lives. He could not lie his way out of a decisive election loss, but his attempt to do so undermined faith in our democracy.

For me, the low point of that awful year came on June 1, when the president marched across the North Lawn of the White House and through Lafayette Square and held up a bible in front of St. John's Episcopal Church in a photo op that will go down in infamy. I was on the North Lawn before the president's fateful walk and heard the explosions of the flash-bang grenades being lobbed at the protestors gathered in front of the church. I saw the puffs of smoke. I heard the distressed sounds of the protestors as they were hit with pepper spray. And I was there as the president walked out of the White House with an entourage that included the secretary of defense and the chairman of the Joint Chiefs of Staff.

As he walked back into the White House, I shouted a question at the president. I wanted to know if it was worth it. Was it worth it to violently break up a peaceful protest so he could pose for pictures? The protestors were gathered as part of a national movement in the wake of the horrific killing of George Floyd by a police officer. It was a time when the nation needed to come together—and in fact, there were protests all across the country, bringing together people from all walks of life to express horror at what had happened to George Floyd and so many others.

The image of Donald Trump holding the Bible aloft (but not reading from it) at the very spot where people had just minutes before been peacefully protesting racial injustice instantly became a defining image of the Trump presidency. At a critical moment for America, he chose division over unity. The image itself was a lie. It wasn't his bible. And he didn't open it. If he had, he could have found words to heal, but what he really wanted was an image to divide.

Amidst the pain and the suffering and the deception, the final acts of the Trump presidency included some of the highest and lowest points of his time in office. He and most of the people around him were infected by COVID-19. The disease hit Trump hard as he was forced to use supplemental oxygen and medevaced on Marine One to one of the best hospitals in the world. Thanks in part to an aggressive experimental treatment, he not only recovered but he then embarked on an exhausting campaign tour, drawing some of the biggest crowds he had ever seen. These events were dangerous and almost certainly contributed to a national spike in coronavirus illnesses. They also showed just how fervent his supporters were—showing up, often in freezing temperatures, at outdoor rallies, despite the real risk of sickness.

Even in loss, Trump could have been remembered, in part, as the political outsider who scored the greatest upset victory in the history of American politics (2016) and as somebody who sparked one of the biggest grassroots political movements of our time. He had also succeeded by the metric he valued most, indisputably becoming the most famous person in the world.

But the Trump Show ended as a mix of tragedy and farce. There was tragedy in his relentless efforts to convince people that the election was stolen from him. He undermined faith in the world's greatest democracy. Thanks to his lies about the election, millions of people will be forever convinced that our elections are rigged. And there was farce in the way it all went down, especially the comical ineptitude of his legal team, which held the two most outlandish press conferences ever convened by anybody representing a president of the United States. One of those press conferences was held in the outskirts of Philadelphia at a location between a crematorium and a sex shop, the other in Washington, DC, at the national headquarters of the Republican party.

It was an inglorious end to the Trump presidency. The man who hates losing and hates losers will go down not just as a loser, but as the sorest loser in the history of American politics. It didn't have to end that way, but somehow it all seemed inevitable.

The Trump Show may not be entirely over, but I suspect it is destined to a future of reruns on right-wing media outlets and speaking tours that resemble the kind of nostalgic concert tours old rock stars embark on—playing the old hits, reliving past glories, and, in Trump's version, harkening back to his greatest lie of all: that his presidency had been stolen from him.

If our paths cross again, I suspect our next encounter will be a lot like our first one, decades ago at Trump Tower. Even after the unimaginable events that landed Donald Trump in the White House and led to his decisive defeat in 2020, he never really changed, and probably never will.

ACKNOWLEDGMENTS

Exactly one week after the 2016 presidential election I lost my stepfather, Howard Shaff. A year later, I lost my father, Wayne Karl. These two towering influences on my life made this book, and so much more, possible. I have tears in my eyes as I write these words, aware that neither of them is here to read it. They were as different as two human beings could be, but in their support of me and in the pride they took in my work, they were identical.

My father began his days reading the local newspapers (obituaries first), but he didn't read *The New York Times* or *The Wall Street Journal*. His national paper of choice was the New York *Daily News*. At least it was until I went to work at the *New York Post* in 1994. After that, and for the rest of his life, it was the *Post*. He would have rather watched NASCAR than national news, but he read every article I ever wrote and watched just about every time I appeared on CNN or ABC. In his final years, he would call me right after I got off the air—unless I managed to reach him first.

He was the kind of guy who would not hesitate to race into a burning building to save a stranger. After serving in the naval reserves, he became a volunteer firefighter. For ten years, he was the chief of the Noroton Heights Fire Department. He was a patriot. He would never miss a Memorial Day or Fourth of July parade. He proudly flew his American flag wherever he was, and when he was told by a home-owners' association he could not install a flagpole at his home in Florida, he fought back hard. When he lost, he put the house up for sale and moved to a place where he could have his flagpole.

My stepfather, Howard, didn't care much for parades. He served in the air force during the Korean War, and when he returned home, he became a cabdriver in Brooklyn, near the Crown Heights neigh-borhood where he grew up. Like my dad, he never went to college, but he wrote a half-dozen novels (still unpublished), and together with my mom, he wrote the definitive biography of Gutzon Borglum, the sculptor of Mount Rushmore. Howard taught me to value learning over school. When I was ten years old, we picked up in the middle of the school year and moved from Connecticut to South Dakota, where we lived in two adjoining rooms in the Circle S Motel, just outside of Hill City. From this unlikely base of operations, Howard and my mom set out to track down anybody who was still alive and had worked on Mount Rushmore. Those interviews became an oral his-tory project you can still access at the University of South Dakota.

I made some great friends in Hill City—especially Todd Surdez and Renae Schrier—who welcomed the city kid, taught me about true friendship, and made it impossible for me to ever take myself too seriously, preparing me for life as a reporter and, especially, for the experiences described in this book.

I missed a fair amount of school in those days, traveling the West and watching Howard and my mom pry stories out of the workers who created Mount Rushmore. They were miners, not artists, but they had been recruited by Borglum to turn his vision of a mountain carving into a reality. Howard showed me the key to a good interview is to listen. In a good interview, he would tell me, you shouldn't even notice the interviewer is there.

I raced to Howard's hospital bedside a few days after the 2016 election. After a long battle with Parkinson's disease, he had taken a sharp turn for the worse. He was staring at the news on the television in his hospital room, but he wasn't really responding to those of us around him. I leaned over and asked him the one thing I believed could get a rise out of him.

"Howard, what are we going to do about Trump?"

Sure enough, he perked up; turned to me, eyes wide; and said his last words to me.

"That's your problem."

He died three days later.

Howard had been pleading with me to write a book for years and years and years. Oh, how I wish he could have been around to read each of my drafts of this one. He would have challenged me. He would have encouraged me. He would have made it a better book.

Without Douglas Kennedy this book simply would not have been written. Thank you, DK, for your friendship, your counsel, your humor, and for never hesitating to tell me when I am wrong. More than a generation ago, we set out to write a postpartisan manifesto for Generation X. Through all the twists and turns since then, Douglas has been as loyal a friend as the world has ever known. Most excellent.

My friends and colleagues at ABC News helped me every step of the way as I embarked on this project. Rick Klein and Chris Donovan read every word and made invaluable edits, corrections, and suggestions. Donovan suggested things to add to the book; Rick told me what to take out. I don't think I would have survived the experiences described here without working side by side with Cecilia Vega, Mary Bruce, Devin Dwyer, Justin Fishel, John Santucci, Jordyn Phelps,

Karen Travers, Alex Mallin, Ben Siegel, and Katherine Faulders—all of whom shared recollections with me as I tried to make sense of what we had all experienced. Devin talked me through this project from the beginning and encouraged me when I was discouraged. Justin told me to write chapter 5. John Santucci, who knows and understands Trumpworld better than anybody, opened up his notebooks for me and read my early drafts. Nancy Gabriner, ABC's one-woman warehouse of knowledge, read my manuscript and offered some key corrections. So did the brilliant and generous Cokie Roberts, who was reading my manuscript on her Kindle and still giving me feedback days before she died.

I have had many great experiences working at ABC News over the years; getting to know and work with Cokie Roberts has been right at the top of the list. I miss her. I never met Roone Arledge, but having a chance to work with and learn from some of the legends he brought together—including Peter Jennings, Ted Koppel, Diane Sawyer, Charlie Gibson, Sam Donaldson, and Cokie—has been a thrill far beyond anything I could have imagined when I moved into the Circle S Motel with my mom and Howard all those years ago. Thank you especially to the fearless and tireless Diane Sawyer for making me a better correspondent and encouraging me to challenge the powerful.

One of the greatest things about covering the Trump campaign and the Trump White House has been working with Emily Cohen, who produced too many of my stories to count. She is patient, passionate, funny, and a damn good journalist. Emily also read my manuscript and helped make it better. My senior producer, Claire Brinberg, did too. Claire loves politics even more than I do. I envision us trading stories about these days many years from now, perhaps over a glass of burgundy on the banks of the Seine.

Barbara Fedida encouraged me and supported me on this project as she has on so much else. So did James Goldston, who has led ABC

News through this era by urging all of us to be tough and unafraid in our reporting, but to never take sides. Julie Townsend and Kerry Smith read my rough drafts and helped make them less rough.

Nobody had more enthusiasm for this project than Ben Sherwood. Ben, who helped me through so much at ABC, read my manuscript, raved about it, and then helped me make it better.

ABC News Washington Bureau Chief Jonathan Greenberger supported the project from the beginning and helped me find a way to write the book while also continuing to cover the Trump White House for ABC. I couldn't have done any of it without the help of the incredibly talented and hardworking journalists of ABC News, who supported me while I juggled my day job with writing this book, including Avery Miller, Chris Vlasto, John Parkinson, Meridith McGraw, Tom Shine, Alisa Wiersema, George Sanchez, Michael Corn, Almin Karamehmedovic, Pete Austin, Kirstyn Crawford, Meredith Nettles, MaryAlice Parks, Liz Alesse, Imtiyaz Delawala, Mitch Alva, Marc Burstein, Bob Murphy, Ali Rogin, Wendy Fisher, Treavor Hastings, Heather Riley, Cindy Smith, and Matt Hosford. These are just a few of the many great people at ABC whom I owe more than I can ever repay. Some of my ABC colleagues have left and are now my competitors (I am talking about you, Arlette Saenz), but I owe them too.

I have benefited immensely from working with George Stephanopoulos throughout virtually all the events described in this book. George's influence goes back to when he wrote *All Too Human*, one of the best insider accounts of life in the West Wing ever written. David Muir has also been along for every step of the way and generously shared his recollections as I was writing this book.

I have been fortunate to call Mike Allen a friend since I first bumped into him in Iowa in 1999, during the early days of the 2000 presidential campaign. Since then, I have compared notes with Mike on just about every major political story I have covered, including, of course, the stories recounted in this book. I was really only able to start writing it after talking it through with Mike and Jeff Nussbaum over lunch at the Bombay Club restaurant in Washington—the way so many projects have begun.

Sal and Maryann Catalano boosted me throughout this project—and way before it started too. So did the ever generous and gracious Franco Nuschese. Michael Feldman's counsel was invaluable, as it always is. The brilliant Robin Sproul's too. I have many friends who offered encouragement and suggestions along the way, including Don Rockwell, Mary Ann Gonser, Scott Alexander, and Frank Luntz. Brian Brown pushed me to challenge my own assumptions and to think big. We have had some intense debates on politics, media, and culture, and those debates helped make this a better book. Paul and Karen Freitas kept me sane when the world around me didn't seem that way. Pete Madej and Rich Dawson have been there for me since the glory days of *Communiqué,* the underground newspaper I started in high school.

David Larabell of CAA started pushing me to write a book before anybody thought Donald Trump would run for president. After Trump was elected, Larabell's appeals became urgent. Finally, one morning in late 2017, David met me for breakfast at the Hay-Adams hotel near the White House and slid a note to me across the table. The note read: "Front Row at the Trump Show: The President, the Press and the Truth."

Alan Berger voraciously devoured every chapter of this book as I wrote it. If my pace slowed, I'd get a call. He believed in this book from the start—sometimes more than I did.

Allison Pecorin helped me with the research. Allie started working at ABC News as an intern in the Pennsylvania Avenue unit during the first year of the Trump presidency. I get the sense she may be running the whole network someday. Kristopher Schneider helped me research the first part of the book, unearthing some lost gems from the ABC archives. The meticulous and thoughtful Chris Good helped me get to the bottom of the phrase "enemy of the people." Jon Garcia opened up his archive of White House emails and pool reports. The man saves everything that comes out of 1600 Pennsylvania Avenue (and makes good guacamole too).

Like every other American, I have benefited immensely from the work of the White House press corps. Reporters like Peter Baker, Maggie Haberman, Josh Dawsey, Phil Rucker, Ashley Parker, Jonathan Swan, and Abby Phillip are among the best ever to cover the beat. This also applies to the excellent work of my NBC colleagues Kristen Welker, Peter Alexander, and Hallie Jackson, with whom I have traveled all over the world covering this story. I am especially grateful to my friends and colleagues on the board of the White House Correspondents' Association: Zeke Miller, Steve Portnoy, Tamara Keith, Anita Kumar, Doug Mills, Todd Gillman, Francesca Chambers, and Fin Gomez. Steve Thomma and George Lehner too.

Above all, this has been a family project. My mom read everything and was even more impatient than Alan Berger when the pace of my writing slowed. When I first started working in television, my mom was happy for me, but she also admonished me: "TV is fine, but you can't stop writing." Mom, this book is for you.

My brother Allan, better known as WorldRider, showed me the way by writing *Forks,* his book about his journey around the world on a motorcycle. Allan encouraged me on this project from the start, reading my drafts and offering feedback even as he was traveling through the Balkans on his motorcycle.

John Parsley of Dutton helped shape this book with his advice, and his edits made it better. I was also fortunate to have the eagle-eyed Aja Pollock on the team; she is a great copy editor and much more. Thank you to Cassidy Sachs too for shepherding this project from start to finish.

Parsley is one of the best editors in the business, but, as I am sure he will understand, there are two editors on this project who were more important: Anna and Emily Karl. Emily was born the year I started working at CNN, Anna three years later. They have been with me every step of the way. Emily asked her first question of a senator during Take Your Daughter to Work Day when she was five years old. A few years later, Anna briefly disappeared while visiting me on Capitol Hill—she was tagging along with John McCain as he bounced between meetings.

They have had their own front-row seats to history. Anna has already met two presidents. Emily has met three. They have both worked as reporters and have firm convictions about what makes good journalism. When I asked them to read the first draft of this book, they took it seriously, editing it line by line. Anna's comments and suggestions caused me to go back and rewrite some of the chapters. She saw things that I'd missed and helped me write a more compelling story. Emily corrected errors that had slipped by everybody else and helped me write with greater clarity. I love you both and I am incredibly proud of you. I knew you were brilliant, but I had no idea the two of you were such good editors.

Finally, the biggest acknowledgment of all goes to my wife, Maria. You have been with me throughout this unbelievable ride. You have tolerated the long hours and ridiculous travel. On this project, as with just about everything I have written since my senior-year college papers, you were the very first person to read what I had written. Even more important, you have loved me even during those times when the stress of this project made me decidedly unlovable.

INDEX